Code Factory

100+ Programming Solutions

Navigating the wonders beyond binary brilliance

Shikha Jain

Kavita Pandey

www.bpbonline.com

First Edition 2024

ISBN: 978-93-55519-115

Distributors:

BPB PUBLICATIONS
20, Ansari Road, Darya Ganj
New Delhi-110002
Ph: 23254990/23254991

DECCAN AGENCIES
4-3-329, Bank Street,
Hyderabad-500195
Ph: 24756967/24756400

MICRO MEDIA
Shop No. 5, Mahendra Chambers,
150 DN Rd. Next to Capital Cinema,
V.T. (C.S.T.) Station, MUMBAI-400 001
Ph: 22078296/22078297

To View Complete BPB Publications Catalogue Scan the QR Code:

Published by Manish Jain for BPB Publications, 20 Ansari Road, Darya Ganj, New Delhi-110002 and Printed by him at Manipal Technologies, Manipal

www.bpbonline.com

Dedicated to

*My son, **Vidit**, for igniting the idea behind this book*

My husband, parents, and siblings for their endless support and blessings

—Shikha Jain

*My dearest daughter, **Sachi**, your love fuels every word in this book*

My husband and the Almighty God, for their guidance and inspiration, without whom this book would not have been possible

—Kavita Pandey

About the Authors

- **Shikha Jain** is an Assistant Professor at Jaypee Institute of Information Technology (JIIT), NOIDA, INDIA. She has more than twenty years of research and academic experience. She has received her PhD in computer science from Jaypee Institute of Information Technology, Noida, India. She has contributed significantly to the field, publishing numerous research papers in prestigious journals and conferences.

  She was a guest editor for the notable Advances in Computational Intelligence and its Applications issue in the International Journal of Information Retrieval Research. She is an active reviewer of many International Journals and a technical program committee member of various International Conferences. Her research area includes Affective Computing, Emotion Modelling, Cognitive Affective Architectures, Machine Learning, and Soft Computing. She also takes on the editor role for the book Artificial Intelligence, Machine Learning, and Mental Health in Pandemics: A Computational Approach.

- **Kavita Pandey** is an Assistant Professor (Senior Grade) at Jaypee Institute of Information Technology (JIIT), Noida. She has more than 20 years of academic experience. She received her B.Tech. in Computer Science and Engineering from M.D. University in 2002 and M.Tech. (CS) from Banasthali Vidyapeeth University in 2003. She obtained her Ph.D. (CS) from JIIT, Noida, India, in January 2017. Presently, she is guiding two Ph.D. students. She has mentored 16 M.Tech. thesis/industrial projects and 57 + undergraduate projects.

  She is an editor of a book named Artificial Intelligence, Machine Learning, and Mental Health in Pandemics: A Computational Approach. She has published one patent. She also contributed to IGNOU study material titled Data Communications and Computer Network. Her research interests include Soft Computing, Machine Learning, Vehicular Ad hoc Networks, the Internet of Things, and Optimization Techniques. She has published 60+ articles in International journals and conferences, including Wiley, IEEE, Springer, Inderscience, etc. She was a guest editor of the special issue Advances in Computational Intelligence and Applications in the International Journal of Information Retrieval Research (IJIRR), IGI Global, ESCI, and Web of Science. She is working as an Academic Editor on the Editorial Board of the International Journal of Distributed Sensor Networks, Hindawi. She was a reviewer in many international journals of renowned publishers, including Elsevier, Inderscience, and IEEE Access, among others. She is an active TPC member of many conferences, such as FSDM, REDSET, IC3, UPCON, TEAMC, ICTCS, and many more. She is also a senior member of the IEEE Society.

About the Reviewer

Sachin Jain, a seasoned professional with over two decades of experience in the IT industry, stands as a testament to the fusion of passion and expertise. Born with a natural inclination towards technology, he embarked on a journey that has defined him as a master in his field. He pursued his academic aspirations with a Master's in Computer Applications, laying the foundation for an illustrious career.

With an impressive 20-plus years of experience, Sachin has become a stalwart in the IT industry, contributing significantly to developing and designing large-scale enterprise applications. His coding prowess and innovative approach have set him apart, making him a go-to technology expert.

Beyond the world of coding and algorithms, Sachin finds solace in his passion for travel and cinema. Exploring new landscapes and immersing himself in diverse cultures fuels his creativity and broadens his perspective. Amid intricate lines of code, Sachin discovers balance through the magic of storytelling, whether on the screen or in the pages of a good book.

Sachin Jain's journey is a testament to the harmonious blend of technical understanding and a rich, multifaceted life. As he continues to push the boundaries of what is possible in the IT landscape, Sachin remains a true connoisseur of the digital age.

Acknowledgement

Alone we can do so little; together we can do so much.

—Helen Keller

We humbly acknowledge the divine presence that has guided and inspired the creation of this book. We sincerely thank Almighty God for providing wisdom, strength, and inspiration throughout this journey.

A heartfelt thanks go to the entire team of BPB Publishers for their unwavering support in bringing our dream to fruition.

We are grateful to known and unknown individuals whose contributions have enriched our pool of knowledge, enabling us to author this book.

We sincerely appreciate the reviewers whose insightful suggestions and feedback significantly enhanced the quality of this book.

Lastly, we express our gratitude to all the readers for their interest in our book. Your encouragement is invaluable.

Preface

Welcome to Code Factory. This is specially designed for new entrants in the programming world. The main objective of the book is to trigger and nurture logic-building skills among students. It provides a comprehensive introduction to the fundamental programming concepts through the lens of two powerful languages—C and Python. The book will help the reader develop problem-solving and logic-building abilities with the help of algorithms and flowcharts. It will also teach how to transform the flowchart/algorithm into a program. Simultaneously, engaging with flowcharts, algorithms, and programming enhances the reader's ability to comprehend the translation of a given problem into logical solutions and subsequently into executable programs. By working in parallel with these components, readers gain a holistic perspective on the problem-solving process. It reinforces the connection between the problem statement, the logical constructs devised in algorithms, and their representation in a programming language.

The book is structured to introduce concepts gradually, ensuring a smooth learning curve. Each chapter presents challenges of increasing difficulty, allowing students to build on their skills progressively. One book chapter is designed to expose real-world examples of applying learned concepts to solve coding problems, enhancing their ability to tackle programming challenges in various domains.

This book will help the readers develop a well-rounded skill set covering flowcharts, algorithmic thinking, and practical implementation in both C and Python languages. It will provide a holistic foundation for anyone aspiring to become fearless in coding. I hope this guide will empower you to embark on a fulfilling journey into coding.

Chapter 1: Simple Input Output Program – It provides a comprehensive understanding of the fundamental concepts and techniques involved in handling input and output operations in programming. It aims to offer a thorough comprehension of fundamental algorithms flowcharts and Python and C code implementations. These programs help users grasp crucial concepts, including user input, data manipulation, and result display. Consider this chapter a foundational step for constructing more intricate applications in subsequent book sections.

Chapter 2: Conditional Statements – It covers the concept of decision statements(if-else), elucidating them through flowcharts, algorithms, and coding. Using numerous examples, it has effectively illustrated the various facets of conditional statements such as simple if, if-else, if-else if-else, and so on. Decision statements enable the execution of specific code blocks based on certain conditions. They provide the logic for making choices within a program, making them a fundamental building block.

Chapter 3: Simple Loops – It discusses the basic loop statements such as while-loop and for-loop. In programming, a loop is a fundamental control structure that allows you to execute a block of code repeatedly as long as a specific condition is met. Loops are essential for automating repetitive tasks, iterating over certain statements, and performing various computational tasks efficiently. It optimizes the code as well. Overall, the chapter underscores the significance of loops as essential tools for improving code automation and computational efficiency in programming

Chapter 4: Complex Loops – It delves into the intricate applications of loops, showcasing their capacity to address complex problems. Loops are not confined to essential repetition; they can be seamlessly integrated with multiple conditional statements to devise sophisticated solutions. Furthermore, the chapter elevates their significance in handling certain challenges that demand the utilization of multiple loops, either sequentially or in the form of nested loops.

Chapter 5: Complex Problem Solving – It presents the complex logic building using various programming constructs (as discussed in previous chapters). The main focus of the chapter is on solving challenging problems by thinking of some logic. The chapter presents the problems or challenges that require creative and intricate solutions. These problems often go beyond simple algorithmic steps and may involve multiple steps, conditional logic, loops, lists, and matrices. The chapter discusses creating a logical flow for solving complex problems, including algorithms and flowcharts, to plan solutions before writing executable code.

Chapter 6: Real World Problems – It guides readers to navigate the intersection of real-world problems and programming constructs. The primary emphasis lies in strategically mapping these tangible challenges to previously studied concepts. By aligning real-world problems with established programming principles, the chapter seeks to demystify complex issues and demonstrate how simple programming constructs can be ingeniously applied.

Errata

We take immense pride in our work at BPB Publications and follow best practices to ensure the accuracy of our content to provide with an indulging reading experience to our subscribers. Our readers are our mirrors, and we use their inputs to reflect and improve upon human errors, if any, that may have occurred during the publishing processes involved. To let us maintain the quality and help us reach out to any readers who might be having difficulties due to any unforeseen errors, please write to us at :

errata@bpbonline.com

Your support, suggestions and feedbacks are highly appreciated by the BPB Publications' Family.

Piracy

If you come across any illegal copies of our works in any form on the internet, we would be grateful if you would provide us with the location address or website name. Please contact us at **business@bpbonline.com** with a link to the material.

If you are interested in becoming an author

If there is a topic that you have expertise in, and you are interested in either writing or contributing to a book, please visit **www.bpbonline.com**. We have worked with thousands of developers and tech professionals, just like you, to help them share their insights with the global tech community. You can make a general application, apply for a specific hot topic that we are recruiting an author for, or submit your own idea.

Reviews

Please leave a review. Once you have read and used this book, why not leave a review on the site that you purchased it from? Potential readers can then see and use your unbiased opinion to make purchase decisions. We at BPB can understand what you think about our products, and our authors can see your feedback on their book. Thank you!

For more information about BPB, please visit **www.bpbonline.com**.

Join our book's Discord space

Join the book's Discord Workspace for Latest updates, Offers, Tech happenings around the world, New Release and Sessions with the Authors:

https://discord.bpbonline.com

Table of Contents

Chapter 1
Simple Input Output Program

Introduction

The ability to process input and generate output is a fundamental aspect of programming. In this chapter, we delve into the world of simple input-output programs. It comprehensively explains basic algorithms, flowcharts, Python, and C code implementations. These programs allow users to grasp essential concepts such as user input, data manipulation, and result display. This chapter will be a building block for developing more complex applications in further book chapters.

Whether you are a novice programmer seeking to strengthen your fundamental abilities or an experienced developer looking for practical examples, this chapter offers a diverse range of simple programs to explore. A basic understanding of the program would be built by studying the algorithms and visualizing the flowcharts. In addition, the Python and C code will give you valuable insights into the core principles of input-output operations in these languages. Overall, the skills necessary to solve real-world programming challenges would be gained. The basic building blocks of a flowchart are shown in *Figure 1.1*:

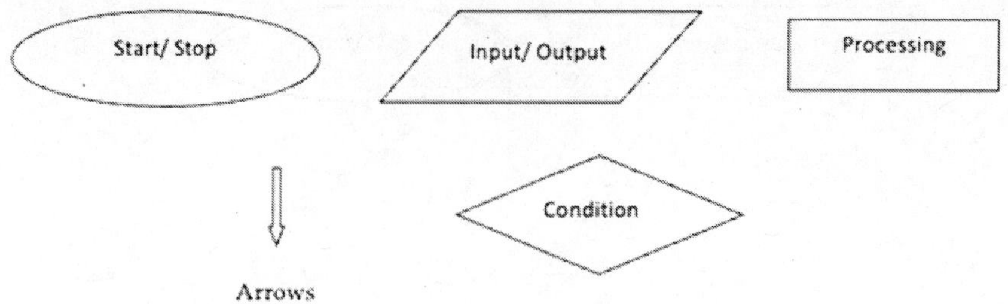

Figure 1.1: The basic building blocks of a flowchart

Let us embark on this journey through simple input-output programs and discover the power of these fundamental building blocks.

Structure

In this chapter, there are a total of 21 programs, and four sub-topics complement each program. The following topics will be covered with each program:

- Understand the program objective with sample input and outputs. It will give the user an understanding of what kind of user input is expected and what result will be projected for a particular program.
- Understand the program with an algorithm. This will help the user to understand the methodology behind writing the sequence of steps required to solve a program.
- Visualize the program flow with flowcharts. Program objectives can be understood easily with the flowchart representation. Users will understand which symbols to use in which context throughout different program's flowchart representations.
- Python source code of each program. Each program's source code in Python programming language is provided to the user so the user can understand the basic operations of the language. An explanation of each code is also provided.
- C implementation of each program. Users can learn the basic concepts of C language with the provided C language code and its explanation for every program.

Objectives

In this chapter, the reader will learn the fundamentals of input-output operations and their significance in program development. We will discuss designing algorithms to perform basic input and output operations. We will acquire the skills to create visual representations of program flow using flowcharts and the ability to implement simple input-output programs using Python and C programming languages. With the sample codes, users can gain hands-on experience. We will also gain problem-solving skills related to simple basic problems, such as accepting user input, performing calculations, and displaying results.

Program 1.1: Print your name

Take your name as input and print **`Hello name`**.

Sample input output

Test case #1:

Input: `Neo`

Output: **`Hello Neo`**

Test case #2:

Input: `Sam`

Output: **`Hello Sam`**

Test case #3:

Input: `John Will`

Output: **`Hello John Will`**

Algorithm

To run the above program, the following steps are needed to be followed:

Step 1. **`Start`**

Step 2. **`Enter your name in name`**

Step 3. **`Print "Hello" name`**

Step 4. **`Stop`**

Flowchart

Figure 1.2 illustrates the program in the form of a flowchart:

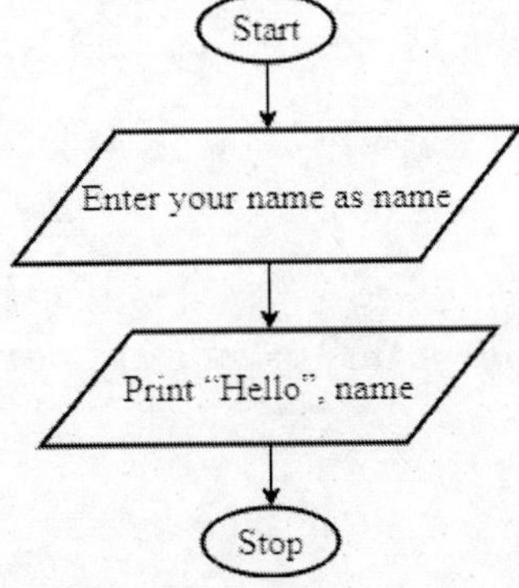

***Figure 1.2:** Flowchart illustrating program 1.1*

Python code

Python code for the *program 1.1* is as follows:

```
# read a input from the user
name= input("Enter your name: ")
# print the name on the screen
print("Hello ", name)
```

Python code explanation

The program prompts the user to enter the name and then prints a greeting message containing the name.

`name = input("Enter your name: ")`: This line prompts the user to enter the name by printing the string **`Enter your name:`**. The **`input()`** function is used to read the user's input as a string and assign it to the variable name.

`print("Hello", name)`: This line uses the **`print()`** function to print the string **`Hello`** followed by the value of the name variable.

Python is an indentation-sensitive language. Indentation is used to mark the block of code.

Any statement preceded by **#** is a comment which does not execute. These comments are ignored by the compiler and used only for the user to understand the code.

C code

The C code of *program 1.1* is specified below:

```
#include <stdio.h>

int main()  //The execution of C program starts with main function
{
    char name[100]; //declared a variable of character type of size 10
    printf("Enter your name: ");
    gets(name);  // read a input from the user
    printf("Hello %s", name);   // print the name on the screen
    return 0;   // The main() function returns an integer value 0
}
```

C code explanation

`stdio.h` is a header file that should be included in the program to use various input-output functions. `Main()` function serves as the starting point for program execution. It is mandatory to write a main function in every C program. Here, **`int`** is written before **`main()`**. This means that the function **`main()`** will return an integer value after completing the program's execution. The last statement `return 0` returns a value 0 on successful execution of the program.

A variable **`name`** is declared as an array of 100 characters. **`gets()`** is an input function used to read a string. Referring to test *case #3*, **`gets()`** function also allows the space between words. Also, C uses **`%s`** as the format specifier for strings. Finally, we use **`printf()` `function`** to output the greeting message with the user's name.

Unlike Python, indentation is not important in C language. Each block of code is enclosed between parentheses.

Program 1.2: Print your lucky number

Take a number as input and print the number as **`Number entered by you is: number`**.

Sample input output

Test case #1:

Input: `10`

Output: **`Number entered by you is: 10`**

Test case #2:

Input: 55

Output: **`Number entered by you is: 55`**

Algorithm

The below steps illustrate the working of *program 1.2*:

Step 1. **`Start`**

Step 2. **`Enter a number in n`**

Step 3. **`Print "Number entered by you is : " n`**

Step 4. **`Stop`**

Flowchart

Figure 1.3 depicts the program in the form of a flowchart as follows:

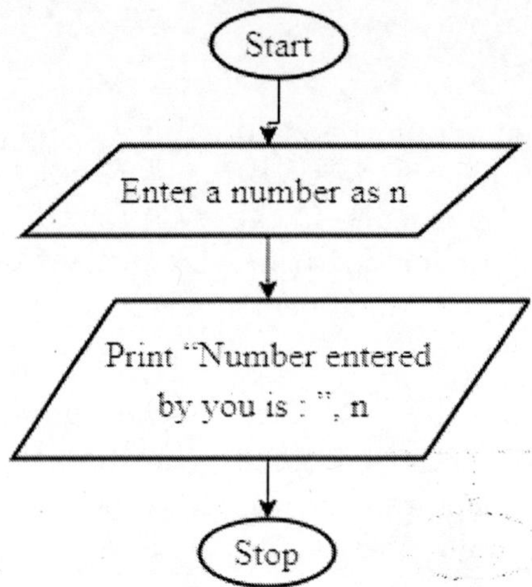

Figure 1.3: Flowchart for program 1.2

Python code

Python code for the *program1.2* is as follows:

```
# read an integer input from the user
n=int(input("Enter a number "))
#print the output on the screen
print("Number entered by you is: ", n)
```

Python code explanation

The first line of this code uses the **input()** function to prompt the user to enter a number. The **input()** function reads the user input as a string, so **int()** function is used to convert the input to an integer. The resulting integer is then assigned to the variable **n**.

The second line of the code uses the **print()** function to output a message to the user. The message includes the string **Number entered by you is:** and the value of the variable **n**. The **print()** function automatically adds a new line character at the end of the output, so the message is printed on a new line.

C code

C code for the *program 1.2* is as follows:

```
#include <stdio.h>
int main() {
    int n;  //declared a variable of integer type
```

```
    printf("Enter a number: ");
    scanf("%d", &n); // read a input from the user
    printf("Number entered by you is: %d\n", n); // print the output on the screen
    return 0; // The main() function returns an integer value 0
}
```

C code explanation

This code prompts the user to enter a number, reads the user's input in a variable **n**, and then prints out the entered number. C uses **%d** as the format specifier for integers.

Program 1.3: Print your details

Take the name, age, address, and class 12th marks as input and print its **name is age years old, lives in address, and scored marks in 12th**.

Sample input output

Test case #1:

Input:

```
Enter your name: Shikha
Enter your age: 42
Enter your address: Delhi
Enter your marks: 40
```

Output:

```
Shikha is 42 years old, lives in Delhi, and scored 40 marks in 12th.
```

Test case #2:

Input:

```
Enter your name: John Gill
Enter your age: 10
Enter your address: Noida, UP
Enter your marks: 30
```

Output:

```
John Gill is 10 years old, lives in Noida, UP, and scored 30 marks in 12th.
```

Algorithm

Steps to execute the *program 1.3* are mentioned as follows:

Step 1. **Start**

Step 2. **Enter your name, age, address, and marks as n, age, address, m**

Step 3. **Print n, " is ", age, " years old, lives in ", address, " and scored ", m, " marks in 12th."**

Step 4. **Stop**

Flowchart

The flowchart of the algorithm is illustrated in *Figure 1.4*:

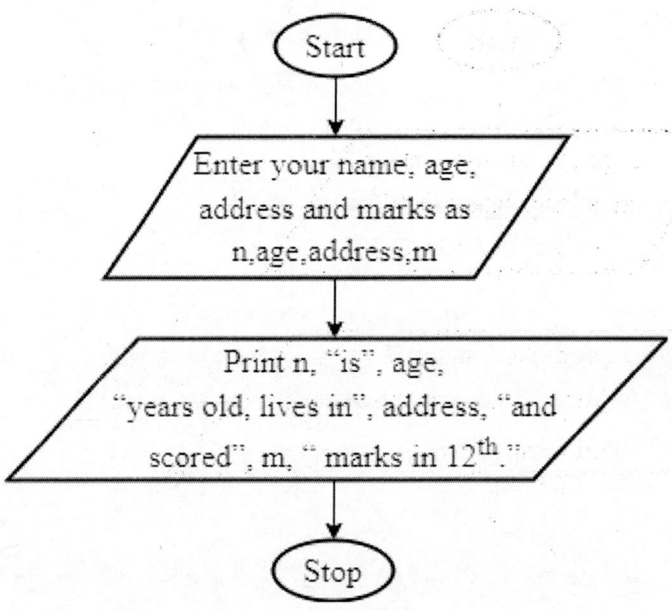

***Figure 1.4**: Flowchart illustrating program 1.3*

Python code

The following describes the Python code for *program 1.3*:

```
#read name and address as string input
n=input("Enter your name: ")
address=input("Enter your address: ")
#read age as integer input
age=int(input("Enter your age: "))
```

```
m=int(input("Enter your marks: "))
# print the output
print( n, "is", age, "years old, lives in ", address, " and scored ",
m, " marks in 12th.")
```

Python code explanation

The first four lines of this code use the **input()** function to prompt a message and take input from the user in variables **n**, **age**, **address**, and **m**.

Then, the **print()** function is used to output a message to the user. The message includes the variables **n**, **age**, **address**, and **m** along with some strings that provide context for the values.

C code

The following describes the C code for *program1.3*:

```
/* Take the name, age, address, and class 12th marks as input
and print as name is age years old, lives in address, and
scored marks in 12th. */

#include <stdio.h>

int main() {
//declared two variable of character type of each of size 100
    char n[100], address[100];
    int age, m; //declared two variable of integer type

    printf("Enter your name: ");
    gets(n); // read a string as input from the user

    printf("Enter your age: ");
    scanf("%d", &age); // read an integer input from the user

    fflush(stdin); //function to clear input buffer
    printf("Enter your address: ");
    gets(address); // read a string as input from the user
```

```

    printf("Enter your marks: ");
    scanf("%d", &m);  // read an integer input from the user

    // print the output on the screen
     printf("%s is %d years old, lives in %s, and scored %d marks in 12th.\n", n, age, address, m);

    return 0;
}
```

C code explanation

In this C code, the variables **n**, **age**, **address**, and **m** are first declared. Since **n** and **address** are strings; we declare them as character arrays with a fixed size 100. The **age** and **m** variables are declared as integers.

Next, **printf()** function prompts the user to enter their name, age, address, and marks. For string-type variables, we have used the **gets()** function so that it can take multiple words together. Before the second use of the **gets()** function, the **fflush()** function is used as it clears the buffer and helps in the smooth handling of the **gets()** function. For integer-type input, the **scanf()** function reads the user's input and stores it in the appropriate variable.

Finally, the **printf()** function prints an output message to the user, including their name, age, address, and marks. We use placeholders like **%s** (for string) and **%d** (for integer) to substitute the values of the variables in the message.

Program 1.4: Find sum of two numbers

Take two numbers as input and print their **sum**.

Sample input output

Test case #1:

Input:

```
Enter first number: 56
Enter second number: 34
```

Output:

```
Sum = 90
```

Test case #2:

Input:

```
Enter first number: -23
Enter second number: 45
```

Output:

```
Sum = 22
```

Test case #3:

Input:

```
Enter first number: -198
Enter second number: -23
```

Output:

```
Sum = -221
```

Algorithm

To run the *program 1.4,* the following steps are needed to be followed:

Step 1. `Start`

Step 2. `Enter two numbers as n and m`

Step 3. `sum = n+m`

Step 4. `Print "Sum=" sum`

Step 5. `Stop`

Flowchart

The flowchart of the algorithm is illustrated in *Figure 1.5*:

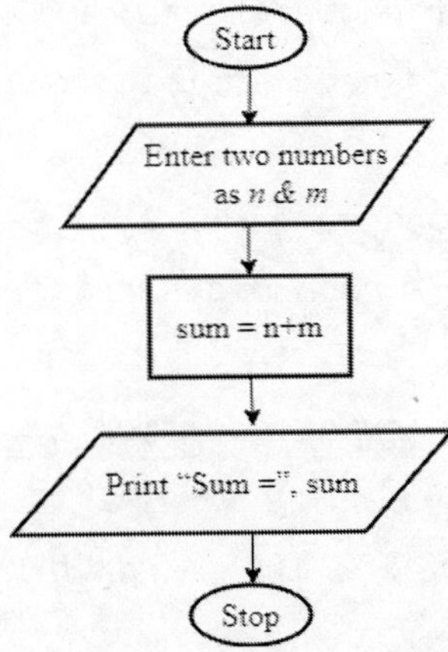

***Figure 1.5**: Flowchart for summation of two numbers*

Python code

Here is the Python source code for *program1.4*:

```
#read two integer inputs from the user
n=int(input("Enter first number: "))
m=int(input("Enter second number: "))
#performed addition of two numbers
sum= n+m
#print the output on the screen
print("Sum =", sum)
```

Python code explanation

This code prompts the user to enter two numbers, **n**, and **m** using the **input()** function preceded by the **int()** function. It calculates their sum and prints it to the console using print() function.

C code

Here is the C source code for *program 1.4*:

```
#include <stdio.h>

int main() {
    int n, m, sum; //declared three variable of integer type


    printf("Enter first number: ");
    scanf("%d", &n); // read an integer input from the user

    printf("Enter second number: ");
    scanf("%d", &m); // read another integer input from the user

    sum = n + m; //performed addition of two numbers

    printf("Sum = %d\n", sum);  // print the output on the screen

```

```
    return 0;
}
```

C code explanation

In this C code, we first declare **n**, **m**, and **sum** as integers. **Printf()** and **scanf()** functions prompt a message and take the input from the user.

The sum of **n** and **m** is calculated and stored in the variable **sum**. Finally, the output is printed using **printf() function**.

Program 1.5: Find product of two numbers

Take two numbers as input and print their **product**.

Sample input output

Test case #1:

Input:

```
Enter first number: 20
Enter second number: 56
```

Output:

```
Product = 1120
```

Test case #2:

Input:

```
Enter first number: -34
Enter second number: 67
```

Output:

```
Product = -2278
```

Test case #3:

Input:

```
Enter first number: -12
Enter second number: -32
```

Output:

```
Product = 384
```

Algorithm

The stages for running *program 1.5* are shown below:

Step 1. **Start**

Step 2. **Enter two numbers as n and m**

Step 3. **p = n * m**

Step 4. **Print "Product =", p**

Step 5. **Stop**

Flowchart

The flowchart of *program 1.5* is shown in *Figure 1.6*:

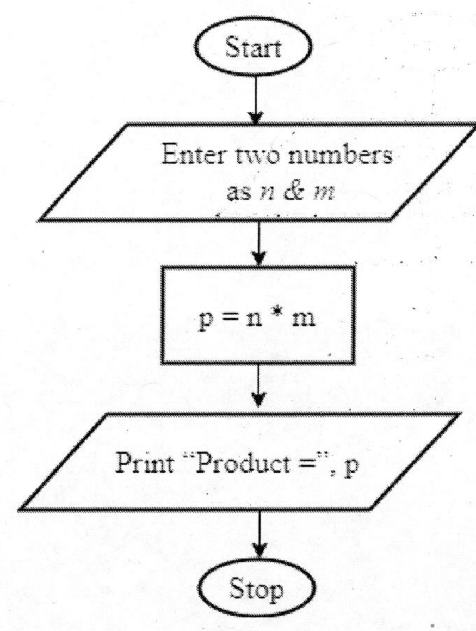

***Figure 1.6**: Flowchart for product of two numbers*

Python code

The Python source code for *program 1.5* is available here:

```
#read two integer inputs from the user
n=int(input("Enter first number: "))
m=int(input("Enter second number: "))
#performed multiplication of two numbers
p= n  * m
```

```
#print the output on the screen
print("Product =", p)
```

Python code explanation

This code prompts the user to enter two numbers, **n**, and **m** using the **input()** function preceded by the **int()** function. It calculates their product and prints it to the console.

C code

The C source code for *program 1.5* is available here:

```
#include <stdio.h>

int main() {
    int n, m, p;

    printf("Enter first number: ");
    scanf("%d", &n); // read an integer input from the user

    printf("Enter second number: ");
    scanf("%d", &m); // read an integer input from the user

    p = n * m; //performed multiplication of two numbers

    printf("Product = %d\n", p); // print the output on the screen

    return 0;
}
```

C code explanation

This C code prompts the user to enter two numbers, **n**, and **m** then calculates their product and prints it to the console.

It declares three integer variables (**n, m,** and **p**). Then, use the **scanf()** function to read the values of **n** and **m** from the console.

It then calculates its product, stores it in the variable **p**, and finally prints out the **p** value using the **printf()** function.

Program 1.6: Perform division

Take two numbers (dividend and divisor) as input and print the **`quotient and remainder`**.

Sample input output

Test case #1:

Input:

```
Enter first number: 98
Enter second number: 3
```

Output:

```
Quotient = 32 Remainder = 2
```

Test case #2:

Input:

```
Enter first number: 936
Enter second number: 6
```

Output:

```
Quotient = 156 Remainder = 0
```

Test case #3:

Input:

```
Enter first number: 56
Enter second number: 76
```

Output:

```
Quotient = 0 Remainder = 56
```

Algorithm

The following are the steps for running *program 1.6*:

Step 1. **`Start`**

Step 2. **`Enter two numbers as n and m`**

Step 3. **`p = n/m`**

Step 4. **`r = n%m`**

Step 5. **`Print "Quotient =", p, " Remainder = ", r`**

Step 6. **`Stop`**

Flowchart

Figure 1.7 shows an illustration of the *program 1.6* flowchart:

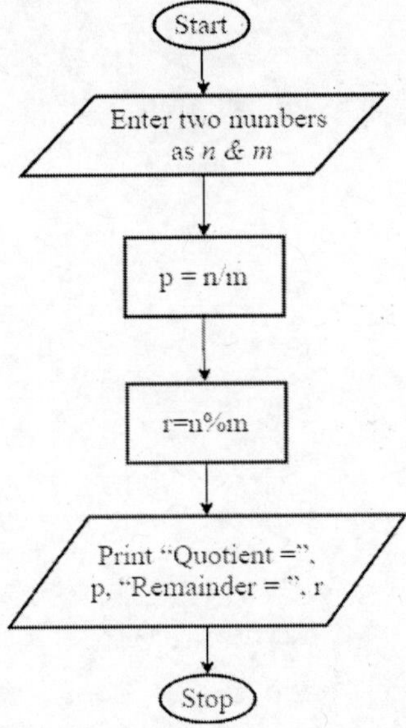

Figure 1.7*: Flowchart illustrating program 1.6*

Python code

The *program 1.6* source code in Python is available here:

```
#read two integer inputs from the user
n=int(input("Enter first number: "))
m=int(input("Enter second number: "))
#performed division to obtain quotient
p= n// m
#obtained remainder using % operator
r=n%m
#print the output on the screen
print("Quotient =", p, "Remainder = ", r)
```

Python code explanation

This code prompts the user to enter two numbers, **n**, and **m** using the **input()** function preceded by the **int()** function. It calculates their quotient and the remainder and prints it to the console.

In line three, the// operator is used for integer division to generate a quotient. In line four, the `%` operator is used to find the remainder.

C code

The *program 1.6* source code in C is available here:

```
#include <stdio.h>

int main() {
     int n, m, p, r;

     printf("Enter first number: ");
     scanf("%d", &n); // read an integer input from the user

     printf("Enter second number: ");
     scanf("%d", &m); // read an integer input from the user

     p = n / m; //performed division to obtain quotient
     r = n % m; // obtained remainder using % operator

     printf("Quotient = %d Remainder = %d\n", p, r); // print the output on the screen

     return 0;
}

```

C code explanation

This C code prompts the user to enter two numbers, **n**, and **m**, then calculates their quotient and remainder and prints them to the console. It does this by declaring four integer variables (**n**, **m**, **p**, and **r**) and then using the **`scanf()`** function to read the values of **n** and **m** from the console.

It then calculates their quotient and remainder using the **/** and **%** operators and stores them in the variables **p** and **r**. Finally, it prints out the values of **p** and **r** using the **`printf()`** function.

Program 1.7: Print equivalent rational numbers

Print three equivalent rational numbers of a given rational number.

Sample input output

Test case #1:

Input:

```
Enter numerator: 3
Enter denominator: 6
```

Output:

```
Equivalent fractions are:  6 / 12, 9 / 18, 12 / 24
```

Test case #2:

Input:

```
Enter numerator: 9
Enter denominator: 4
```

Output:

```
Equivalent fractions are:  18 / 8,  27 / 12,  36 / 16
```

Algorithm

The following steps are provided for running *program 1.7*:

Step 1. `Start`

Step 2. `Enter numerator and denominator as n and m`

Step 3. `Print "Equivalent fractions are: ", n*2, /, m*2, ,,n*3, /, m*3, ,, n*4, /,m*4`

Step 4. `Stop`

Flowchart

Figure 1.8 illustrates the algorithm flowchart:

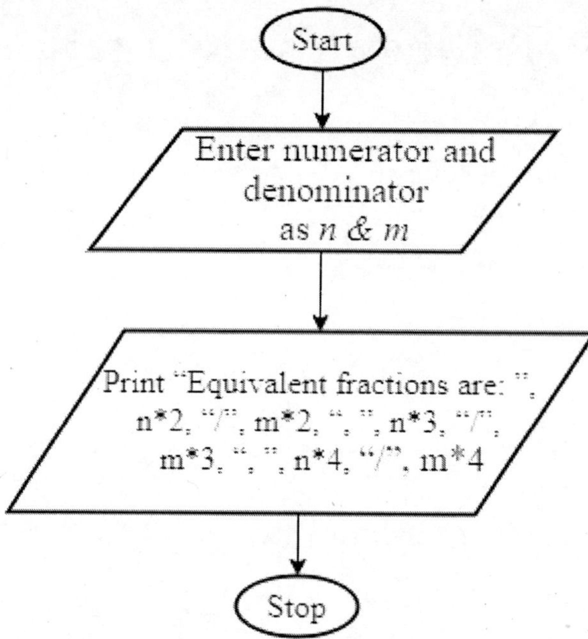

Figure 1.8: *Flowchart to obtain the equivalent rational numbers*

Python code

The source code for *program 1.7* in Python is provided below:

```
#read two integer inputs from the user
n=int(input(" Enter numerator: "))
m=int(input(" Enter denominator: "))

#print the output on the screen
#it is obtained by multiplying numerator & #denominator by 2, the 3 and then 4
print(" Equivalent fractions are : ", n*2, "/", m*2, ", ", n*3, "/", m*3, ", ", n*4, "/", m*4)
```

Python code explanation

This code prompts the user to enter two numbers, **n** and **m**, representing the numerator and denominator of a fraction using the **input()** function preceded by the **int()** function.

It then calculates three equivalent fractions by multiplying the numerator and denominator by **2**, **3**, and **4**, respectively, and prints them using the **print()** function.

C code

The source code for *program 1.7* in C is provided below:

```
#include <stdio.h>

int main() {
    int n, m;

    printf("Enter numerator: ");
    scanf("%d", &n); // read an integer input from the user

    printf("Enter denominator: ");
    scanf("%d", &m); // read an integer input from the user

    // print the output on the screen
    //it is obtained by multiplying numerator & denominator by 2, the 3 and then 4
     printf("Equivalent fractions are: %d/%d, %d/%d, %d/%d\n",  n*2, m*2, n*3, m*3, n*4, m*4);

    return 0;
}
```

C code explanation

This C code prompts the user to enter two numbers, `n` and `m`, representing the numerator and denominator of a fraction, respectively.

It then calculates three equivalent fractions by multiplying the numerator and denominator by **2**, **3**, and **4**, respectively, and prints them to the console using the **`printf()`** function.

Program 1.8: Swapping using temporary variable

Swap two variables provided by the user using a temporary variable.

Sample input output

Test case #1:

Input:

```
Enter first number: 65
Enter second number: 92
```

Output:

```
Numbers after swapping are 92 65
```

Test case # 2:

Input:

```
Enter first number: 34
Enter second number: 98
```

Output:

```
Numbers after swapping are 98 34
```

Algorithm

Follow these steps to run the *program1.8*:

Step 1. **Start**

Step 2. **Enter two numbers as n and m**

Step 3. **temp = n**

Step 4. **n=m**

Step 5. **m= temp**

Step 6. **Print "Numbers after swapping are ", n, m**

Step 7. **Stop**

Flowchart

The flowchart of the algorithm is illustrated in *Figure 1.9*:

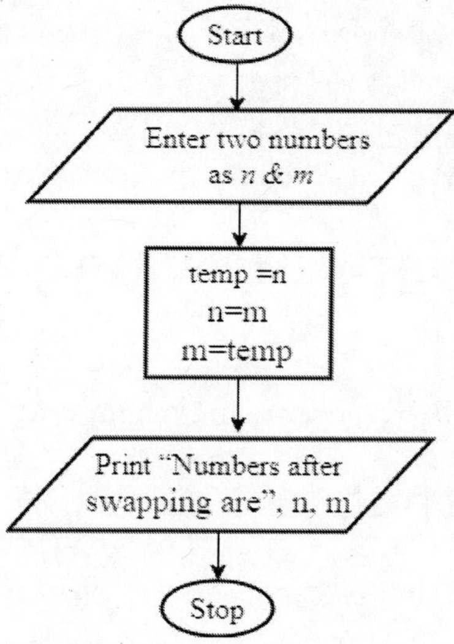

***Figure 1.9**: Flowchart for swapping two numbers using temporary variable*

Python code

The Python source code for *program 1.8* is provided here:

```
#read two integer inputs from the user
n=int(input("Enter first number: "))
m=int(input("Enter second number: "))
temp = n #store the value of n in a temporary variable
n=m #copy second variable to first one
m = temp #copy the value of first variable form temporary variable to second variable

#print the output on the screen
print("Numbers after swapping are ", n, m)
```

Python code explanation

The code takes two numbers as input from the user in **n** and **m** variables. It then stores the value of **n** in **temp**, assigns the value of **m** to **n**, and finally assigns the value of **temp** to **m**.

Finally, the interchanged values are displayed in the console.

C code

The C source code for *program 1.8* is provided here:

```
#include <stdio.h>

int main() {
    int n, m, temp;

    printf("Enter first number: ");
    scanf("%d", &n); // read an integer input from the user

    printf("Enter second number: ");
    scanf("%d", &m); // read an integer input from the user

   temp = n; //store the value of n in a temporary variable
   n = m;  //copy second variable to first one
```

```
    m = temp; // copy the value of first variable form temporary variable to second variable.

    // print the output on the screen
    printf("Numbers after swapping are : n = %d, m = %d\n", n, m);

    return 0;
}
```

C code explanation

This C code prompts the user to enter two numbers, **`n`**, and **`m`**, then swaps their values using a temporary variable **`temp`**. It does this by declaring three integer variables (**`n, m`**, and **`temp`**) and then using **`scanf()`** to read the values of **`n`** and **`m`** from the console. It then stores the value of **`n`** in **`temp`**, assigns the value of **`m`** to **`n`**, and finally assigns the value of **`temp`** to **`m`**.

This has the effect of swapping the values of **`n`** and **`m`**. Finally, the code prints out the new values of **`n`** and **`m`** using **`print()`**.

Program 1.9: Swapping without temporary variable

Swap two variables provided by the user without using a temporary variable.

Sample input output

Test case #1:

Input:

```
Enter first number: 66
Enter second number: 99
```

Output:

```
Numbers after swapping are 99 66
```

Test case #2:

Input:

```
Enter first number: 34
Enter second number: 123
```

Output:

```
Numbers after swapping are 123 34
```

Algorithm

The following steps are provided for running *program1.9*:

Step 1. **`Start`**

Step 2. **`Enter two numbers as n and m`**

Step 3. `n= n+m`

Step 4. `m= n-m`

Step 5. `n= n-m`

Step 6. **`Print "Numbers after swapping are ", n, m`**

Step 7. **`Stop`**

Flowchart

Figure 1.10 depicts the *program1.9* flowchart:

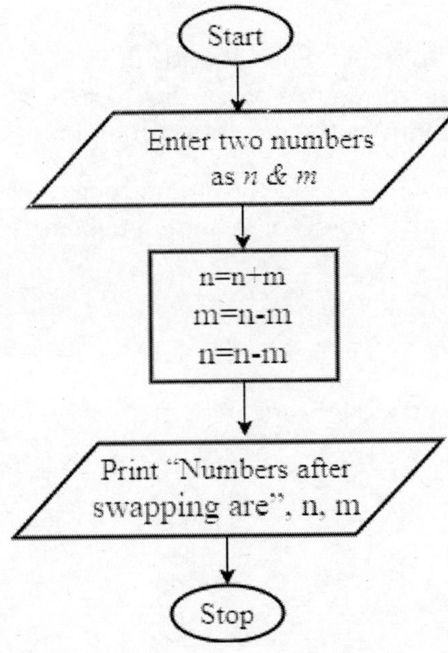

***Figure 1.10**: Flowchart illustrating program 1.9*

Python code

The following describes the Python code for *program 1.9*:

```
#read two integer inputs from the user
n=int(input("Enter first number: "))
```

```
m=int(input("Enter second number: "))

#to swap to numbers without temporary variable
#some simple arithmetic is applied

n = n+m
m = n-m
n = n-m

#print the output on the screen
print("Numbers after swapping are ", n, m)
```

This code takes two integers as input from the user and stores them in variables **n** and **m** respectively. It then swaps the values of these variables without using a temporary variable.

It asks the user to enter two numbers. First, it adds the values of **n** and **m** and assigns the result to **n**. Then, it assigns the difference of **n** and **m** to **m**. Since **n** now contains the sum of the original **n** and **m**, **m** now contains the original value of **n**.

Finally, it assigns the difference of **n** and **m** to **n**. Since **m** now contains the original value of **n**, **n** now contains the original value of **m**, the values are swapped. Then, it prints the swapped values.

C code

The following describes the C code for *program 1.9*:

```
#include <stdio.h>

int main() {
    int n, m, temp;

    printf("Enter first number: ");
    scanf("%d", &n); // read an integer input from the user

    printf("Enter second number: ");
    scanf("%d", &m); // read an integer input from the user

```

```
    //to swap to numbers without temporary variable
    // some simple arithmetic is applied

    n = n + m;
    m = n - m;
    n = n - m;

    // print the output on the screen
    printf("Numbers after swapping are %d %d\n", n, m);

    return 0;
}
```

C code explanation

This C code prompts the user to enter two numbers, `n`, and `m`, and then swaps their values without using a temporary variable. It does this by declaring two integer variables (`n` and `m`) and then using `scanf()` to read the values of `n` and `m` from the console.

It then performs the swap using arithmetic operations: First, it adds `n` and `m` together and stores the result in `n`. Then, it subtracts the original value of `m` from the new value of `n` and assigns the result to `m`.

Finally, it subtracts the new value of `m` from the new value of `n` and assigns the result to `n`. This has the effect of swapping the values of `n` and `m`. Finally, the code prints out the new values of `n` and `m` using `printf()`.

Program 1.10: Find square of a number

Take a number as input and print the square of the number as **`Square of the number is number`**.

Sample input output

Test case #1:

Input:

```
Enter a number 8
```

Output:

```
Square of 8 is 64
```

Test case # 2:

Input:

`Enter a number: 34`

Output:

`Square of 34 is 1156`

Algorithm

The following are the steps for running *program 1.10*:

Step 1. **`Start`**

Step 2. **`Enter a number in n`**

Step 3. **`Print "Square of ", n, " is ", n*n`**

Step 4. **`Stop`**

Flowchart

The flowchart for *program1.10* is shown in *Figure 1.11*:

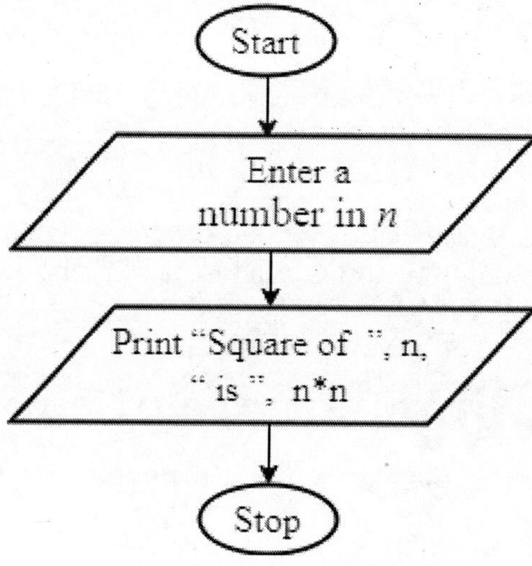

***Figure 1.11**: Flowchart for finding the square of a number*

Python code

The Python code for *program 1.10* is as follows:

```
#read an integer input from the user
n=int(input("Enter a number "))
```

```

#print the square of the number on the screen
print("Square of  ", n, " is ",  n*n)
```

Python code explanation

This code takes an integer input from the user using the **`input()`** function and stores it in the variable **`n`**. It then calculates the square of the input number by multiplying **`n`** with itself and prints the result using the **`print()`** function.

C code

The C code for *program 1.10* is as follows:

```c
#include <stdio.h>

int main() {
    int n;

    printf("Enter a number ");
    scanf("%d", &n); // read an integer input from the user

    // print the square of the number on the screen
    printf("Square of %d is %d\n", n, n*n);

    return 0;
}
```

C code explanation

This C code prompts the user to enter a number, **`n`**, and then calculates and prints its square. It does this by declaring an integer variable **`n`** and then using **`scanf()`** to read the value of**`n`** from the console. It then calculates the square of **`n`** using the **`*`** operator.

Finally, the code prints out the result using **`printf()`** function using format specifiers **`%d`**.

Program 1.11: Find cube of a number

Take a number as input and print the cube of the number as the **`Cube of the number is number`**.

Sample input output

Test case #1:

Input:

```
Enter a number 7
```

Output:

```
Cube of 7 is 343
```

Test case #2:

Input:

```
Enter a number 21
```

Output:

```
Cube of 21 is 9261
```

Algorithm

To run the *program 1.11*, the following steps are formulated as an algorithm:

Step 1. **Start**

Step 2. **Enter a number in n**

Step 3. **Print "Cube of ", n, " is ", n*n*n**

Step 4. **Stop**

Flowchart

Figure 1.12 depicts the flowchart of *program 1.11*:

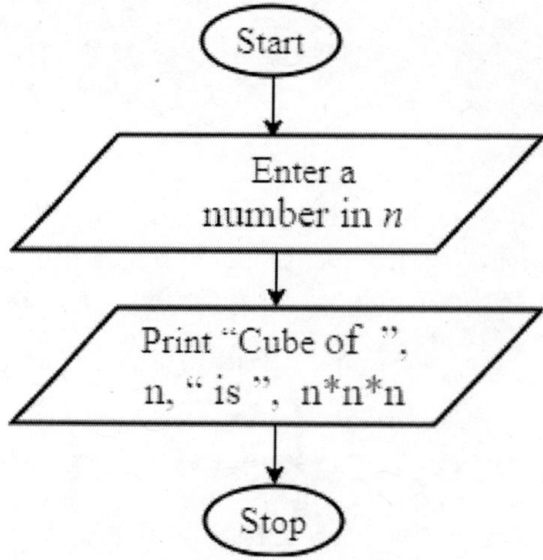

***Figure 1.12**: Flowchart to find the cube of a number*

Python code

The *program 1.11* source code in Python is specified as follows:

```
#read an integer input from the user
n=int(input("Enter a number "))
#print the cube of the number on the screen
print("Cube of ", n, " is ",  n*n*n)
```

Python code explanation

This code takes an integer input from the user using the **input()** function and stores it in the variable **n**. It then calculates the cube of the input number by multiplying **n** with itself three times **(n*n*n)** and prints the result using the **print()**function.

C code

The *program 1.11* source code in C is specified as follows:

```
#include<stdio.h>
void main()
{
int n;
printf("Enter a number ");
scanf("%d", &n); // read an integer input from the user

// print the cube of the number on the screen
printf("Cube of %d is %d", n, n*n*n);
}
```

C code explanation

This C code takes an integer input from the user and calculates the cube of the input number using the formula **n*n*n**. The output is then printed to the console using the **printf()** function.

Program 1.12: Find average

Take three numbers as input and print their **average**.

Sample input output

Test case #1:

Input:

```
Enter first number 23
Enter second number 33
Enter third number 65
```

Output:

```
Average = 40.333333333333336
```

Test case #2:

Input:

```
Enter first number 7
Enter second number 3
Enter third number 4
```

Output:

```
Average = 4.6666666667
```

Algorithm

To run the *program 1.12,* the algorithm is as follows:

Step 1. **Start**

Step 2. **Enter three numbers as n, m, and p**

Step 3. **a = (n+m+p)/3**

Step 4. **Print "Average = ", a**

Step 5. **Stop**

Flowchart

The flowchart of the *program 1.12* is illustrated in *Figure 1.13*:

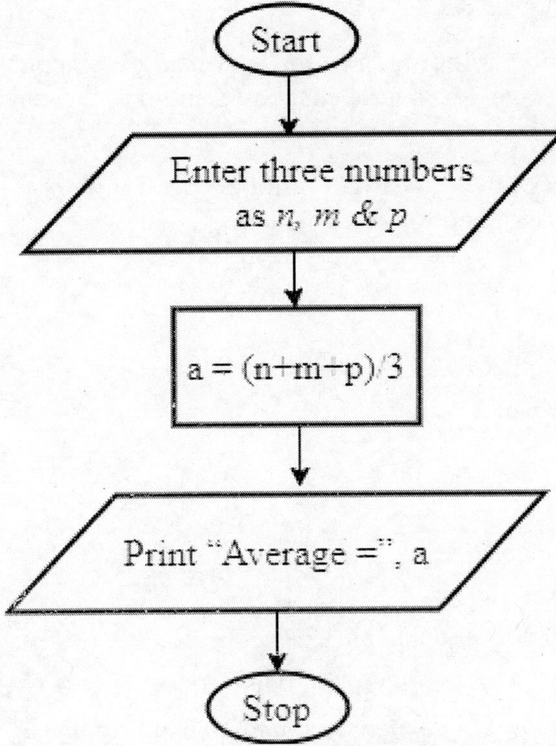

***Figure 1.13**: Flowchart illustrating program 1.12*

Python code

Here is the Python source code for *program 1.12*:

```
#read three integer inputs from the user
n=int(input("Enter first number "))
m=int(input("Enter second number "))
p=int(input("Enter third number "))

#find average
a = (n+m+p)/3

#print the output on the screen
print("Average = ", a)
```

Python code explanation

This code takes three integer inputs from the user using the **input()**and **int()**functions and calculates their average. The average is then printed to the console using the **print()** function.

It calculates the average of the three input numbers by adding **n**, **m**, and **p** and dividing the sum by **3**. The result is assigned to the variable **a**.

C code

Here is the C source code for *program 1.12*:

```
#include<stdio.h>
void main()
{
int n,m, p;
float a;
printf("Enter three numbers");
scanf("%d%d%d",& n,&m, &p); // read three integer inputs from the user
//find the sum of three numbers and divide it by 3
a = (n+m+p)/3.0;
// print the output on the screen
printf("Average =%f", a);
}
```

C code explanation

This code takes three integer inputs from the user using the **scanf()** function and calculates their average. The average is then printed to the console using the **printf()** function.

Here, the sum of three numbers is divided by **3.0**. In C, dividing an integer value by an integer value gives an integer result. However, an average of three numbers can be a real number. Hence, the **sum** is divided by a float number (**3.0**).

Program 1.13: Find percentage marks

Take your marks in 5 subjects as input and print the **percentage marks**.

Sample input output

Test case #1:

Input:

```
Enter marks in first subject 20
Enter marks in 2nd subject 21
Enter marks in 3rd subject 21
Enter marks in 4th subject 21
Enter marks in 5th subject 21
```

Output:

```
Percentage = 20.8
```

Test case #2:

Input:

```
Enter marks in first subject 70
Enter marks in 2nd subject 80
Enter marks in 3rd subject 90
Enter marks in 4th subject 85
Enter marks in 5th subject 75
```

Output:

```
Percentage = 80
```

Algorithm

The following steps are expressed as an algorithm to execute *program 1.13*:

Step 1. **Start**

Step 2. **Enter marks in 5 subjects as s1, s2, s3, s4 and s5**

Step 3. **a= (s1+s2+s3+s4+s5)***100/500

Step 4. **Print "Percentage = ", a**

Step 5. **Stop**

Flowchart

Figure 1.14 shows the flowchart of *program 1.13*:

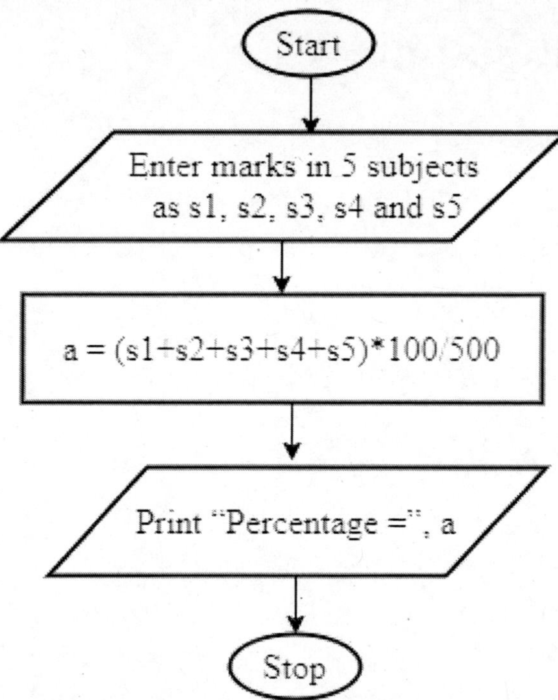

***Figure 1.14**: Flowchart illustrating program 1.13*

Python code

The following describes the Python source code for *program 1.13*:

```
#read marks in five subjects as inputs from the user

s1=int(input(" Enter marks in first subject "))
s2=int(input("Enter marks in 2nd subject "))
s3=int(input("Enter marks in 3rd subject "))
s4=int(input("Enter marks in 4th subject "))
s5=int(input("Enter marks in 5th subject "))

#find percentage marks
a = (s1+s2+s3+s4+s5)*100/500

#print the output on the screen
print ("Percentage =", a)
```

Python code explanation

This code prompts the user to enter marks in five different subjects and calculates the percentage of marks obtained by the student. The percentage marks is calculated by dividing the sum of all the marks by 500 and multiplying the result by 100. The result is stored in the variable **a**. Finally, the output is printed on the console.

C code

The following describes the Python source code for *program 1.13*:

```
#include<stdio.h>
void main()
{
int s1, s2, s3, s4, s5;
float a;
printf("Enter marks in 5 subjects ");
scanf("%d%d%d%d%d",&s1,&s2, &s3, &s4, &s5); // read five integer inputs from the user
//calculate the percentage of marks in 5 subjects
a = (s1+s2+s3+s4+s5)*100/500.0;
// print the output on the screen
printf ("Percentage = %f ", a);
}
```

C code explanation

This code prompts the user to enter marks in five different subjects, and entered values are stored in five different variables. The next line calculates the total marks obtained by adding marks in all five subjects and then multiplying the **sum** by **100/500.0** to get the percentage of marks. The result is stored in the variable **a** and displayed using the **printf()**function. It should be noted that the sum is divided by **500.0** to obtain the real value as result of the division.

Program 1.14: Convert meter to centimeter

Take length (in meters) as input and print it in **centimeters**.

Sample input output

Test case #1:

Input:

```
Enter length in meters 3.4567
```

Output:

```
Length in cm is 345.67
```

Test case #2:

Input:

```
Enter length in meters 10.5
```

Output:

```
Length in cm is 1050
```

Algorithm

The steps listed below are formed as an algorithm to run *program 1.14*:

Step 1. **Start**

Step 2. **Enter length in meters as m**

Step 3. **cm= m*100**

Step 4. **Print "Length in cm is ", cm**

Step 5. **Stop**

Flowchart

The flowchart of *program 1.14* is shown in *Figure 1.15*:

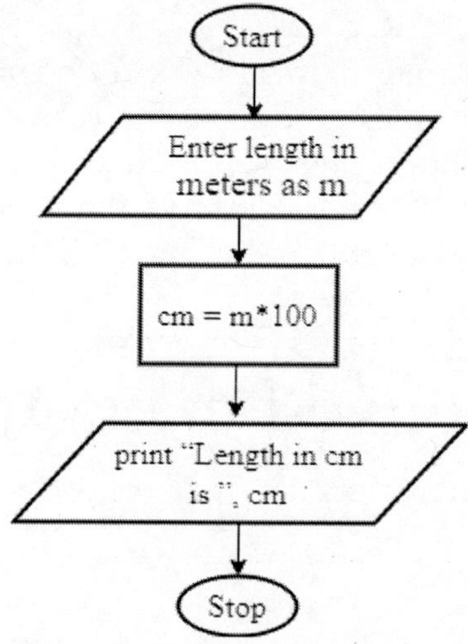

***Figure 1.15**: Flowchart of program 1.14*

Python code

The Python source code for *program 1.14* is as follows:

```
#read float type input from the user
m=float(input("Enter length in meters  "))
#convert cm to m by multiplying by 100
cm = m*100
#print the output on the screen
print("Length in cm is ", cm)
```

Python code explanation

This code prompts the user to enter a length in meters, then calculates and prints the equivalent length in centimeters. This program converts this by multiplying the m value by `100`, which is the conversion factor from meters to centimeters.

C code

The C source code for *program 1.14* looks as follows:

```
#include<stdio.h>
void main()
{
float m, cm;
printf("Enter length in meters");
scanf("%f",&m); // read a float input from the user
//to convert meter in cm, multiply it by 100
cm = m*100;
// print the output on the screen
printf("Length in cm is %f", cm);
}
```

C code explanation

This C language code is a simple example of converting a length measurement from one unit (meters) to another (centimeters) by multiplying the value of `m` by `100`, using input and output functions to interact with the user.

Program 1.15: Convert degree F to degree C

Take temperature (in degree F) as input and print it in **`degree C`**.

Sample input output

Test case #1:

Input:

```
Enter temperature in degree F: 98.4
```

Output:

```
Temperature in degree Celsius is 36.888888888888886
```

Test case #2:

Input:

```
Enter temperature in degree F: 32
```

Output:

```
Temperature in degree Celsius is 0.0
```

Algorithm

The steps to run *program 1.15* are listed below:

Step 1. **`Start`**

Step 2. **`Read temperature in degree F as F1`**

Step 1. **`C1=(F1-32)*5/9`**

Step 2. **`Print "Temperature in degree Celsius is ", C1`**

Step 3. **`Stop`**

Flowchart

Figure 1.16 shows an illustration of the *program 1.15* in a flowchart:

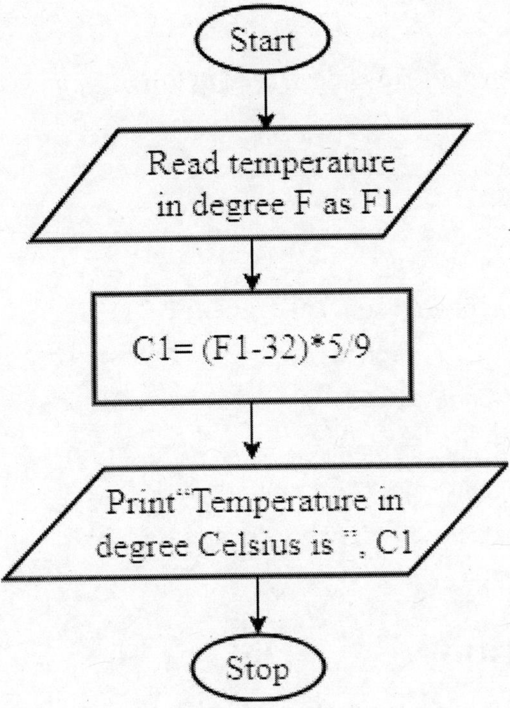

Figure 1.16: Flowchart of program 1.15

Python code

The Python source code for *program 1.15* is described below:

```
#read float type input from the user
F1 = float(input("Enter temperature in degree F: "))
#convert temp in F to C
C1 = (F1 - 32) * 5 / 9
#print the output on the screen
print("Temperature in degree Celsius is ", C1)
```

Python code explanation

This code prompts the user to enter a temperature in Fahrenheit and reads the input value as an integer, which is stored in the variable **F1**. Then, it converts the temperature in Fahrenheit to Celsius using the formula **(F1 - 32) * 5/9**, where **F1** is the temperature in Fahrenheit.

The result is stored in the variable **C1**. Finally, it prints the converted temperature in Celsius to the console.

C code

The C source code for *program 1.15* is described below:

```
#include<stdio.h>
void main()
{
float F1, C1;
printf("Enter temperature in degree F ");
scanf("%f",&F1); // read a float input from the user
//convert temp on F to C
C1= (F1-32)*5/9.0;
// print the output on the screen
printf("Temperature in degree Celsius is %f", C1);
}
```

C code explanation

This C program takes an input temperature in Fahrenheit and converts it to Celsius using the formula **`(F1-32)*5/9`**. Since temperature can be a real number, **`F1`** and **`C1`** are declared float, and the **`%f`** format specifier is used. Again, to obtain a real number as a result of division, **`9.0`** (a real number) is used in the denominator.

Program 1.16: Convert inch to feet

Take height (in inches) as input. Convert it into feet and display it as **`Your height is 5 feet 2 in`**.

Sample input output

Test case #1:

Input:

`Enter height in inches 63.5`

Output:

`Your height is 5.0 feet 3.5 in`

Test case #2:

Input:

`Enter height in inches 55.0`

Output:

```
Your height is 4.0 feet 7.0 in
```

Algorithm

The following steps are provided for running *program 1.16*:

Step 1. **`Start`**

Step 2. **`Read height in inches as i`**

Step 3. **`f = i/12`**

Step 4. **`in = i%12`**

Step 5. **`Display "Your height is ", f, " feet ",in, " inch. "`**

Step 6. **`Stop`**

Flowchart

Here, the flowchart of*program 1.16* is shown in *Figure 1.17*:

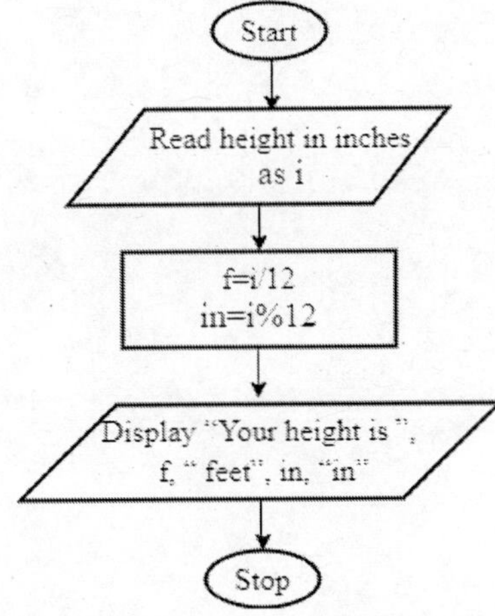

***Figure 1.17**: Flowchart illustrating program 1.16*

Python code

The Python source code of *program 1.16* is described as follows:

```
#read float type input from the user
i=float(input("Enter height in inches "))
#convert inch to feet-inch
f=i//12
```

```
inch = i%12
#print the output on the screen
print("Your height is ", f, " feet", inch, "in")
```

Python code explanation

This Python program takes an input height in inches in variable **i** and converts it to feet and inches. It calculates the number of whole feet in height by dividing **i** by **12** using the integer division operator **//** and stores the result in the variable **f**.

Then, it calculates the number of remaining inches by dividing the remainder of **i** by **12** using the modulus operator % and stores the result (remainder) in the variable **inch**. Also, note that the conversion to feet and inches is not rounded, so the output may include a fractional part for the inches.

C code

The C source code of *program 1.16* is described as follows:

```
#include<stdio.h>
void main()
{
int i, in, f;

printf("Enter height in inches ");
scanf("%d",&i); // read a float input from the user
//convert height given in inches to feet, inches
f=i/12;
in = i%12;
// print the output on the screen
printf("Your height is %d feet %d in", f, in);
}
```

C code explanation

This program takes an input height in inches in variable **i** and converts it to feet and inches. It declares two float variables, **in** and **i**, to hold the height in inches and remaining inches, respectively, and an integer variable **f**, to hold the number of feet in the height.

First, it calculates the number of whole feet in height by dividing **i** by **12**. Then, it calculates the remaining inches by taking the remainder of dividing **i** by **12** using % operater and then stores the result in the variable **in**. It finally prints the result to the console.

Program 1.17: Find area of a rectangle

Read two sides of a **`rectangle (in meters)`** as input and calculate its **`area`**.

Sample input output

Test case #1:

Input:

`Enter length of the rectangle` **`(in meters)`** `3.5`

`Enter breadth of the rectangle` **`(in meters)`** `5`

Output:

`Area of (3.5 X 5.0) is 17.5 sq meter`

Test case #2:

Input:

`Enter length of the rectangle` **`(in meters)`** `4`

`Enter breadth of the rectangle` **`(in meters)`** `5`

Output:

`Area of (4.0X 5.0) is 20 sq meter`

Algorithm

The action listed below is an algorithm to execute *program 1.17*:

Step 1. **`Start`**

Step 2. **`Read two sides (in meters) of a rectangle as l and b`**

Step 3. **`area=l*b`**

Step 4. **`Display "Area of (", l, " X ", b, ") is “, area`**

Step 5. **`Stop`**

Flowchart

Program 1.17 flowchart is depicted in *Figure 1.18*:

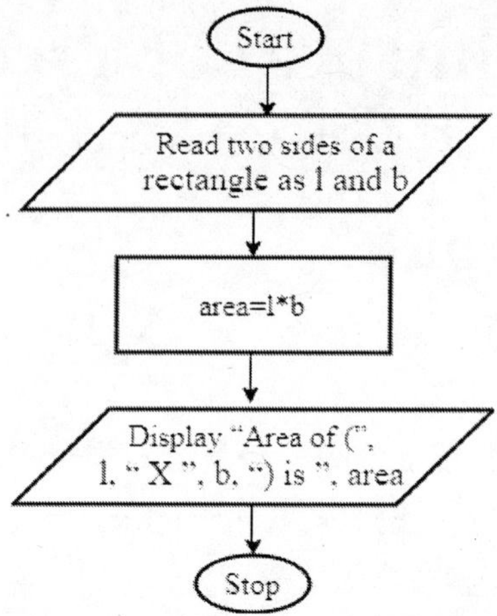

Figure 1.18: The flowchart of program 1.17

Python code

The Python source code for *program 1.17* is as follows:

```
#read float type inputs from the user
l=float(input("Enter length of the rectangle "))
b=float(input("Enter breadth of the rectangle "))
#obtain area
area=l*b
#print the output on the screen
print("Area of (", l, " X ", b, ") is ", area)
```

Python code explanation

The code reads the length and breadth of a rectangle, calculates its area by multiplying length and breadth, and then prints the area to the console.

C code

The C source code for *program 1.17* is as follows:

```
#include<stdio.h>
void main()
{
float l,b, area;
```

```
printf("Enter two sides of a rectangle (in meters)");
scanf("%f%f",&l, &b); // read two float inputs from the user
//obtain area by multiplying length and breath
area = l*b;
// print the output on the screen
printf("Area of ( %f X %f) is %f sq meter",l,b, area);
}
```

C code explanation

This program takes the sides of a rectangle as input. The area of the rectangle is calculated by multiplying the **`length (l)`** and **`breadth (b)`** of the rectangle, and the result is stored in the **`area`** variable.

Finally, the **`printf()`** function is used to display the area of the rectangle on the screen, along with the values of **`l`** and **`b`**.

Program 1.18: Find area of a circle

Read the radius of a **`circle`** as input and calculate its **`area`**.

Sample input output

Test case #1:

Input:

`Enter the radius of circle 4.5`

Output:

`Area of circle is 63.585`

Test case #2:

Input:

`Enter the radius of circle 2.4`

Output:

`Area of circle is 18.09`

Algorithm

Program 1.18 can be executed using the algorithm listed below:

Step 1. **`Start`**

Step 2. **`Read the radius of circle as r`**

Step 3. **pie=3.14**

Step 4. **area=pie*r*r**

Step 5. **Display "Area of circle is ", area**

Step 6. **Stop**

Flowchart

Figure 1.19 depicts the flowchart of *program 1.18*:

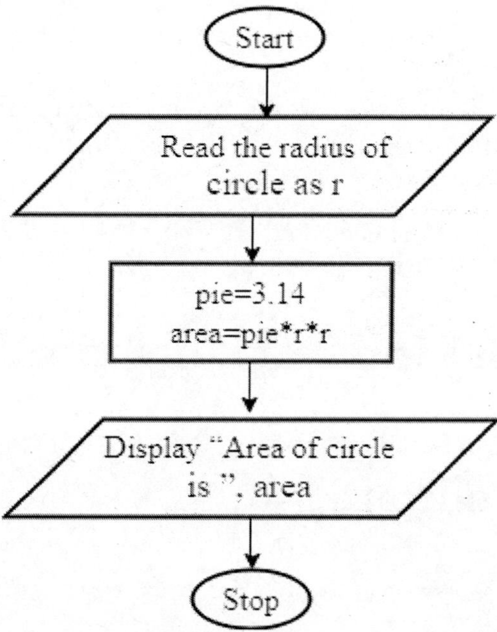

***Figure 1.19**: Flowchart for computing the area of a circle*

Python code

Here is the Python source code for *program 1.18*:

```
#read float type input from the user
r=float(input("Enter the radius of circle "))

#define constant value of Pie
pie=3.14

#obtain area
```

```
area=pie*r*r

#print the output on the screen
print("Area of circle is ", area)
```

Python code explanation

This code reads the radius of a circle from the user and calculates its area. The program starts with the user entering the circle's radius value using the **input()** function. The input value is read as a string and converted to float using the **float()** function.

The area of the circle is calculated using the formula $A = \pi r^2$, where **r** is the radius of the circle. The result is displayed on the screen using the **print()** function, along with a message that says **Area of circle is**.

C code

Here is the C source code for *program 1.18*:

```
#include<stdio.h>
void main()
{
float r, pie,area;
printf("Enter the radius of circle");
scanf("%f", &r); // read a float input from the user
//define value of pie
pie=3.14;
//find area of circle
area=pie*r*r;
// print the output on the screen
printf("Area of circle is %f", area);
}
```

C code explanation

The program calculates the area of a circle. The program starts with including the standard input-output header file using the **#include** directive. Three variables are declared in the main function: **r**, **pie**, and **area**. These variables are of type float. The value of the mathematical constant **pi** is assigned to a variable called **pie**.

The area of the circle is calculated using the formula **A = πr²**, where **r** is the radius of the circle. Finally, the **printf()** function is used to display the area of the circle on the screen, along with a message that says **Area of circle is**.

Program 1.19: Find area of parallelogram

Read the base and height of a **parallelogram** as area and compute its **area**.

Sample input output

Test case #1:

Input:

```
Enter base of a parallelogram 6.5
Enter height of a parallelogram 3.5
```

Output:

```
Area of (6.5 X 3.5) is 22.75
```

Test case #2:

Input:

```
Enter base of a parallelogram 3.5
Enter height of a parallelogram 4.5
```

Output:

```
Area of (3.500000 X 4.500000) is 15.750000
```

Algorithm

Program 1.19 can be executed using the steps listed below:

Step 1. **Start**

Step 2. **Read base and height of a parallelogram as b and h**

Step 3. **area=b*h**

Step 4. **Display "Area of (", b, " X ", h, ") is ", area**

Step 5. **Stop**

Flowchart

Figure 1.20 illustrates the flowchart of *program 1.19*:

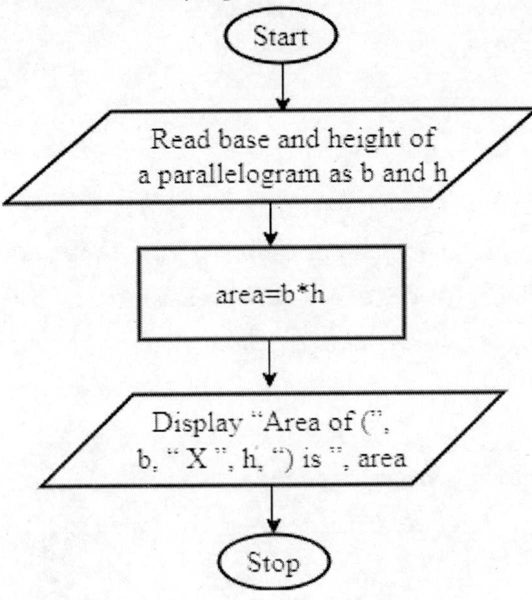

***Figure 1.20**: Flowchart illustrating program 1.19*

Python code

The source code in Python of *program 1.19* is available here:

```
#read float type inputs from the user
b=float(input("Enter base of a parallelogram"))
h=float(input("Enter height of a parallelogram"))
#obtain area
area=b*h
#print the output on the screen
print("Area of (", b, " X ", h, ") is ", area)
```

Python code explanation

The given Python code reads the base and height of a parallelogram from the user, calculates its area using the formula **`area = base * height`**, and then prints the area on the console.

C code

The source code in C of *program1.19* is available here:

```
#include<stdio.h>
void main()
{
float b, h, area;
printf("Enter base of a parallelogram ");
scanf("%f",&b); // read a float input from the user
printf("Enter height of a parallelogram ");
scanf("%f",&h); // read a float input from the user
//obtain area
area = b*h;
// print the output on the screen
printf("Area of ( %f X %f) is %f",b,h, area);
}
```

C code explanation

The code takes the base and height of a parallelogram from the user, calculates its area using the formula **`area = base * height`**, and then prints the area to the console. Format specifier **`%f`** is used to handle real numbers.

Program 1.20: Find distance between two points

Find the distance between two points **`P1 = (x1, y1)`** and **`P2 = (x2, y2)`** using the Manhattan distance and Euclidean distance formula.

Sample input output

Test case #1:

Input:

```
Enter x-point 1 3
Enter y-point 1 6
```

```
Enter x-point 2 4
Enter y-point 2 5
```

Output:

```
Manhattan distance is 2
Euclidean distance is 1.4142135623730951
```

Test case #2:

Input:

```
Enter x-point 1 4
Enter y-point 1 5
Enter x-point 2 10
Enter y-point 2 20
```

Output:

```
Manhattan distance is 21
Euclidean distance is 16.155
```

Algorithm

The following steps execute *program 1.20*:

Step 1. **Start**

Step 2. **Enter point 1 as x1, y1**

Step 3. **Enter point 2 as x2, y2**

Step 4. **man_dis = abs(x1-x2) + abs (y1-y2)**

Step 5. **eucl_dis = sqrt((x1-x2)* (x1-x2) + (y1-y2)* (y1-y2))**

Step 6. **Display "Manhattan distance is ", man_dis**

Step 7. **Display "Euclidean distance is ", eucl_dis**

Step 8. **Stop**

Flowchart

The *program 1.20* flowchart is shown in *Figure 1.21*:

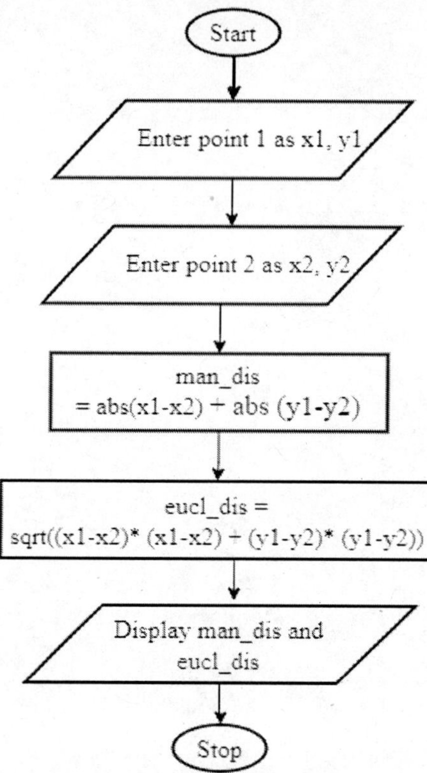

Figure 1.21: *Flowchart depicting program 1.20*

Python code

The Python source code for *program 1.20* is provided below:

```
import math

#read coordinates (x, y) as input from the user
x1=int(input("Enter x-point 1 "))
y1=int(input("Enter y-point 1 "))
x2=int(input("Enter x-point 2 "))
y2=int(input("Enter y-point 2 "))
#obtain Manhattan distance
man_dis = abs(x1-x2) + abs (y1-y2)
#obtain Euclidean distance
eucl_dis = math.sqrt((x1-x2)* (x1-x2) + (y1-y2)* (y1-y2))
```

```
#print the output on the screen
print("Manhattan distance is ",man_dis)
print("Euclidean distance is ", eucl_dis)
```

Python code explanation

This code reads in the **x** and **y** coordinates of two points and then calculates the Manhattan and Euclidean distances between them. The Manhattan distance is the sum of the absolute differences between the **x** and **y** coordinates, while the Euclidean distance is the square root of the sum of the squared differences of the **x** and **y** coordinates. Finally, the code prints out the calculated distances. Here, the math library is imported at the beginning to calculate the square root.

C code

The C source code for *program 1.20* is provided below:

```
#include<stdio.h>
#include<math.h>
void main()
{
float x1,y1,x2,y2,man_dis, eucl_dis;
printf("Enter x1, y1, x2, y2");
scanf("%f%f%f%f", &x1, &y1, &x2, &y2); // read four float inputs from the user
//calculate  Manhattan distance
man_dis = abs(x1-x2) + abs (y1-y2);
//calculate  Euclidean distance
eucl_dis = sqrt((x1-x2)* (x1-x2) + (y1-y2)* (y1-y2));
// print the output on the screen
printf("Manhattan distance is %f",man_dis);
printf("\nEuclidean distance is %f",eucl_dis);
}
```

C code explanation

<math.h> is a library of C where **sqrt()** function is defined. Thus, it is used in this program. The user is asked to read the **x** and **y** coordinates of two points and then it calculates the Manhattan distance and Euclidean distance between them. The Manhattan distance is the sum of the absolute differences between the **x** and **y** coordinates, while the

Euclidean distance is the square root of the sum of the squared differences of the **x** and **y** coordinates. Finally, the code prints out the calculated distances.

Program 1.21: Obtain logical truth table

Print the **truth table** of logical operators **AND**, **OR**, and **NOT**.

Sample input output

x	y	x and y	x or y	Not x
0	0	0	0	True
0	1	0	1	True
1	0	0	1	False
1	1	1	1	False

Algorithm

The algorithm listed below is used to execute *program 1.21*:

Step 1. **Start**

Step 2. **Print("x y (x and y) (x or y) (not x)")**

Step 3. **x=0, y=0**

Step 4. **Print (x, y, x&&y, x||y, !x)**

Step 5. **x=0, y=1**

Step 6. **Print (x, y, x&&y, x||y, !x)**

Step 7. **x=1, y=0**

Step 8. **Print (x, y, x&&y, x||y, !x)**

Step 9. **x=1, y=1**

Step 10. **Print (x, y, x&&y, x||y, !x)**

Step 11. **Stop**

Flowchart

The flowchart of the algorithm is illustrated in *Figure 1.22*:

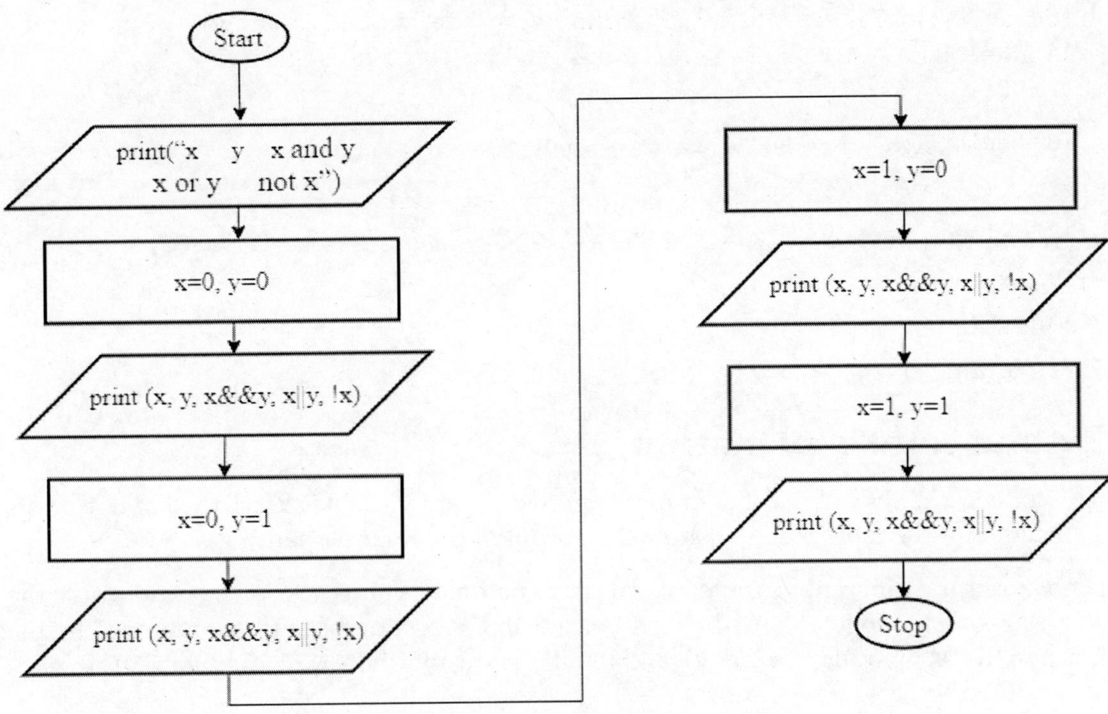

Figure 1.22: *Flowchart depicting program 1.21*

Python code

The Python source code for *program 1.21* is written as follows:

```
print("x y x and y x or y not x")
#first time value of x & y is 0
x=0
y=0
# and is to perform bitwise ANd operation, or #performs OR operation,
not perform NOT operation
print (x, y, x and y, x or y, not x)

#then, values of x & y are set to 0 & 1
x=0
y=1
print (x, y, x and y, x or y, not x)

```

```
#then, values of x & y are set to 1 & 0
x=1
y=0
print (x, y, x and y, x or y, not x)

#then, values of x & y are set to 1 & 1
x=1
y=1
print (x, y, x and y, x or y, not x)
```

Python code explanation

This code is a series of logical operations on two binary variables **x** and **y**. First, it prints the header for the table that will show the output of the logical operations.

Then, it sets the different possible logical combination of values to **x** and **y** and prints the values of **x** and **y**, followed by the result of the **AND** operation (**x and y**), followed by the result of the **OR** operation (**x or y**), and finally the result of the **NOT** operation (**not x**).

C code

The C source code for *program 1.21* is written as follows:

```
#include<stdio.h>
void main()
{
int x,y;
printf("x y x and y x or y not x");
//first time value of x & y is 0
x=0;
y=0;
// && is to perform bitwise ANd operation, || performs OR operation, ! perform NOT operation
printf ("\n%d %d %d %d %d",x, y, x&&y, x||y, !(x));
//then, values of x & y are set to 0 & 1
x=0; y=1;
printf ("\n%d %d %d %d %d",x, y, x&&y, x||y, !(x));
//then, values of x & y are set to 1 & 0
```

```
x=1; y=0;
printf ("\n%d %d %d %d %d",x, y, x&&y, x||y, !(x));
//then, values of x & y are set to 1 & 1
x=1; y=1;
printf ("\n%d %d %d %d %d",x, y, x&&y, x||y, !(x));
}
```

C code explanation

This code is a series of logical operations on two binary variables **`x`** and **`y`**. First, it prints the header for the table that will show the output of the logical operations.

Then, it sets the different possible logical combination of values to **`x`** and **`y`** and prints the values of **`x`** and **`y`**, followed by the result of the **`AND`** operation (**`x and y`**), followed by the result of the **`OR`** operation (**`x or y`**), and finally the result of the **`NOT`** operation (**`not x`**).

In C language, **&&** is used for **`AND`** operation, **`||`** is used for **`OR`** operation, and **`!`** is a unary not operation.

Conclusion

This chapter has provided a comprehensive understanding of the fundamental programming concepts and techniques for handling input and output operations. Readers have learned how to break down given problems into manageable steps and visualize the program flow using the presented algorithms and flowcharts as visual aids. Python and C programming languages have allowed for hands-on experience in implementing input-output programs, reinforcing concepts such as user input handling, data processing, and result display.

The next chapter on programs with conditional statements will discuss the interesting realm of conditional statements, exploring how programming languages use decision-making constructs to control the execution flow.

Points to remember

- Use clear and precise language while writing the steps of the algorithm. To check the correctness of the algorithm, test it with different input combinations.
- While drawing the flowchart, use standard symbols such as oval for mentioning start and end points, parallelogram for input/output, rectangle for process steps, and arrows for flow direction.
- Import the required modules using **`import`** in Python.

- Every C program begins with a main function, and every line in a C program ends with a semicolon.
- All variables to be used in a C program are to be declared at the beginning of the program, whereas explicit variable declaration is not required in Python language.
- Include relevant header files using **`#include`** in a C program.
- Use **`scanf()`** and **`printf()`** functions to accept user input from the standard input stream and display the output to the standard output stream in C language.
- In Python, utilize the **`input()`** function to accept user input from the standard input stream and **`print()`** function to display the output to the standard output stream.

Questions

1. Write a Python and C codes for the program, which takes two numbers as input and prints the subtracted value.
2. Draw a flowchart and write the algorithm, which takes four numbers as input and prints their product.
3. Write an algorithm and Python code for the program that takes temperature (in degree Celsius) as input and prints it in degree Fahrenheit.
4. Draw a flowchart and write the C code for the program that takes length (in km) as input and print it in meters.
5. Write the code in Python and C for the program, which takes the base and height of a triangle (in cm) as input and computes its area.

Join our book's Discord space

Join the book's Discord Workspace for Latest updates, Offers, Tech happenings around the world, New Release and Sessions with the Authors:

https://discord.bpbonline.com

CHAPTER 2

Conditional Statements

Introduction

Certain variations of conditional statements, such as the first type, involve taking action only if the condition is true. The second type deals with taking action 1 if the condition is true; otherwise, it proceeds to take action 2. The third type takes action 1 if condition 1 is true. If condition 1 is false, it checks condition 2. If condition 2 is true, then action 2 is executed; otherwise, it resorts to taking action 3. The fourth type requires both condition 1 and condition 2 to be true for action 1 to be executed. If any of the conditions is false, it leads to executing action 2. The fifth type calls for taking action 1 if either condition 1 or condition 2 or both are true. However, if both conditions are false, action 2 is carried out. The final type involves checking condition 1 first. If condition 1 is true, it proceeds to check condition 2. If both conditions are true, action 1 is taken.

In programming, the combinations of if-else statements are used to make decisions based on certain conditions. It allows the program to execute code blocks depending on whether a given condition is true or false. Here **`if`**, **`else-if`**, **`else`**, **`elif`** are the keywords.

Here is a breakdown of how the if-else statement works:

- The condition is a logical expression that evaluates to either true or false.
- If the condition is true, the code within the if block is executed.
- If the condition is false, the code within the else block is executed (if present).

- The else block is optional. If it is not included, the program will simply skip the code within the else block if the condition is false.
- The code within the if and else blocks can consist of a single statement or multiple statements enclosed within curly braces {} (in C program) or indented towards the right side (in Python program).
- Multiple if-else statements can be nested to handle more complex conditions. The else-if (elif, in Python) construct can also specify additional conditions to check if the initial condition is false.

Structure

In this chapter, there are a total of 18 programs, and five sub-sections complement each program:

- Understand the program objective with sample test cases consisting of inputs and outputs. It will give the user an understanding of what kind of user input is expected and what result will be projected for a particular program.
- Understand the program with an algorithm. This will help the user to understand the logic and methodology behind writing the sequence of steps required to solve a program.
- Visualize the program flow with flowcharts. Program objectives can be understood easily with the flowchart representation. User will understand which symbols to use in which context throughout different program's flowchart representations.
- Python source code of each program. Each program's source code in Python programming language is provided to the user so the user can understand the basic operations of the language. An explanation of each code is also provided.
- C implementation of each program. Users can learn the basic concepts of C language with the provided C language code and its explanation for every program.

Objectives

This chapter provides readers with a comprehensive understanding of conditional statements and their importance in the development of programs. It covers the fundamental concepts behind conditional statements and how they enable decision-making within algorithms through if-else constructs. Additionally, the chapter imparts the skills necessary for visual representations of conditional statements in program flow using flowcharts, facilitating a clearer and more intuitive grasp of their functionality.

Moreover, the chapter focuses on practical application by demonstrating how to implement conditional statements in Python and C programming languages. Sample codes are provided to offer hands-on experience, allowing readers to practice and gain confidence in effectively utilizing conditional statements in real-world coding scenarios. By the end of this chapter, readers will have acquired the knowledge and skills to leverage conditional statements in their programming.

Program 2.1: Find absolute value of a number

Print the absolute value of a number entered by the user.

Sample input output

Test case #1:

Input: `Enter the value of n: -23`

Output: `23`

Test case #2:

Input: `Enter the value of n: 56`

Output: `56`

Test case #3:

Input: `Enter the value of n: 0`

Output: `0`

Algorithm

To run the above program, the following steps are needed to be followed:

Step 1. **`Start`**

Step 2. **`Declare variable n`**

Step 3. **`Read n`**

Step 4. **`if n >= 0`**

 `i. print n`

Step 5. **`else`**

 `i. print n*(-1)`

Step 6. **`Stop`**

Flowchart

Figure 2.1 illustrates the program in the form of a flowchart:

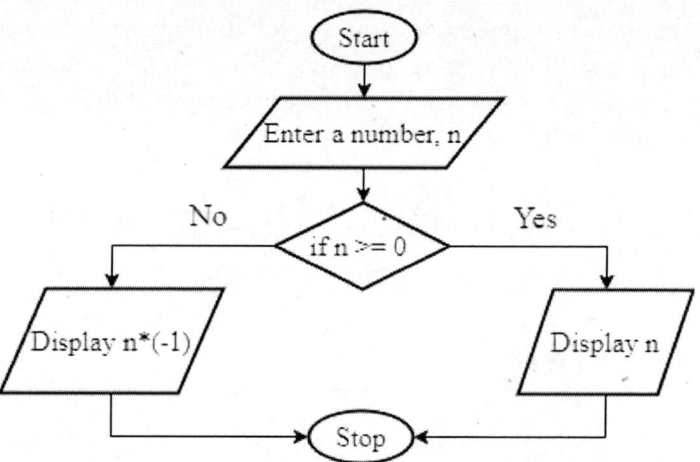

Figure 2.1: Flowchart illustrating the program 2.1

Python code

Python code for the *program 2.1* is as follows:

```
n=int(input("Enter n: "))
if n >= 0:
        print( n)
else:
        print(-1*n)
```

Python code explanation

The given code asks the user to enter a number, which is taken as the input using the **`input()`** function, and then the value is converted to an integer using the **`int()`**function. In Python, the block of **`if`** and **`else`** statements are indented towards the right. **`if`** and **`else`** are the keywords. Here, **`if-else`** statement is used to check if **`n`** is greater than **`0`**. If the number is greater than **`0`**, it is called a positive number. Otherwise, it is called a negative number. **`if`** keyword is followed by the condition (**`n >= 0`**). If the condition is true, the next statement in the program **`print(n)`** will execute and print the value of **`n`**. Otherwise, this statement will be skipped, and a block of **`else`** will execute. It will multiply the value of **`n`** after multiplying it with **`-1`**.

C code

C code for the *program 2.1* is as follows:

```c
#include<stdio.h>
#include<math.h>
int main()
{
int n;
printf("Enter the value of n: ");
scanf("%d", &n);
if(n >= 0)    //check if n is a positive number
printf("%d", n);
else          //Else block will execute only if n is a negative number
printf("%d",-1*n);
return 0;
}
```

C code explanation

The given code prompts the user to enter a value for **n**, reads the input, and then checks whether the value of **n** is positive. If the number is greater than **0**, it is called a positive number. Otherwise, it is called a negative. An **if-else** statement is used to check whether **n** is greater than **0**. If it is greater than or equal to zero, the value of n is displayed as it is. If the value of n is less than zero, it is multiplied by **-1** to make it positive, and then the resultant value is displayed.

The **if** and **else** are the keywords used for the **if-else** statement. The condition is enclosed in parentheses **()**. It is a logical expression that evaluates to either true or false. If the condition is true, the code block follows the **if** statement and is executed. If the condition is false, the code block immediately following the **else** statement is executed (if present).

Unlike Python, the code block associated with the **if** statement is enclosed in curly braces **{}**. It contains one or more statements executed if the condition is true. The else part is optional. If it is present, it is followed by a code block enclosed in curly braces **{}**. This code block contains one or more statements executed if the condition is false.

Program 2.2: Check if you are an adult?

Ask the user to enter the name and the age. Check if the age is **>=18**, then print the message **Abc is an adult**.

Sample input output

Test case #1:

Input:

`Enter your name: Neo`

`Enter your age: 98`

Output:

`Neo is an adult`

Test case #2:

Input:

`Enter your name: John`

`Enter your age: 10`

Output:

Algorithm

The steps to be followed to write the program are:

Step 1. **`Start`**

Step 2. **`Enter your name and age as n, a`**

Step 3. **`if a>=18:`**

Step 4. **`print(n, " is an adult")`**

Step 5. **`Stop`**

Flowchart

Figure 2.2 illustrates the flowchart of the program:

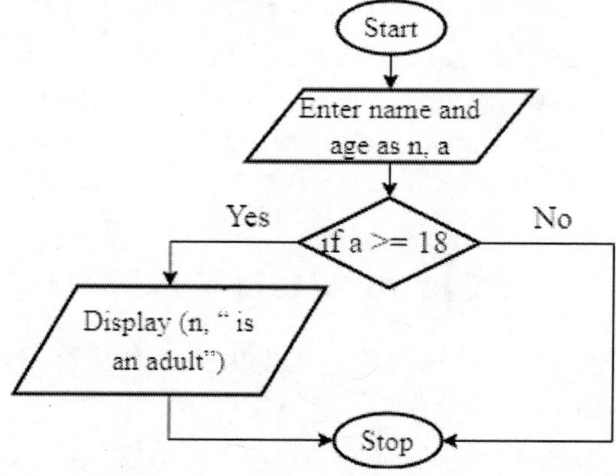

***Figure 2.2**: Flowchart illustrating the program 2.2*

Python code

Python code for the program is as follows:

```
n=input("Enter your name: ")
a=int(input("Enter your age: "))
if a>=18:
    print(n, " is an adult")
```

Python code explanation

This code prompts the user to enter their name and age as **n** and **a**. By default, Python reads the input as a string. So, age, **a**, is converted to a number using the **int()** function. Using the **if** condition, it checks if the entered age is greater than or equal to **18**. If the condition is true, it prints the entered name followed by the message **is an adult**. It should be noticed that **else** block is not mentioned in the code. Hence, if the condition fails (as in *test case#* 2), the program will terminate without generating any output.

C code

C code for the program is as follows:

```
#include<stdio.h>
void main()
{
char n[100];
int a;
printf("Enter your name: ");
gets(n);
fflush(stdin);
printf("Enter your age: ");
scanf("%d", &a);
if (a>=18)
printf("%s  is an adult", n);
}
```

C code explanation

This C code starts with the necessary header files. It includes the header file **stdio.h**, which provides input and output functionality. Within the **main()** function, it declares a character array **n** of size **100** to store the user's name and an integer variable **a** to store the user's age. It asks the user to enter their name and age. It reads the user's input as a string using the **gets()** function and stores it in the **n** variable. In C code, sometimes, string input creates problems with the **scanf()** or **gets()** function. To avoid these issues, **fflush()** is used to clear the input stream. Then, it takes age as the input. It checks if the value of **a** is greater than or equal to **18**. If the condition is true, it prints the value of **n** followed by the message **is an adult**. Since the **else** part is optional, it is not used. Hence, if the condition fails (as in test case number 2), the program will terminate without generating any output.

Program 2.3: Check if number is even or odd

Ask the user for a number (3-digit integer). Print out an appropriate message to the user, depending on whether the number is even or odd.

Sample input output

Test case #1:

Input: `Enter a number: 45`

Output: **`Number is ODD`**

Test case #2:

Input: `Enter a number: 68`

Output: **`Number is EVEN`**

Algorithm

The steps to be followed to write the program are:

Step 1. **`Start`**

Step 2. **`Enter a number as n`**

Step 3. **`if n%2 ==0:`**

```
print("number is EVEN")
```

Step 4. **`else:`**

```
print("number is ODD")
```

Step 5. **`Stop`**

Flowchart

Figure 2.3 illustrates the flowchart of the program:

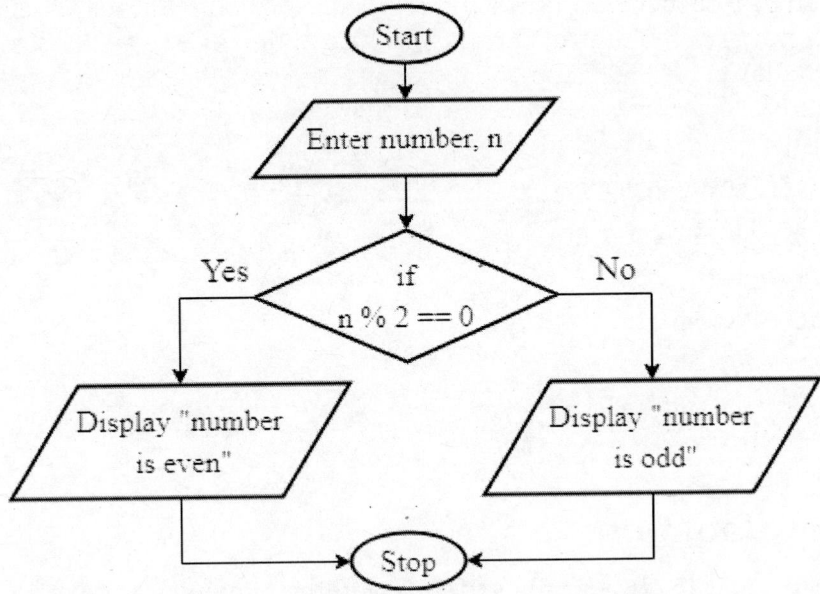

Figure 2.3: Flowchart illustrating the program 2.3

Python code

Python code for the program is as follows:

```
n=int(input("Enter a number : "))
if n%2 ==0:
    print("number is EVEN")
else:
    print("number is ODD")
```

Python code explanation

The Python code prompts the user to enter a number and reads the input as an integer, storing it in the variable `n`. It checks if the value of `n` is divisible by `2` or not. For that, the modulo operator (%) is used, which calculates the remainder when `n` is divided by `2`. If the remainder is `0`, it means the number is even and prints the message **`number is EVEN`**. Otherwise, it executes the **`else`** block and prints the message **`number is ODD`**.

C code

C code for the program is as follows:

```
#include<stdio.h>
void main()
{
int n;
printf("Enter a number : ");
scanf("%d",&n);
if (n%2 ==0)
printf("Number is EVEN");
else
printf("Number is ODD");
}
```

C code explanation

This C code includes the header file **`stdio.h`**, and the remaining code is written within curly brackets **`{}`** of the **`main()`** function. It declares an integer variable **`n`** to store the user's number, reads the user's input as an integer using the **`scanf()`** function, and stores it in the **`n`** variable.

It checks if the value of **`n`** is divisible by **`2`** or not. The modulo operator (**`%`**) calculates the remainder when **`n`** is divided by **`2`**. If the remainder is **`0`**, it means the number is even and prints the message **`Number is EVEN`**. Otherwise, it executes the **`else`** block and prints the message **`Number is ODD`**. Since, here, **`if`** and **`else`** blocks contain only one statement, there is no need to enclose the block within **`{}`** brackets. However, if the number of statements in the if-else block is more than one, they must be placed within **`{}`** brackets.

Program 2.4: Check type of integer

Check if the input number is positive, negative, or zero.

Sample input output

Test case #1:

Input: `Enter a number 56`

Output: **`Number is positive`**

Test case #2:

Input: `Enter a number -98`

Output: **`Number is negative`**

Algorithm

The steps needed to be followed to write the program are:

Step 1. **`Start`**

Step 2. **`Declare variable x`**

Step 3. **`Read x`**

Step 4. **`If (x<0)`**

```
        print "Number is negative"
```

Step 5. **`else if (x ==0)`**

```
        print "Number is zero"
```

Step 6. **`else`**

```
        print "Number is positive"
```

Step 7. **`Stop`**

Flowchart

Figure 2.4 illustrates the flowchart of the program:

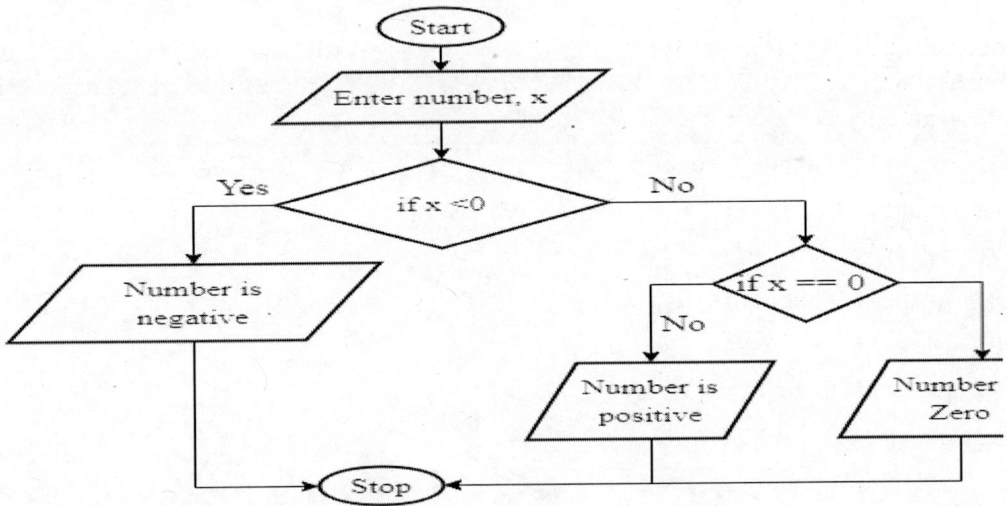

***Figure 2.4**: Flowchart illustrating the program 2.4*

Python code

Python code for the program is as follows:

```
x=int(input("Enter a number: "))
if x < 0:
```

```
3.     print("Number is negative")
4. elif x == 0:
5.     print("Number is zero")
6. else:
7.     print("Number is positive")
```

Python code explanation

The code prompts the user to enter a number and stores the input as an integer in the variable **x**. It checks if the value of **x** is less than **0**. If the condition in *line 2* is true (**x** is negative), it prints the message **Number is negative**. If the condition in *line 2* is false, it checks the next condition. It checks if the value of **x** is equal to **0**. If the condition in *line 4* is true (**x** is zero), it prints the message **Number is zero**. If both the conditions in *line 2* and *line 4* are false, it executes the else block and prints the message **Number is positive**.

C code

C code for the program is as follows:

```
1. #include<stdio.h>
2. void main()
3. {
4. int x;
5. printf("Enter a number ");
6. scanf("%d", &x);
7. if (x < 0)
8. printf("Number is negative");
9. else if (x == 0)
10. printf("Number is zero");
11. else
12. printf("Number is positive");
13. }
```

C code explanation

The code prompts the user to enter a number and stores the input in an integer variable **x**. It checks if the value of **x** is less than **0**. If the condition in *line 2* is true (**x** is negative), it prints the message **Number is negative**. If the condition in *line 2* is false, it checks the next condition. It checks if the value of **x** is equal to **0**. If the condition in *line 4* is true (**x** is zero), it prints the message **`Number is zero`**. If both the conditions in *line 2* and *line 4* are false, it executes the else block and prints the message **`Number is positive`**.

Program 2.5: Validate a triangle

Take the sides of a triangle as input and check whether a triangle can be formed or not using if else.

Hint: For a valid triangle, the sum of the two sides should be greater than the third side of the triangle.

Sample input output

Test case #1:

Input: `Enter the three sides of a triangle: 6`

`7`

`8`

Output: **`It is a valid triangle`**

Test case #2:

Input: `Enter the three sides of a triangle: 1`

`1`

`3`

Output: **`It is not a valid triangle`**

Algorithm

The steps needed to be followed to write the program are:

```
Step 1. Start
Step 2. Declare variable x1,x2,x3
Step 3. Read x1,x2,x3
Step 4. if (x1+x2) > x3   and (x1+x3) > x2  and (x2+x3) > x1
            print "It is a valid triangle"
Step 5. else
            print "It is not a valid triangle"
Step 6. Stop
```

Flowchart

Figure 2.5 illustrates the flowchart of the program:

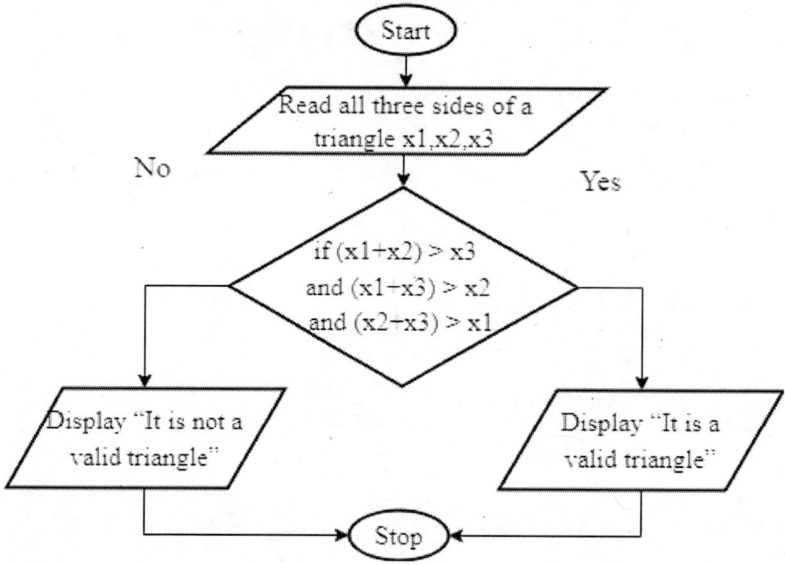

***Figure 2.5**: Flowchart illustrating the program 2.5*

Python code

Python code for the program is as follows:

```
1. x1=int(input("Enter first side of triangle: "))
2. x2=int(input("Enter second side of triangle: "))
3. x3=int(input("Enter third side of triangle: "))
4. if((x1+x2) > x3  and (x1+x3) > x2  and (x2+x3) > x1):
5.     print ("It is a valid triangle")
6. else:
7.     print ("It is not a valid triangle")
```

Python code explanation

This Python code takes 3 sides of a triangle as input from the user and converts them into an integer using the **`int()`** function. For a triangle to be valid, the sum of two sides should be greater than the third side of the triangle based on the triangle inequality theorem. So, there are three such conditions, and if all three conditions are true, then only the triangle can be considered valid. Hence, in *step 4*, three conditions are combined using **and** operator. The **`if`** statement is true only if all the three conditions are individually true and *step 5* executes. If any one of them is false, **`else`** block executes and prints the message **`It is not a valid triangle`**.

Note: The block of if-else is indented towards the right side.

C code

C code for the program is as follows:

```
#include<stdio.h>
void main()
{
int x1, x2, x3;
printf("Enter the three sides of a triangle: ");
scanf("%d%d%d", &x1,&x2,&x3);
if((x1+x2) > x3  && (x1+x3) > x2  && (x2+x3) > x1)
printf("It is a valid triangle");
else
printf("It is not a valid triangle");
}
```

C code explanation

This C code takes three sides of a triangle as input from the user in variables **`x1`**, **`x2`**, **`x3`**. For a triangle to be valid, the sum of two sides should be greater than the third side of the triangle based on the triangle inequality theorem. So, there are three such conditions, and if all three conditions are true, then only the triangle can be considered valid. Hence, in *step 8*, three conditions are combined using the **`&&`** operator. In C, **`&&`** is the logical **`AND`** operator. The **`if`** statement is true only if all three conditions are individually true and *step 9* executes. It prints the message **`It is a valid triangle`**. If any one of them is false, **`else`** block executes and prints the message **`It is not a valid triangle`**.

Program 2.6: Check divisibility by 7 and 5

Read a number from the user and check if the number is divisible by 7 and 5.

Hint: A number is divisible by 7 and 5 if the remainder is zero on dividing the number by 7 and 5.

Sample input output

Test case #1:

Input: `Enter a number 35`

Output: **`Number is divisible by 7 and 5`**

Test case #2:

Input: `Enter a number 63`

Output: **`It is not divisible by 7 and 5`**

Algorithm

The steps needed to be followed to write the program are:

Step 1. **`Start`**

Step 2. **`Declare variable x`**

Step 3. **`Read x`**

Step 4. **`if (x%7 ==0) && (x%5==0)`**

i. **`Print "Number is divisible by 7 and 5 both"`**

Step 5. **`else`**

i. **`Print "It is not divisible by 7 and 5 both"`**

Step 6. **`Stop`**

Flowchart

Figure 2.6 illustrates the flowchart of the program:

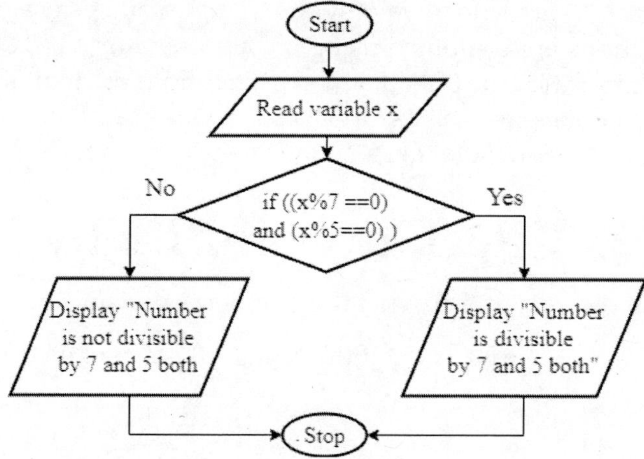

***Figure 2.6**: Flowchart illustrating the program 2.6*

Python code

Python code for the program is as follows:

```
1. x= int(input("Enter a number: "))
2. if (x%7 ==0) and (x%5==0):
3.     print("Number is divisible by 7 and 5 both")
4. else:
5.     print("It is not divisible by 7 and 5 both ")
```

Python code explanation

The code takes a number as input using **input()** and **int()** functions. Since a number is divisible by 7 and 5, if the remainder is zero on dividing the number by 7 and 5, there are 2 conditions to be true. So, in *step 2*, both the conditions are checked and combined using **and** operator. **If** statement is true only if both the conditions are individually true and *step 3* executes. It prints the message **Number is divisible by 7 and 5 both**. If any of them is false, **else** block executes and prints the message: **It is not divisible by 7 and 5 both**.

C code

C code for the program is as follows:

```
1. #include<stdio.h>
2. void main()
3. {
4. int x;
5. printf("Enter a number: ");
6. scanf("%d", &x);
7. if ((x%7 ==0) && (x%5==0))
8. printf("Number is divisible by 7 and 5 both");
9. else
10. printf("It is not divisible by 7 and 5 both ");
11. }
```

C code explanation

The C code takes an integer number as input using **scanf()** function. Since a number is divisible by 7 and 5, if the remainder is zero on dividing the number by 7 and 5, there are two conditions to be true. So, in *step 7*, both the conditions are checked and combined using the **&&** operator. It checks if the value of `x` is divisible by 7 (`x%7 == 0`) and divisible by 5 (`x%5 == 0`). `if` statement is true only if both the conditions are individually true and *step 8* executes. It prints the message `Number is divisible by 7 and 5 both`. If any of them is false, `else` block executes and prints the message `It is not divisible by 7 and 5 both`.

Program 2.7: Check if character is a vowel or consonant

Check whether an entered letter is a vowel or consonant.

Hint: In English, out of 26 alphabets, 5 (a, e, i, o, u) are vowels, and the rest are consonants.

Sample input output

Test case #1:

Input: `Enter a character a`

Output: `a is a vowel`

Test case #2:

Input: `Enter a character p`

Output: `p is a consonant`

Algorithm

The steps needed to be followed to write the program are:

Step 1. `Start`

Step 2. `Read input as c`

Step 3. `If c== 'a' or c== 'e' or c== 'i' or c== 'o' or c== 'u' then`

`print "entered character is a vowel"`

Step 4. `else`

`print "entered character is a consonant"`

Step 5. `Stop`

Flowchart

Figure 2.7 illustrates the flowchart of the program:

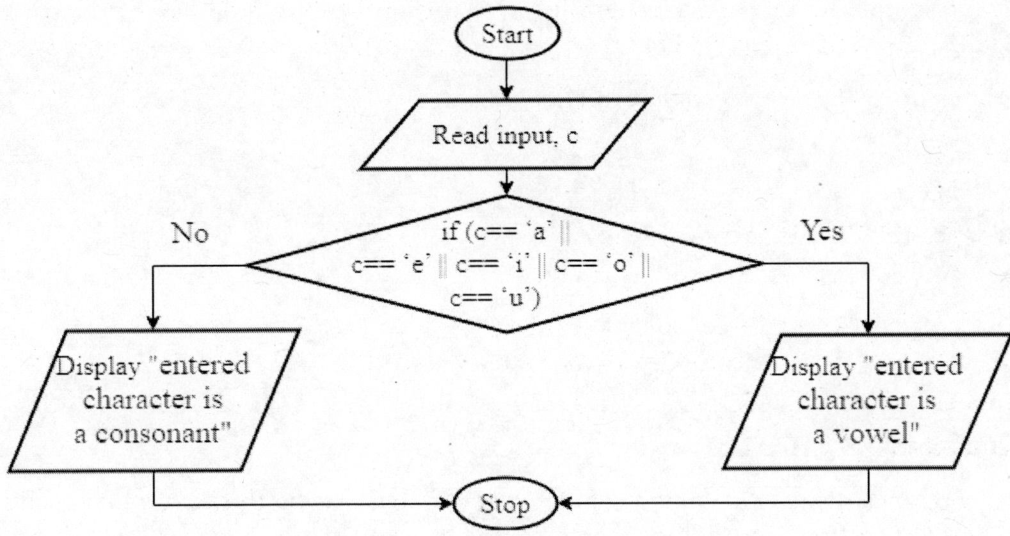

Figure 2.7: Flowchart illustrating the program 2.7

Python code

Python code for the program is as follows:

```
1. c=input("Enter a character: ")
2. if c== 'a' or c== 'e' or c== 'i' or c== 'o' or c== 'u':
3.     print( "Entered character is a vowel")
4. else:
5.     print( "The character is a consonant")
```

Python code explanation

The code prompts the user to enter a character in variable c using the **input()** function. Here, if the entered character is any one of the characters (**a**, **e**, **i**, **o**, or **u**), then **if** condition should be true. Since, in this program, at least one condition should be true, the **or** operator is used. So, in *step 2*, out of 5 conditions, if anyone is true, the **if-block** executes. It prints the message **it is a vowel**. If all the conditions are false, it executes the **else** block. In the **else** block, it prints the message **it is a consonant**.

C code

C code for the program is as follows:

```
#include<stdio.h>
void main()
```

```
3. {
4. char c;
5. printf("Enter a character ");
6. scanf("%c", &c);
7. if(c== 'a' || c== 'e' || c== 'i' || c== 'o' || c== 'u')
8. printf("%c is a vowel", c);
9. else
10. printf("%c is a consonant", c);
11. }
```

C code explanation

The C code asks the user to enter a character in variable **`c`** using the **`%c`** format specifier in the **`scanf()`** function. Here, if the entered character is any of the characters (**a**, **e**, **i**, **o**, or **u**), then the **`if`**-condition should be true. Since, in this program, at least one condition should be true, the **`||`** operator is used. **`II`** is **`or`** operator in the C program. So, in *step 7*, out of five conditions, if anyone is true, the **`if`**-block executes. It prints the message **`it is a vowel`**. If all the conditions are false, it executes the **`else`** block. In the **`else`** block, it prints the message **`it is a consonant`**.

Program 2.8: Check if you can sit in exam?

A student will not be allowed to sit in the end-term exam if the attendance is less than 80%. Take the input: number of classes held and number of classes attended. Print the percentage of classes attended. Then, decide whether a student is allowed to sit in the exam or not.

Sample input output

Test case #1:

Input:

```
Enter total number of classes held 42
Enter total number of classes attended 20
```

Output:

```
You are debarred. Attendance is 47.619049
```

Test case #2:

Input:

```
Enter total number of classes held 10
```

```
Enter total number of classes attended 9
```

Output:

```
Not debarred. Attendance is 90
```

Algorithm

The steps needed to be followed to write the program are:

Step 1. **Start**

Step 2. **Declare variable class_held, class_att, Percent_att**

Step 3. **Read class_held, class_att**

Step 4. **Percent_att = (class_att / class_held) *100**

Step 5. **if Percent_att>=80**

print "Not Debarred"

Step 6. **else**

print "You are debarred"

Step 7. **print "attendance is " +Percent_att**

Step 8. **Stop**

Flowchart

Figure 2.8 illustrates the flowchart of the program:

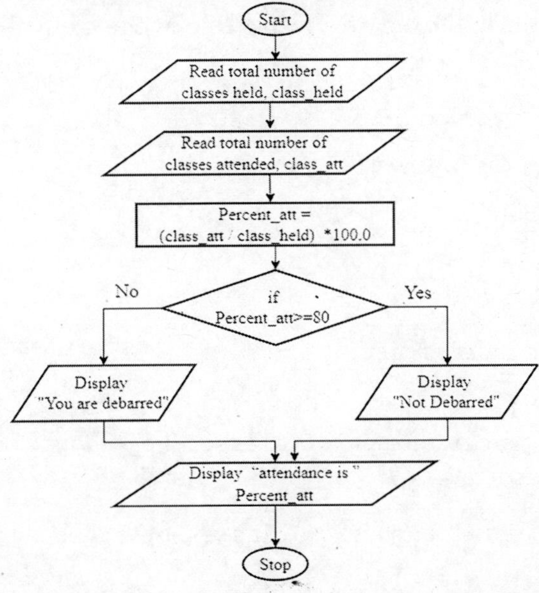

Figure 2.8*: Flowchart illustrating the program 2.8*

Python code

Python code for the program is as follows:

```
1. class_held = int(input("Total number of classes held: "))
2. class_att= int(input("Total number of classes attended: "))
3. Percent_att = (class_att / class_held)  *100
4. if(Percent_att>=80):
5.     print( "Not Debarred")
6. else:
7.     print( "You are debarred")
8.
9. print("Attendance is ",round(Percent_att,2), "%")
```

Python code explanation

The Python program reads the number of classes held and the total number of classes attended values from the user. *Step 3* calculates the attendance percentage by dividing the number of classes attended by the total classes held, multiplied by 100. If attendance percentage is greater than or equal to 80, it prints the message **`Not Debarred`**. Otherwise, it executes the **`else`** block and prints the message **`You are debarred`**. In *step 9*, it prints the attendance percentage. The decimal number is rounded up to 2 places after decimal.

Note: The indentation of the statement 9. It is left indented, which means it is outside the if and else block and will execute irrespective of the condition.

C code

C code for the program is as follows:

```
#include<stdio.h>
void main()
{
int class_held, class_att;
float Percent_att;
printf("Enter total number of classes held ");
scanf("%d", &class_held);
printf("Enter total number of classes attended ");
scanf("%d", &class_att);
Percent_att = (class_att / (float)(class_held))  *100.0;
```

```
11.
12. if(Percent_att>=80)
13. printf( "Not Debarred");
14. else
15. printf( "You are debarred. ");
16.
17. printf("Attendance is %f", Percent_att);
18. }
```

C code explanation

The C code calculates the percentage of attendance based on the total number of classes held and attended and determines if the student is debarred or not based on a threshold of 80%. It provides the appropriate output message indicating the result and displays the attendance percentage. The Python program reads the number of classes held and the total number of classes attended values from the user. In *step 10*, it calculates the attendance percentage by dividing the number of classes attended by the total classes held, multiplied by 100. Here, **`float`** is written before **`class_held`** to convert the nature of the variable from integer to floating point. If attendance percentage is greater than or equal to 80, it prints the message **`Not Debarred`**. Otherwise, it executes the **`else`** block and prints the message **`You are debarred`**. In *step 17*, it prints the attendance percentage. Note that this statement is outside the **`if`** and **`else`** block and will execute irrespective of the condition.

Program 2.9: Check if you can sit in exam (extended)?

Modify the *program 2.8* to allow students to sit if they have a medical case. Ask the user if they have a medical case or not (**`Y`** or **`N`**) and print accordingly.

Sample input output

Test case #1:

Input:

```
Enter total number of classes held 42
Enter total number of classes attended 39
If there is some medical case enter y n
```

Output:

```
Not Debarred
Attendance is 92.857140
```

Test case # 2:

Input:

```
Enter total number of classes held 42
Enter total number of classes attended 20
If there is some medical case enter y n
```

Output:

```
You are debarred
Attendance is 47.619049
```

Test case # 3:

Input:

```
Enter total number of classes held 42
Enter total number of classes attended 20
If there is some medical case enter y y
```

Output:

```
Not Debarred
Attendance is 47.619049
```

Algorithm

The steps needed to be followed to write the program are:

Step 1. **Start**

Step 2. **Declare variable class_held, class_att, Percent_att, medical_case**

Step 3. **Read class_held, class_att, medical_case**

Step 4. **Percent_att = (class_att / class_held) *100**

Step 5. **if Percent_att>=80**

```
print "Not Debarred"
```

Step 6. **Else if medical_case== 'Y'**

```
print "Not Debarred"
```

Step 7. **else**

```
print "You are debarred"
```

Step 8. **print "attendance is " +Percent_att**

Step 9. **Stop**

Flowchart

Figure 2.9 illustrates the flowchart of the program:

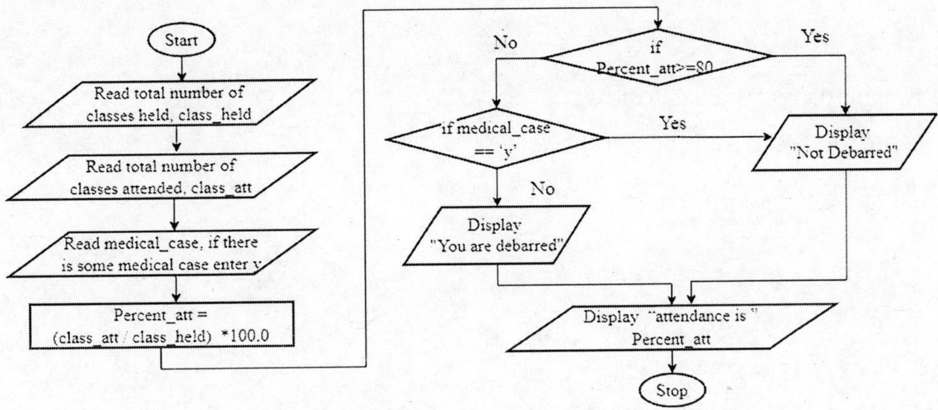

***Figure 2.9**: Flowchart illustrating the program 2.9*

Python code

Python code for the program is as follows:

```
1.  class_held = int(input("Total number of classes held "))
2.  class_att= int(input("Total number of classes attended "))
3.  medical_case = input("if there is some medical case enter y ")
4.
5.  Percent_att = (class_att / class_held)  *100
6.  if Percent_att>=80 :
7.      print("Not Debarred")
8.  elif medical_case== 'y':
9.      print("Not Debarred")
10. else:
11.     print("Debarred")
12. print("Attendance is ", round(Percent_att,2))
```

Python code explanation

This program is an extension of the previous program with an extra condition of medical case. So, if the attendance percentage is less than 80%, the student is checked for medical cases. If the student has some medical case, the condition in *step 8* becomes true, and the corresponding block is executed. Otherwise, it prints the message **You are debarred** as the attendance percentage is below 80, and there is no medical case. Finally, it displays the attendance percentage irrespective of condition (note the indentation of the statement).

C code

C code for the program is as follows:

```
1. #include<stdio.h>
2. void main()
3. {
4. int class_held, class_att;
5. float Percent_att;
6. char medical_case;
7. printf("Enter total number of classes held ");
8. scanf("%d", &class_held);
9. printf("Enter total number of classes attended ");
10. scanf("%d", &class_att);
11. fflush(stdin);
12. printf("If there is some medical case enter y ");
13. scanf("%c", &medical_case);
14. Percent_att = (class_att / (float)class_held)  *100.0;
15.
16. if(Percent_att>=80)
17. printf( "Not Debarred");
18. else if (medical_case== 'y')
19. printf( "Not Debarred");
20. else
21. printf( "You are debarred");
22.
23. printf("\nAttendance is %f", Percent_att);
24. }
```

C code explanation

This program is an extension of the previous program with an extra condition of medical case. So, if the attendance percentage is less than 80%, the student is checked for medical cases. If the student has some medical case, the condition in step 18 becomes true, and the corresponding block is executed. Otherwise, it prints the message **`You are debarred`** as the attendance percentage is below 80, and there is no medical case. Finally, it displays the attendance percentage irrespective of condition as this statement in outside **`if-else if-else`** blocks.

Program 2.10: Who spent more money?

You purchased some toffees, each costing $2. Your sister purchased some chocolates, each costing $10. Check that who spent more money. Take the number of toffees and chocolates as input from the user.

Sample input output

Test case #1:

Input:

```
Enter no of your toffees 25
Enter no of sister toffee 2
```

Output:

```
I spent more money
```

Test case #2:

Input:

```
Enter no of your toffees 10
Enter no of sister toffee 3
```

Output:

```
She spent more money
```

Test case #3:

Input:

```
Enter no of your toffees 10
Enter no of sister toffee 2
```

Output:

```
We spent equal money
```

Algorithm

The steps needed to be followed to write the program are:

Step 1. **`Start`**

Step 2. **`Declare variable no_my_toffee, no_sis_choco, my_rs, sis_rs`**

Step 3. `Read no_my_toffee, no_sis_choco`

Step 4. `my_rs = 2 *no_my_toffee`

Step 5. `sis_rs = 10 * no_sis_choco`

Step 6. `if my_rs>sis_rs`

```
          print "I spent more money"
```

Step 7. `elseifmy_rs==sis_rs`

```
          print "We spent equal money"
```

Step 8. `else`

```
          print "She spent more money"
```

Step 9. `Stop`

Flowchart

Figure 2.10 illustrates the flowchart of the program:

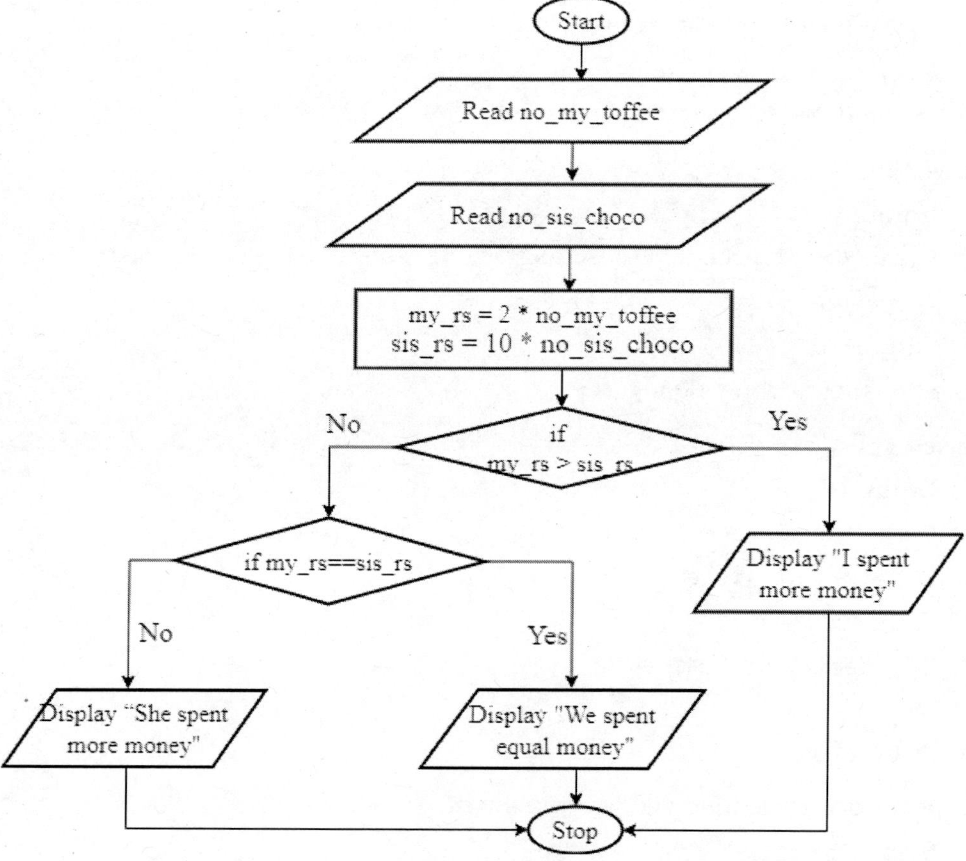

***Figure 2.10**: Flowchart illustrating the program 2.10*

Python code

Python code for the program is as follows:

```
1. no_my_toffee = int(input("Enter number of your toffees "))
2. no_sis_choco = int(input("Enter number of sister's chocolates "))
3. my_rs = 2 *no_my_toffee
4. sis_rs = 10 * no_sis_choco
5. if my_rs>sis_rs:
6.     print("I spent more money")
7. elif my_rs==sis_rs:
8.     print("We spent equal money")
9. else:
10.    print("She spent more money")
```

Python code explanation

This program is similar to the previous one, checking two levels of conditions using **`if-else if- else`** statement. It takes the number of toffees and chocolates as input and then calculates the cost of both (*Steps 3* and *4*). It first calculates the amount of money you spent by multiplying the number of your toffees (**`no_my_toffee`**) by 2 and stores the result in the **`my_rs`** variable. Similarly, it calculates the amount of money your sister spent by multiplying the number of your sister's toffees (**`no_sis_choco`**) by 10 and stores the result in the **`sis_rs`** variable. If the amount of money you spent (**`my_rs`**) is greater than the amount of money your sister spent (**`sis_rs`**), it prints the message **`I spent more money`**. Else if the amount of money you spent (**`my_rs`**) is equal to the amount your sister spent (**`sis_rs`**), it prints the message **`We spent equal money`**. Else (the amount of money your sister spent **`sis_rs`**, is greater than the amount of money you spent **`my_rs`**), it prints the message: **`She spent more money`**.

C code

C code for the program is as follows:

```
#include<stdio.h>
void main()
{
int no_my_toffee, no_sis_choco, my_rs, sis_rs;
printf("Enter no of your toffees ");
scanf("%d", &no_my_toffee);
```

```
7. printf("Enter no of sister toffee ");
8. scanf("%d", &no_sis_choco);
9. my_rs = 2 *no_my_toffee;
10. sis_rs = 10 * no_sis_choco;
11.
12. if(my_rs>sis_rs)
13. printf("I spent more money");
14. else if (my_rs==sis_rs)
15. printf("We spent equal money");
16. else
17. printf("She spent more money");
18. }
```

C code explanation

This program is similar to the previous one, checking two levels of conditions using **`if-else if- else`** statement. It takes the number of toffees and chocolates as input and then calculates the cost of both (*Step 9* and *10*). It calculates the money you spend by multiplying the number of your toffees (**`no_my_toffee`**) by 2 and stores the result in the **`my_rs`** variable. Similarly, it calculates the amount of money your sister spent by multiplying the number of your sister's toffees (**`no_sis_choco`**) by **`10`** and stores the result in the **`sis_rs`** variable. If the amount of money you spent (**`my_rs`**) is greater than the amount of money your sister spent (**`sis_rs`**), it prints the message **`I spent more money`**. Else if the amount of money you spent (**`my_rs`**) is equal to the amount your sister spent (**`sis_rs`**), it prints the message **`We spent equal money`**. Else (the amount of money your sister spent, **`sis_rs`**, is greater than the amount you spent **`my_rs`**), it prints the message: **`She spent more money`**.

Program 2.11: Find type of triangle

Lengths of three sides of a triangle, **`a`**, **`b`**, **`c`**, are given as input. Check if the triangle is isosceles, equilateral, or scalene.

Hint: In an equilateral triangle, three sides are equal. In an isosceles triangle, two sides are equal. In a scalene triangle, three sides are not equal.

Sample input output

Test case #1:

Input: `Enter 3 sides of a triangle: 12 12 4`

Output: **`It is an isosceles triangle`**

Test case #2:

Input: `Enter 3 sides of a triangle: 10 4 9`

Output: **`It is a scalene triangle`**

Test case #3:

Input: `Enter 3 sides of a triangle: 5 5 5`

Output: **`It is an equilateral triangle`**

Algorithm

The steps needed to be followed to write the program are:

```
Step 1. Start
Step 2. Enter three sides of a triangle as a,b,c
Step 3. If a==b==c:
            Print("It is an equilateral triangle")
Step 4. else if a==b or b==c or c==a :
            Print("It is an isosceles triangle")
Step 5. Else:
            Print("It is a scalene triangle")
```

Flowchart

Figure 2.11 illustrates the flowchart of the program:

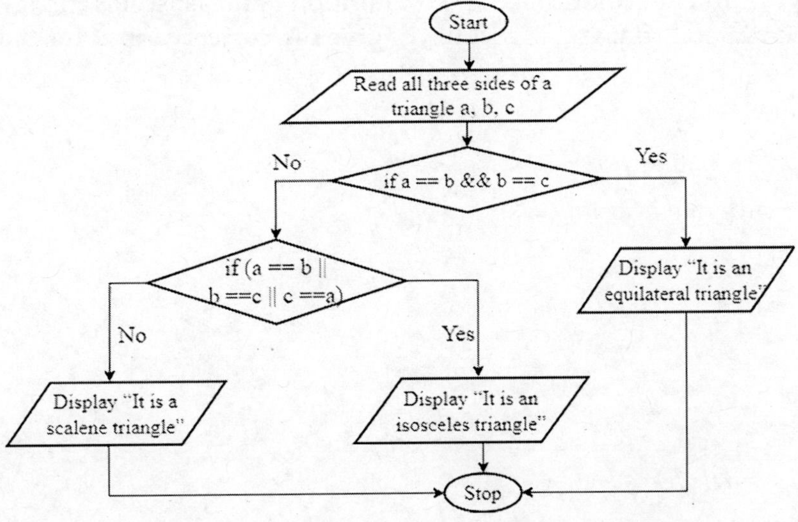

***Figure 2.11**: Flowchart illustrating the program 2.11*

Python code

Python code for the program is as follows:

```
a=int(input("Enter side 1 of a triangle "))
b=int(input("Enter side 1 of a triangle "))
c=int(input("Enter side 1 of a triangle "))
if a==b and b==c:
    print("It is an equilateral triangle")
elif a==b or b==c or c==a :
    print("It is an isosceles triangle")
else:
    print("It is a scalene triangle")
```

Python code explanation

The code prompts the user to enter the lengths of the sides of a triangle, and then it determines the type of triangle (equilateral, isosceles, or scalene). The first condition checks if the first side is equal to the second and the second is equal to the third. Here, both the conditions must be true. Hence, **`and`** operator is used. If both the conditions are true, it prints the message **`It is an equilateral triangle`**. Else if at least two sides of the triangle are equal, it prints the message: **`It is an isosceles triangle`**. Here, only one condition is sufficient to make the statement true, and hence, **`or`** operator is used. If none of the sides are equal, it prints the message: **`It is a scalene triangle`**.

Note: Check the order of conditions. If the condition of the isosceles triangle is checked before the equilateral triangle, it will never give the correct output for the equilateral triangle.

C code

C code for the program is as follows:

```
#include<stdio.h>
void main()
{
int a,b,c;
printf("Enter 3 sides of a triangle: ");
scanf("%d%d%d",&a,&b,&c);
if (a==b && b==c)
printf("It is an equilateral triangle: ");
```

```
else if (a==b || b==c || c==a)
printf("It is an isosceles triangle");
else
printf("It is a scalene triangle");
}
```

C code explanation

The code prompts the user to enter the lengths of the sides of a triangle and determines the type of triangle (equilateral, isosceles, or scalene). The first condition checks if the first side is equal to the second and the second is equal to the third. Here, both conditions must be true. Hence, the **&&** (and) operator is used. If both the conditions are true, it prints the message **`It is an equilateral triangle`**. Else if at least two sides of the triangle are equal, it prints the message: **`It is an isosceles triangle`**. Here, only one condition is sufficient to make the statement true; hence, the **||** (or) operator is used. If none of the sides are equal, it prints the message: **`It is a scalene triangle`**.

Note: Check the order of conditions. If the condition of an isosceles triangle is checked before the equilateral triangle, it will never give the correct output for the equilateral triangle.

Program 2.12: Check if year is a leap year

Check if the year entered is a leap year or not.

Hint: To be a leap year, the year should be divisible by either 400 or 4 but not with 100.

Sample input output

Test case #1:

Input: `Enter year 2024`

Output: **`It is a leap year`**

Test case #2:

Input: `Enter year 2300`

Output: **`It is not a leap year`**

Test case #3:

Input: `Enter year 2000`

Output: **`It is a leap year`**

Algorithm

The steps needed to be followed to write the program are:

```
Step 1. Start
Step 2. input year
Step 3. if year%400 ==0 then
            Print "it is a leap year"
Step 4.  else if year %100 != 0 and year%4 ==0 then
            Print "it is a leap year"
Step 5.  Else
            Print "it is not a leap year"
Step 6. Stop
```

Flowchart

Figure 2.12 illustrates the flowchart of the program:

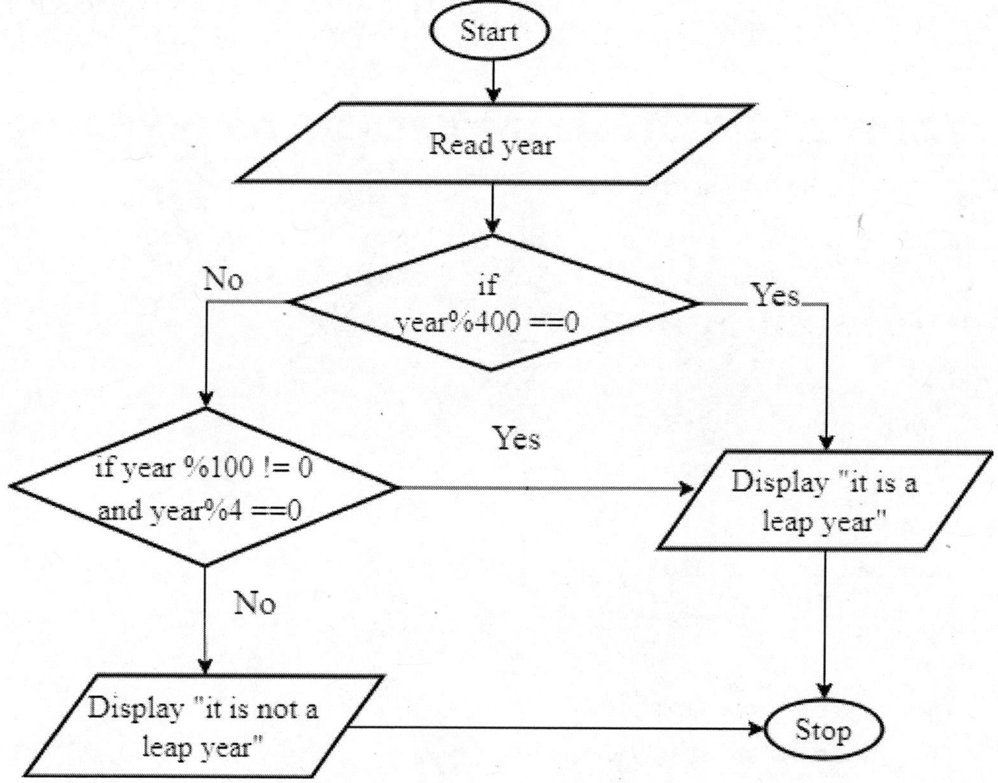

***Figure 2.12**: Flowchart illustrating the program 2.12*

Python code

Python code for the program is as follows:

```
year = int(input("Enter year "))
if year%400 ==0:
    print("it is a leap year")
elif year %100 != 0 and year%4 ==0:
    print("it is a leap year")
else:
    print("it is not a leap year")
```

Python code explanation

The code prompts the user to enter a year and determines if it is a leap year based on the given conditions: If the year is divisible by 400 (**`year%400 == 0`**), it prints the message **`it is a leap year`**. Otherwise, it checks the second condition. If the year is not divisible by 100 (**`year%100 != 0`**) and divisible by 4 (**`year%4 == 0`**), it prints the message **`it is a leap year`**. Else (neither of the above conditions is true), it prints the message **`it is not a leap year`**.

C code

C code for the program is as follows:

```
#include<stdio.h>
void main()
{
int year;
printf("Enter year ");
scanf("%d", &year);
if (year%400 ==0)
printf("it is a leap year");
else if (year %100 != 0 && year%4 ==0)
printf("it is a leap year");
else
printf("it is not a leap year");
}
```

C code explanation

The code prompts the user to enter a year and determines if it is a leap year based on the given conditions: If the year is divisible by 400 (**year%400 == 0**), it prints the message **it is a leap year**. Otherwise, it checks the second condition. That is, if the year is not divisible by 100 (**year%100 != 0**) and divisible by 4 (**year%4 == 0**), it prints the message **it is a leap year**. Else (neither of the above conditions is true), it prints the message **it is not a leap year**.

Program 2.13: Find largest number

Take three numbers as input from the user and print the largest number.

Sample input output

Test case #1:

Input: `Enter 3 numbers: 23 54 87`

Output: **87 is largest**

Test case #2:

Input: `Enter 3 numbers: 12 54 7`

Output: **54 is largest**

Algorithm

The steps needed to be followed to write the program are:

Step 1. **Start**

Step 2. **Declare a,b,c**

Step 3. **Input a,b,c**

Step 4. **If a>b:**

```
        If b>c
            Print a is largest
        Else if a>c
            Pint a is largest
        Else
            Print c is largest
```

Step 5. **Else**

```
        If a>c
            Print b is largest
```

```
Else if b>c
        Print b is largest
Else
        Print c is largest
```

Step 6. **Stop**

Flowchart

Figure 2.13 illustrates the flowchart of the program:

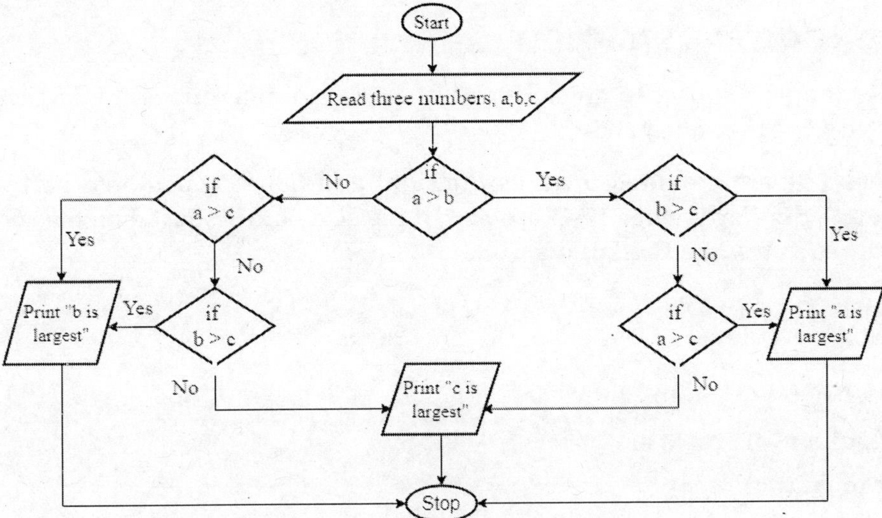

***Figure 2.13**: Flowchart illustrating the program 2.13*

Python code

Python code for the program is as follows:

```
a=int(input("Enter first number"))
b=int(input("Enter first number"))
c=int(input("Enter first number"))
if a>b:
    if b>c:
        print("a is largest")
    elif a>c:
        print("a is largest")
    else:
```

```
10.         print("c is largest")
11. else:
12.     if a>c:
13.         print("b is largest")
14.     elif b>c:
15.         print("b is largest")
16.     else:
17.         print("c is largest")
```

Python code explanation

The code prompts the user to enter three numbers and determines the largest number using nested **if-else** statements.

Note: Steps 5-10 are indented towards the right and hence considered part of if - if-block (step 4). Similarly, steps 12-17 are part of the else - block. Based on the conditions, the appropriate message is displayed.

C code

C code for the program is as follows:

```
#include<stdio.h>
void main()
{
int a, b,c;
printf("Enter 3 numbers: ");
scanf("%d%d%d", &a, &b, &c);
if (a>b)
{
 if (b>c)
  printf( "%d is largest", a);
 else if (a>c)
  printf( "%d is largest", a);
 else
  printf( "%d is largest", c);
}
else
```

```
17. {
18.  if (a>c)
19.   printf( "%d is largest", b);
20.  else if ( b>c)
21.   printf( "%d is largest", b);
22.  else
23.   printf( "%d is largest", c);
24. }
25. }
```

C code explanation

The code prompts the user to enter three numbers and determines the largest number using nested **`if-else`** statements.

Note: The steps 9-14 are enclosed within {} brackets. Hence, they are part of the if-block (step 7). Similarly, steps 18-23 are part of the else - block. Based on the conditions, the appropriate message is displayed.

Program 2.14: Design arithmetic calculator

Design a simple arithmetic calculator.

Sample input output

Test case #1:

Input:

`Enter two numbers: 23 65`

`Enter operator: a for addition, s for subtraction, m for multiplication and d for division a`

Output: 88

Test case #2:

Input:

`Enter two numbers: 12 4`

`Enter operator: a for addition, s for subtraction, m for multiplication and d for division: d`

Output: `3.000000`

Algorithm

The steps needed to be followed to write the program are:

Step 1. **Start**

Step 2. **Read two number as x, y**

Step 3. **Read operator op as a for addition, s for subtraction, m for multiplication and d for division**

Step 4. **if op== 'a' then**

    Print x+y

Step 5. **Else if op== 's' then**

    Print x-y

Step 6. **Else if op== 'm' then**

    Print x*y

Step 7. **Else if op== 'd' then**

    Print x/y

Step 8. **Else**

    Print "entered invalid operator"

Step 9. **Stop**

Flowchart

Figure 2.14 illustrates the flowchart of the program:

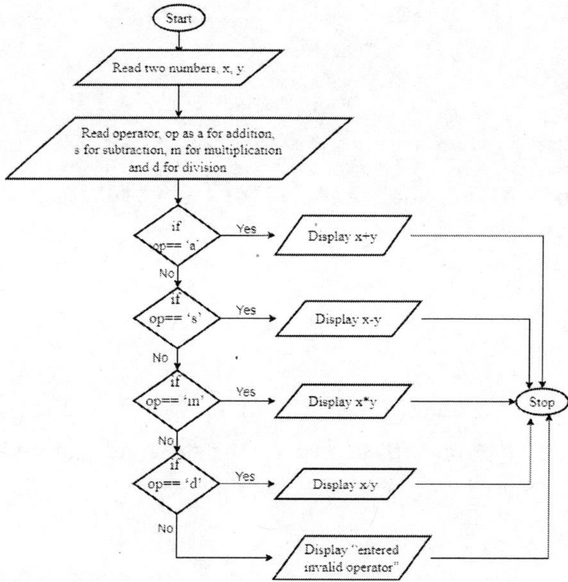

***Figure 2.14**: Flowchart illustrating the program 2.14*

Python code

Python code for the program is as follows:

```
x=int(input("Enter first number "))
y= int(input("Enter second number "))
op=input("Enter operator: a for addition, s for subtraction, m for multiplication and d for division ")
if op== 'a':
    print( x+y)
elif op== 's':
    print( x-y)
elif op== 'm':
    print( x*y)
elif op== 'd':
    print( x/y)
else:
    print("Entered invalid operator")
```

Python code explanation

The code prompts the user to enter two numbers and an operator. It performs the corresponding arithmetic operation based on the operator entered and provides the appropriate output message or result. It should be noted that using multiple **`elif`** statements, many conditions are checked. If none of the conditions match, the **`else`**-block is executed.

C code

C code for the program is as follows:

```
#include<stdio.h>
void main()
{
int x,y;
char op;
printf("Enter two numbers: ");
scanf("%d%d",&x, &y);
fflush(stdin);
```

```
printf("Enter operator: a for addition, s for subtraction, m for multiplication and d for division: ");
scanf("%c", &op);
if (op== 'a')
printf("%d",x+y);
else if (op== 's')
printf("%d", x-y);
else if (op== 'm')
printf("%d", x*y);
else if (op== 'd')
printf("%f", x/(float)y);
else
printf( "Entered invalid operator");
}
```

C code explanation

The code prompts the user to enter two numbers and an operator. It performs the corresponding arithmetic operation based on the operator entered and provides the appropriate output message or result. It should be noted that many conditions are checked by using multiple **`else if`** statements. If none of the conditions match, the **`else`**-block is executed.

Program 2.15: Calculate the grade of a student

Write a program that will take the marks of a student in five subjects: Computer, Social Science, Math, English, and Hindi. It will calculate the percentage and print the grade sheet according to given conditions:

- If percentage >= 90% : Grade A
- If percentage >= 80% : Grade B
- If percentage >= 60% : Grade C
- If percentage >= 40% : Grade D
- If percentage <40%: Grade F

Sample input output

Test case #1:

Input: `Enter marks in 5 subjects 87 89 86 90 92`

Output: `Grade is B`

Test case #2:

Input: `Enter marks in 5 subjects 43 56 73 34 66`

Output: `Grade is D`

Algorithm

The steps needed to be followed to write the program are:

```
Step 1. Start
Step 2. Enter marks in 5 subjects as a,b,c,d,e
Step 3. p=((a+b+c+d+e)/500)*100
Step 4. if  p>=90
              print("grade is A")
Step 5. else if  p>=80
              print("grade is B")
Step 6. else  if  p >=60
              print("grade is C")
Step 7. else  if  p >=40
              print("grade is D")
Step 8. else
              print("grade is F")
Step 9. STOP
```

Flowchart

Figure 2.15 illustrates the flowchart of the program:

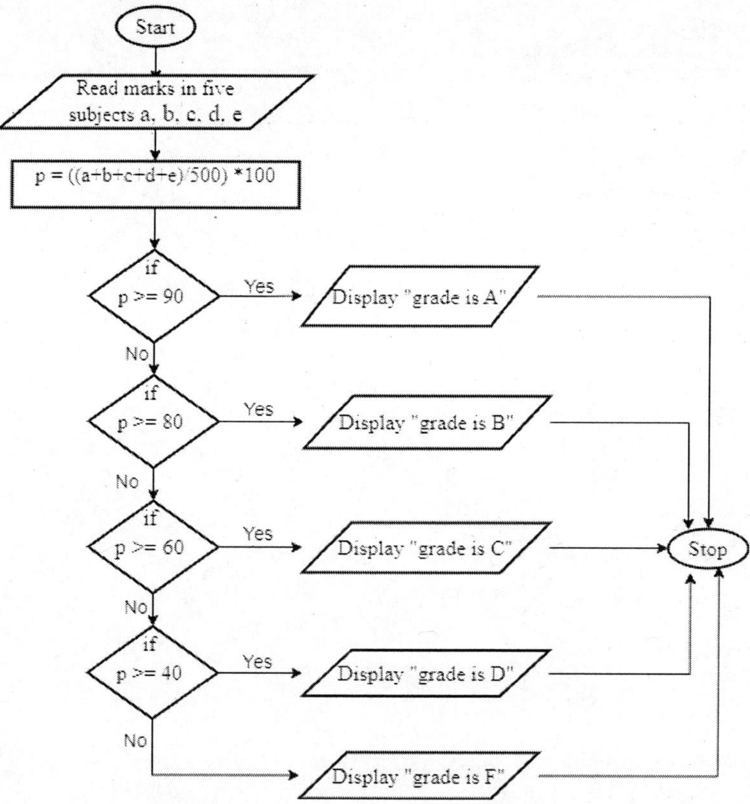

***Figure 2.15**: Flowchart illustrating the program 2.15*

Python code

Python code for the program is as follows:

```
a=int(input("Enter marks in subject 1: "))
b=int(input("Enter marks in subject 2: "))
c=int(input("Enter marks in subject 3: "))
d=int(input("Enter marks in subject 4: "))
e=int(input("Enter marks in subject 5: "))

p=((a+b+c+d+e)/500)*100
if  p >=90:
     print("Grade is A")
elif  p >=80:
     print("Grade is B")
```

```
elif  p >=60:
     print("Grade is C")
elif  p >=40:
     print("Grade is D")
else:
     print("Grade is F")
```

Python code explanation

The code prompts the user to enter marks in five subjects, calculates the percentage, determines the grade based on the percentage, and provides the appropriate output based on the following conditions:

- If the percentage (`p`) is greater than or equal to **`90`**, it prints the message **`Grade is A`**.
- Else if the percentage (`p`) is greater than or equal to **`80`**, it prints the message **`Grade is B`**.
- Else if the percentage (`p`) is greater than or equal to **`60`**, it prints the message **`Grade is C`**.
- Else if the percentage (`p`) is greater than or equal to **`40`**, it prints the message **`Grade is D`**. Else (the percentage is less than 40), it prints the message **`Grade is F`**.

Note: Check the order of the conditions. Try to check the conditions in some other order and observe the difference in the output.

C code

C code for the program is as follows:

```
#include<stdio.h>
void  main()
{
int a,b,c,d,e;
float p;
printf("Enter marks in  5 subjects ");
scanf("%d%d%d%d%d", &a,&b,&c,&d,&e);
p=((a+b+c+d+e)/(float)500)*100;
if (p >=90)
printf("Grade is A");
else  if  (p >=80)
```

```
printf("Grade is B");
else if ( p >=60)
printf("Grade is C");
else if  (p >=40)
printf("Grade is D");
else
printf("Grade is F");
}
```

C code explanation

The code prompts the user to enter marks in five subjects, calculates the percentage, determines the grade based on the percentage, and provides the appropriate output based on the following conditions:

- If the percentage (**p**) is greater than or equal to 90, it prints the message **`Grade is A`**.
- Else if the percentage (**p**) is greater than or equal to 80, it prints the message **`Grade is B`**.
- Else if the percentage (**p**) is greater than or equal to 60, it prints the message **`Grade is C`**.
- Else if the percentage (**p**) is greater than or equal to 40, it prints the message **`Grade is D`**.
- Else (the percentage is less than 40), it prints the message **`Grade is F`**.

Note: The order of conditions. Try to check the conditions in some other order and observe the difference in the output.

Program 2.16: Find gross salary

The gross salary of an employee in a firm is calculated based on the following:

Formula: Gross = Basic + DA+HRA

Take the basic salary of an employee as input and calculate gross salary according to given conditions:

- Basic salary <= 10000 : HRA = 20%, DA = 80%
- Basic salary is between 10001 to 20000 : HRA = 25%, DA = 90%
- Basic salary >= 20001 : HRA = 30%, DA = 95%

Sample input output

Test case #1:

Input: `Enter your basic salary 3000`

Output: **`Gross Salary is 6000.000000`**

Test case #2:

Input: `Enter your basic salary 25000`

Output: **`Gross Salary is 56250.000000`**

Algorithm

The steps to be followed to write the program are:

```
Step 1. Start
Step 2. Enter your basic salary as sal
Step 3. if sal<= 10000 :
            HRA = 0.2 * sal
            DA = 0.8*sal
Step 4. else if sal<= 20000 :
            HRA = 0.25*sal
            DA =0.9*sal
Step 5. else:
            HRA = 0.3*sal
            DA =0.95*sal
Step 6. print(" Gross Salary is", sal+HRA+DA)
Step 7. Stop
```

Flowchart

Figure 2.16 illustrates the flowchart of the program:

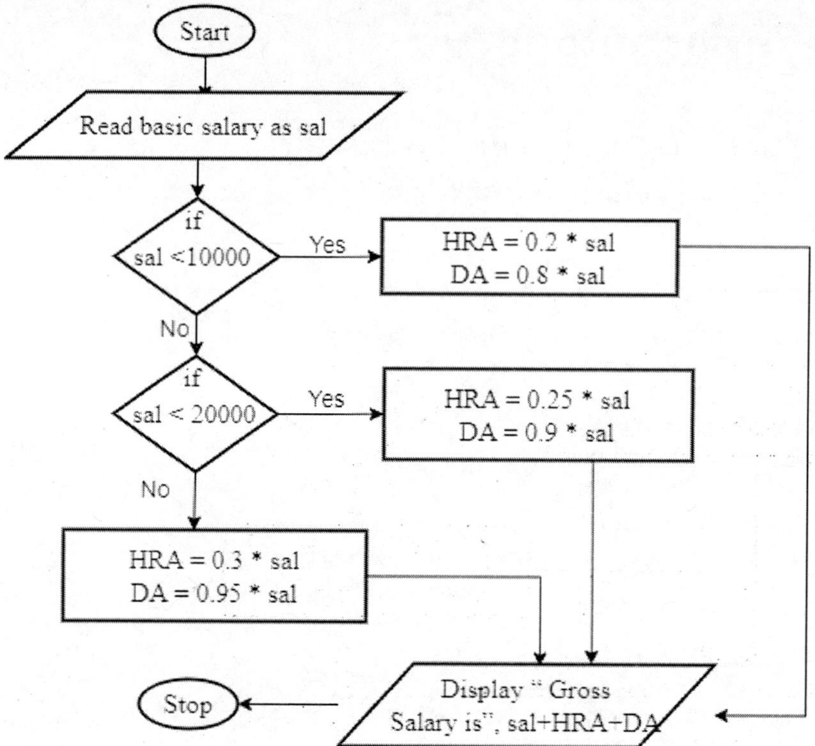

***Figure 2.16**: Flowchart illustrating the program 2.16*

Python code

Python code for the program is as follows:

```
sal=int(input("Enter your basic salary "))
if sal <= 10000 :
    HRA = 0.2 * sal
    DA = 0.8*sal
elif sal <= 20000 :
    HRA = 0.25*sal
    DA =0.9*sal
else:
    HRA = 0.3*sal
    DA =0.95*sal
print("Gross Salary is ", sal+HRA+DA)
```

Python code explanation

The code prompts the user to enter their basic salary, calculates the **House Rent Allowance (HRA)** and **Dearness Allowance (DA)** based on the salary range, and calculates the gross salary by adding the basic salary, HRA, and DA. It then provides the appropriate output message indicating the gross salary. Note the indentation in the code.

C code

C code for the program is as follows:

```
#include<stdio.h>
void main()
{
int sal;
float HRA, DA;
printf("Enter your basic salary ");
scanf("%d", &sal);
if (sal <= 10000)
{
HRA = 0.2 * sal;
DA = 0.8*sal;
}
else if (sal <= 20000)
{
HRA = 0.25*sal;
DA =0.9*sal;
}
else
{
HRA = 0.3*sal;
DA =0.95*sal;
}
printf("Gross Salary is %f", sal+HRA+DA);
}
```

C code explanation

The code prompts the user to enter their basic salary, calculates the HRA and DA based on the salary range, and calculates the gross salary by adding the basic salary, HRA, and DA. It then provides the appropriate output message indicating the gross salary. Note the indentation in the code.

Program 2.17: Generate shopping bill

During the sale hours, a shop prints the following offer:

If you will purchase for more than $1000, you will get a 20% discount. If you purchase for more than $5000, you will get a 50% discount.

Assume that each product costs $120.Take quantity as input and calculate the amount to be paid.

Sample input output

Test case #1:

Input: `Enter no of products you purchased: 3000`

Output: **`Please pay 180000.000000`**

Test case #2:

Input: `Enter no of products you purchased: 350`

Output: **`Please pay 21000.000000`**

Algorithm

The steps to be followed to write the program are:

Step 1. **`Start`**

Step 2. **`Declare variable quantity, amt, x`**

Step 3. **`Read quantity`**

Step 4. **`amt=quantity * 120`**

Step 5. **`if amt>5000`**

```
x= amt - 0.5*amt

print "Pls pay" + x
```

Step 6. **`Else if amt> 1000`**

```
x= amt - 0.2*amt

print "Pls pay" + x
```

Step 7. **else**

```
print "Pls pay" + amt
```

Step 8. **Stop**

Flowchart

Figure 2.17 illustrates the flowchart of the program:

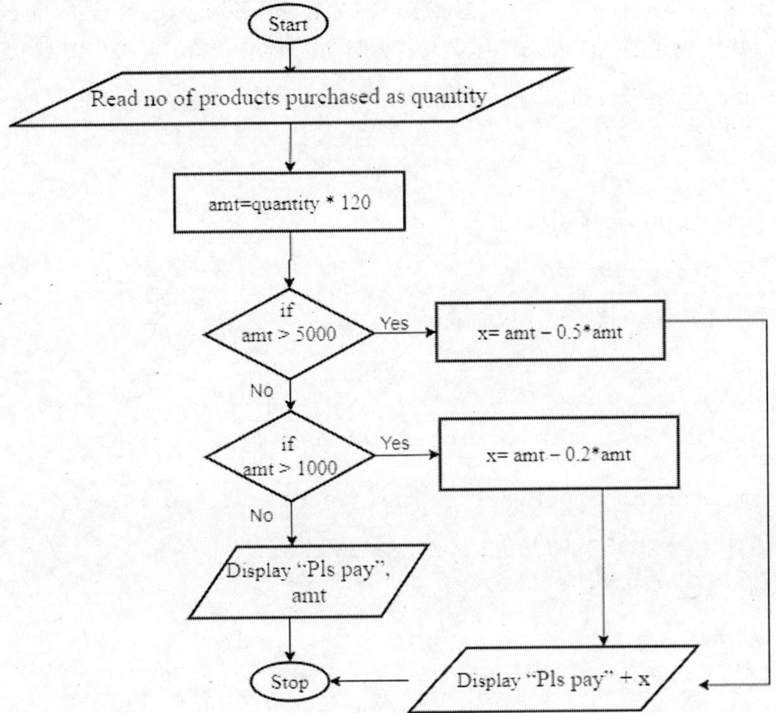

***Figure 2.17**: Flowchart illustrating the program 2.17*

Python code

Python code for the program is as follows:

```
quantity=int(input("Enter no of products you purchased "))
amt=quantity * 120
if amt>5000:
    x= amt-0.5*amt
    print("Pls pay ", x)
elif amt>  1000:
```

```
        x= amt-0.2*amt
        print("Pls pay ", x)
else:
        print("Pls pay ", amt)
```

Python code explanation

The code prompts the user to enter the quantity of products purchased and calculates the total amount by multiplying the quantity by 120. It applies a discount based on the total amount range and provides the appropriate output message indicating the final amount to be paid.

C code

C code for the program is as follows:

```
#include<stdio.h>
void main()
{
int quantity, amt;
float x;
printf("Enter no of products you purchased: ");
scanf("%d", &quantity);
amt=quantity * 120;
if(amt>5000)
{
x= amt-0.5*amt;
printf("Pls pay %f", x);
}
else if (amt>  1000)
{
x= amt-0.2*amt;
printf("Pls pay %f", x);
}
else
{
printf("Pls pay %d", amt);
```

```
22. }
23. }
```

C code explanation

The code prompts the user to enter the quantity of products purchased and calculates the total amount by multiplying the quantity by 120. It applies a discount based on the total amount range and provides the appropriate output message indicating the final amount to be paid.

Program 2.18: Generate shopping bill during sale

A bookshop prints the following discount:

Buy 2, get 3

Two higher MRP book prices would be used to calculate the amount to be paid. For example, you purchased 3 books for $500, $900, and $700. Then, your bill amount will be $1600. Write an algorithm to compute the bill amount.

Sample input output

Test case #1:

Input: `Enter price of 3 books: 300 400 500`

Output: `Please pay 900.000000`

Test case #2:

Input: `Enter price of 3 books: 800 400 1000`

Output: `Please pay 1800.000000`

Algorithm

The steps to be followed to write the program are:

Step 1. **Start**

Step 2. **Declare variable price1, price2, price3**

Step 3. **Read price1, price2, price3**

Step 4. **If (price1 < price2 and price 1< price3)**

amt_paid = price2 + price3

Step 5. **else if (price2 < price 1 and price 2< price 3)**

amt_paid = price1 + price3

Step 6. **else**

amt_paid = price2 + price1

Step 7. **Print" Pls pay" + amt_paid**

Step 8. **Stop**

Flowchart

Figure 2.18 illustrates the flowchart of the program:

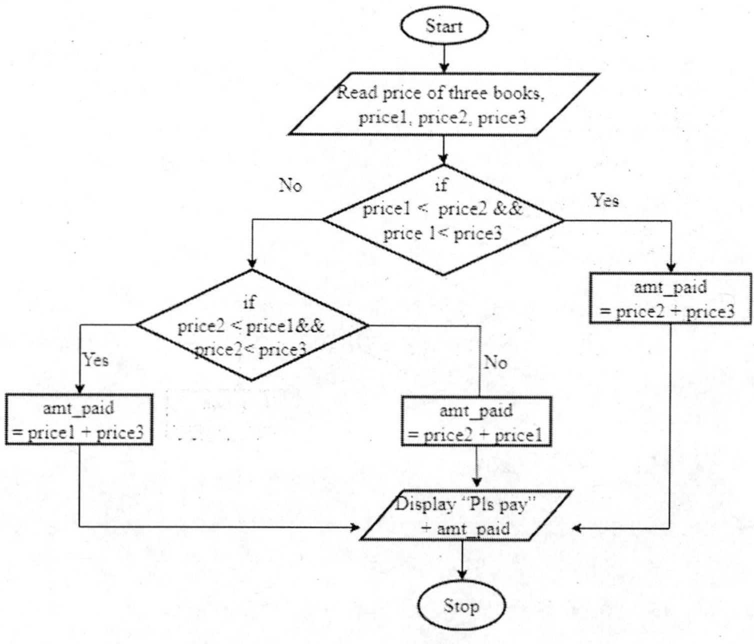

***Figure 2.18**: Flowchart illustrating the program 2.18*

Python code

Python code for the program is as follows:

```
price1=int(input("enter price of book 1 "))
price2=int(input("enter price of book 2 "))
price3=int(input("enter price of book 3 "))

if (price1 <  price2 and price1< price3):
    amt_paid = price2 + price3
elif (price2 < price1 and price2< price3):
```

```
    amt_paid = price1 + price3
else:
    amt_paid = price2 + price1
print("Pls pay",amt_paid)
```

Python code explanation

The code prompts the user to enter the prices of three books and compare them. The conditions are combined using **and** operator. It picks the price of two books with higher MRP than the third one and calculates the amount to be paid based on those two books. It then provides the appropriate output message indicating the amount to be paid.

C code

C code for the program is as follows:

```
void main()
{
float price1, price2, price3;
float amt_paid;
printf("Enter price of 3 books: ");
scanf("%f%f%f",&price1, &price2, &price3);
if ((price1 <  price2) && (price1< price3))
amt_paid = price2 + price3;
else if ((price2 < price1) && (price2 < price3))
amt_paid = price1 + price3;
else
amt_paid = price2 + price1;
printf("Pls pay %f",amt_paid);
}
```

C code explanation

The code prompts the user to enter the prices of three books and compare them. The conditions are combined using **and** operator. It picks the price of two books with higher MRP than the third one and calculates the amount to be paid based on those two books. It then provides the appropriate output message indicating the amount to be paid.

Conclusion

The chapter has discussed decision statements through flowcharts, algorithms, and coding. With the help of several examples, the different flavors of condition statements are presented.

In the next chapter, control flow statements (loops) will be discussed with the help of a good number of solved programs.

Points to remember

- For comparing the values, double equal to sign (`==`) is used.
- In Python, indentation plays an important role in deciding the code block.
- In C, a single line block can be written without special care.
- Multiple line blocks in C should be enclosed within curly `{}` brackets.
- An **`if`** statement within the **`if`** block is known as a nested **`if else`** statement.
- It is possible to check many options one after the other using the **`if- else if - else`** statement.
- Logical operators and (**&&**) / or (**||**) allow us to combine multiple conditions in a single **`if-`** statement.
- While writing the code, the order of checking the conditions should be decided carefully.

Questions

1. Write a program to check if the number entered by the user is divisible by 4 using the **`if`** statement.
2. Extend question 1 to print the appropriate message using the **`else`** statement.
3. Extend question 1. If the number is not divisible by 4, then check whether it is an even number.
4. Further to question 2, if the number is divisible by 4, check if it is divisible by 9.
5. Write a program to check whether the user is an adult male.

CHAPTER 3
Simple Loops

Introduction

In this chapter, the basic loop statements, while-loop and for-loop, are discussed. In programming, a loop is a fundamental control structure that allows you to execute a block of code repeatedly as long as a certain condition is met. Loops are essential for automating repetitive tasks, iterating over certain statements, and performing various computational tasks efficiently. It optimizes the code as well. There are different types of loops in most programming languages, but the two main types are while-loops and for-loops:

- **While-loop**: A while loop repeatedly executes a block of code as long as a specified condition is evaluated to be true. The loop continues to run until the condition becomes false. The loop counter is initialibefore the beginning of the while-loop. It is incremented inside the loop.

- **For-loop**: A for loop is used when you know the number of iterations. It allows you to iterate over a sequence (list, tuple, string) or a range of values. All three operations, initialization, increment, and condition check, are performed using a single statement.

The flowchart presents loops by pointing the edge backward until the loop condition becomes false.

Structure

In this chapter, there are a total of 16 programs, and five sub-sections complement each program:

- Understand the program objective with sample test cases consisting of inputs and outputs. It will give the user an understanding of what kind of user input is expected and what result will be projected for a particular program.
- Understand the program with an algorithm. This will help the user to understand the logic and methodology behind writing the sequence of steps required to solve a program.
- Visualize the program flow with flowcharts. Program objectives can be understood easily with the flowchart representation. Users will understand which symbols to use in which context throughout different program's flowchart representations.
- Python source code of each program. Each program's source code in Python is provided to the user so the user can understand the basic operations of the language. An explanation of each code is also provided.
- C implementation of each program. Users can learn the basic concepts of C language with the provided C language code and its explanation for every program.

Objectives

This chapter provides readers with a comprehensive understanding of control statements and their importance in the development of programs. It covers the fundamental concepts behind control statements and how they can execute the instruction repeatedly using a loop. Additionally, the chapter imparts the skills necessary for visual representations of control statements in program flow using flowcharts, facilitating a clearer and more intuitive grasp of their functionality.

Moreover, the chapter focuses on practical application by demonstrating how to implement control statements (for-loop and while-loop) in Python and C programming languages. Sample codes are provided to offer hands-on experience, allowing readers to practice and gain confidence in effectively utilizing loops in real-world coding scenarios. By the end of this chapter, readers will have acquired the knowledge and skills to leverage control statements in their programming.

Program 3.1: Display '*'

Display *for **n** times.

Sample input output

Test case #1:

Input: `Enter a number: 3`

Output: `* * *`

Test case #2:

Input: `Enter a number: 6`

Output: `* * * * * *`

Algorithm

To run the above program, the following steps are needed:

Step 1. **`Start`**

Step 2. **`Input n`**

Step 3. **`i=1`**

Step 4. **`Repeat if i< = n:`**

```
print "*"
i=i+1
```

Step 5. **`Stop`**

Flowchart

Figure 3.1 illustrates the program in the form of a flowchart:

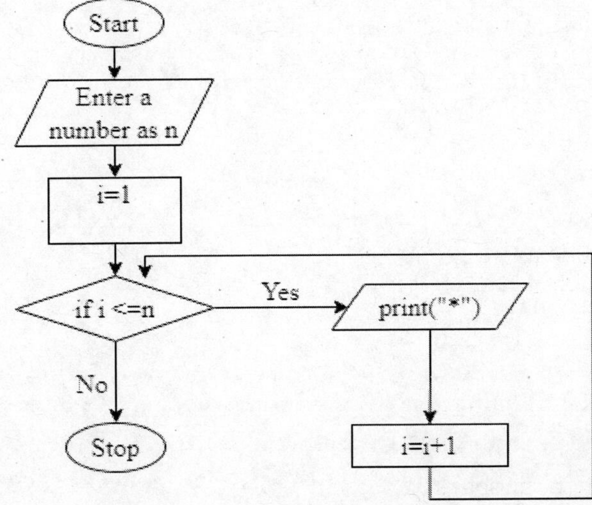

***Figure 3.1**: Flowchart illustrating the program 3.1*

Python code

Python code for the program is as follows:

```
n=int(input("Enter a number: "))
1. i=1
2. while(i<=n):
3.       print("*", end=" ")
4.       i=i+1
```

Python code explanation

This Python code prompts the user to enter a number, and the input function is used to read the input from the user. The input is initially treated as a string, so we use **`int()`** to convert it to an integer and store it in the variable **`n`**. The variable **`i`** is initialized to **`1`**. The variable **`i`** is used to keep track of the current iteration. To repeat statements 4 and 5, while loop is used. The loop will continue executing if the value of **`i`** is less than or equal to **`n`**.

Inside the **`while`** loop, this line prints an asterisk (*) to the console using the print function. The **`end=" "`** argument is used to specify that after printing the asterisk, a space should be added instead of the default newline character. This means that each asterisk will be printed side by side on the same line instead of each one on a new line.

After each execution of the while block, the counter **`i`** is increased by **`1`**. This is essential because it ensures that the loop will eventually reach a point where the condition (**`i<= n`**) becomes false, and the loop will terminate.

So, it should be noted that instead of writing the statement 4 again and again, it is written once, while loop helps repeat the statement n times.

Also, note the indentation in the code. Since *steps* 4and5 are indented towards the right, both belong to the block of **`while`** loop.

C code

C code for the program is as follows:

```
#include<stdio.h>
void main()
{
int i, n;
printf("Enter a number: " );
scanf("%d", &n);
```

```
7. i=1;
8. while(i<=n)
9. {
10. printf ("*");
11. i=i+1;
12. }
13. }
```

C code explanation

This C code prompts the user to enter a number **n** and reads the input from the user using the **scanf()** function. The variable **i** is an integer-type variable that is initialized toequal1. The variable **i** is used to keep track of the current iteration. *Steps 10* and *11* are enclosed within the curly brackets, indicating that it is a block of while-loop. These statements will continue repeating if the value of **i** is less than or equal to **n**.

Inside the **while** loop, this line prints an asterisk (*) to the console using the **printf()** function. After each execution of the while block, the counter **i** is increased by 1. This is essential because it ensures that the loop will eventually reach a point where the condition (`i`<= **n**) becomes false, and the loop will terminate.

Program 3.2: Display natural numbers

Display first n natural numbers.

Sample input output

Test case #1:

Input: `Enter a number: 4`

Output: **`1 2 3 4`**

Test case #2:

Input: `Enter a number: 7`

Output: **`1 2 3 4 5 6 7`**

Algorithm

To run the above program, the following steps are needed:

Step 1. **`Start`**

Step 2. **`Input n`**

Step 3. **i=1**

Step 4. **Repeat if i< = n:**

print i

i=i+1

Step 5. **Stop**

Flowchart

Figure 3.2 illustrates the program in the form of a flowchart:

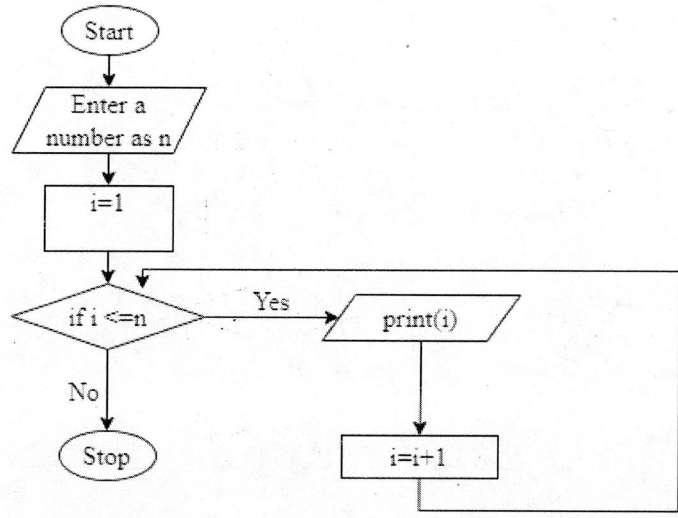

***Figure 3.2**: Flowchart illustrating the program 3.2*

Python code

Python code for the program is as follows:

```
n=int(input("Enter a number: "))
i=1
while(i<=n):
    print(i, end=" ")
    i=i+1
```

Python code explanation

The Python code is to print first n natural numbers (starting from 1). It takes an integer input `n` from the user. The variable `i` is initialized to `1` to keep track of the count of iterations of the loop. Then, it uses a while loop to print numbers from **1** to **n**, separated by spaces in ascending order. The loop stops when the value of **i** becomes more than **n**. Note the indentation of the while-block.

C code

C code for the program is as follows:

```
#include<stdio.h>
void main()
{
int i, n;
printf("Enter a number: " );
scanf("%d", &n);
i=1;
while(i<=n)
{
printf (" %d", i);
i=i+1;
}
}
```

C code explanation

The C code prints first n natural numbers (starting from 1). It takes an integer input **n** from the user. The variable **i** is initialized to **1** to keep track of the count of iterations of the loop. Then, it uses a while loop to print numbers from **1** to **n**, separated by spaces in ascending order. The loop stops when the value of **i** becomes more than **n**. Note the curly **{}** brackets of the while-block.

Program 3.3: Display square of natural numbers

Display the square of the first n natural numbers.

Sample input output

Test case #1:

Input: `Enter a number: 3`

Output: 149

Test case # 2:

Input: `Enter a number: 5`

Output: **1491625**

Algorithm

To run the above program, the following steps are needed:

Step 1. **Start**

Step 2. **Input n**

Step 3. **i=1**

Step 4. **Repeat if i< = n:**

```
print i*i
i=i+1
```

Step 5. **Stop**

Flowchart

Figure 3.3 illustrates the program in the form of a flowchart:

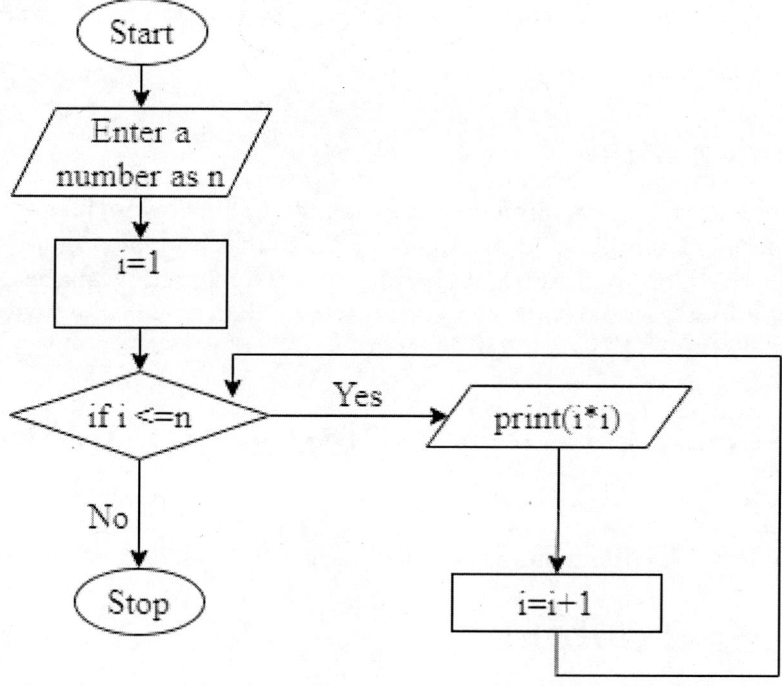

***Figure 3.3**: Flowchart illustrating the program 3.3*

Python code

Python code for the program is as follows:

```
n=int(input("Enter a number: "))
i=1
while(i<=n):
    print(i*i)
    i=i+1
```

Python code explanation

This code takes an integer input from the user, stores it in the variable **n**, and then uses a while loop to calculate and print the square of each number from **1** to **n**. Each square is printed on a new line. The loop iterates from **1** to **n**, inclusive, and **i** is incremented by **1** after each iteration.

C code

C code for the program is as follows:

```
#include<stdio.h>
void main()
{
int i, n;
printf("Enter a number: " );
scanf("%d", &n);
i=1;
while(i<=n)
{
printf (" %d", i*i);
i=i+1;
}
}
```

C code explanation

This C code takes an integer input from the user, stores it in the variable **n**, and then uses a while loop to calculate and print the square of each number from **1** to **n**. Each square is printed on a new line. The loop iterates from **1**to **n**, inclusive, and **i** is incremented by

1 after each iteration. Note the placement of curly brackets. Everything inside the curly brackets of the while-loop is repeated till the condition **i<=n** becomes false.

Program 3.4: Display cube of numbers

Display the cube of numbers between the range **n** and **m** where **n** and **m** are inclusive.

Sample input output

Test case #1:

Input:

```
Enter number1: 5
Enter number2: 9
```

Output: **125216343512729**

Test case #2:

Input:

```
Enter number1: 2
Enter number2: 5
```

Output: **82764125**

Algorithm

To run the above program, the following steps are needed to be followed:

Step 1. **Start**

Step 2. **Input n,m**

Step 3. **i=n**

Step 4. **Repeat if i< = m:**

```
print i*i*i
i=i+1
```

Step 5. **Stop**

Flowchart

Figure 3.4 illustrates the program in the form of a flowchart:

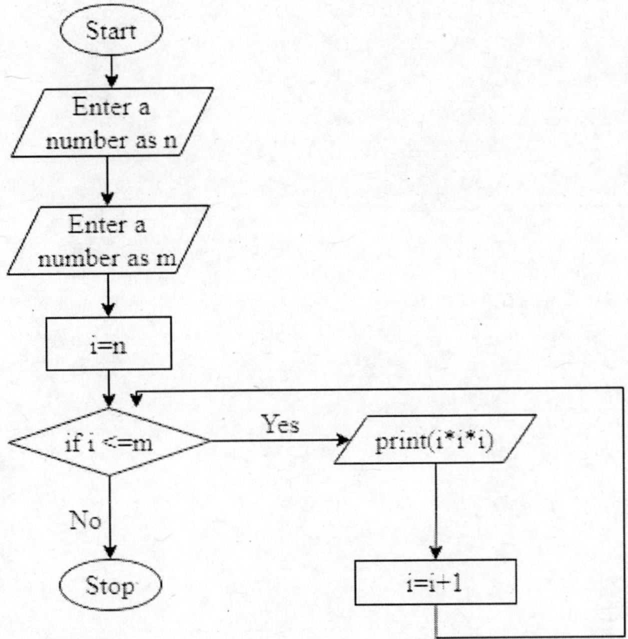

***Figure 3.4**: Flowchart illustrating the program 3.4*

Python code

Python code for the program is as follows:

```
n=int(input("Enter number1: "))
m=int(input("Enter number2: "))

i=n
while(i<=m):
      print(i*i*i)
      i=i+1
```

Python code explanation

This Python code prompts the user to enter two integer numbers, n, and m, and then uses a **`while`** loop to calculate and print the cube of each number from **`n`** to **`m`**. The variable **`i`** is initialized with the value of **`n`**. The loop starts with **`i=n`** and stops when i becomes greater than m. The loop variable **`i`** is incremented by **`1`** after each iteration to ensure the progress of the while-loop. Inside the loop, the cube of the current value **`i`** is calculated and printed on the console.

C code

C code for the program is as follows:

```
#include<stdio.h>
void main()
{
int i, n, m;
printf("Enter two numbers: " );
scanf("%d%d", &n, &m);
i=n;
while(i<=m)
{
printf (" %d", i*i*i);
i=i+1;
}
}
```

C code explanation

This C code asks the user to enter two integer numbers, `n`, and `m`, and then uses a while-loop to calculate and print the cube of each number from `n` to `m`. The variable `i` is initialized with the value of `n`. The loop starts with `i=n` and stops when `i` becomes greater than `m`. The loop variable `i` is incremented by `1` after each iteration to ensure the progress of the while-loop. Inside the loop, the cube of the current value of `i` is calculated and printed on the console.

Program 3.5: Display multiples

Display first `n` multiples of `5`.

Sample input output

Test case #1:

Input: `Enter number: 4`

Output: **`5101520`**

Test case #2:

Input: `Enter number: 6`

Output:**`51015202530`**

Algorithm

To run the above program, the following steps are needed to be followed:

Step 1. **Start**

Step 2. **Input n**

Step 3. **i=1**

Step 4. **Repeat if i< = n:**

```
print 5*i
i=i+1
```

Step 5. **Stop**

Flowchart

Figure 3.5 illustrates the program in the form of a flowchart:

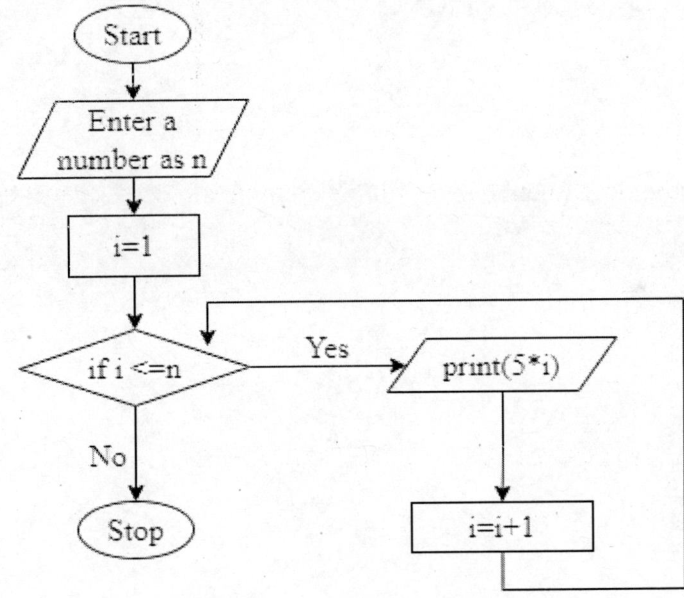

***Figure 3.5**: Flowchart illustrating the program 3.5*

Python code

Python code for the program is as follows:

```
n=int(input("Enter number: "))
i=1
```

```
while(i<=n):
    print(5*i)
    i=i+1
```

Python code explanation

This Python code prompts the user to enter an integer number, n, and then uses a `while` loop to calculate and print the n multiples of 5, such as 5, 10, 15, and so on. The loop iterates from `1` to `n`, inclusive, and the loop variable `i` is incremented by `1` after each iteration. The while-loop continues as long as the value of `i` is less than or equal to `n`. Inside the loop, it calculates the multiple of 5 by multiplying the current value of `i` with 5 and printing the result on the console. The block of the while-loop is presented with indentation.

C code

C code for the program is as follows:

```
#include<stdio.h>
void main()
{
int i, n;
printf("Enter a numbers: " );
scanf("%d", &n);
i=1;
while(i<=n)
{
printf (" %d", 5*i);
i=i+1;
}
}
```

C code explanation

This code prompts the user to enter an integer number, `n`, and then uses a `while` loop to calculate and print the `n` multiples of `5`, such as 5, 10, 15, and so on. The loop iterates from `1` to `n`, inclusive, and the loop variable `i` is incremented by `1` after each iteration. The while-loop continues as long as the value of `i` is less than or equal to `n`. Inside the loop, it calculates the multiple of `5` by multiplying the current value of `i` with `5` and printing the result on the console. The block of the while-loop is presented within curly brackets.

Program 3.6: Find sum and average

Display the sum and average of the first 10 natural numbers.

Sample input output

Test case #1:

Output: `Sum and Average are 55, 5.5`

Algorithm

To run the above program, the following steps are needed to be followed:

Step 1. **`Start`**

Step 2. **`Declare the variables as i,n,s,avg`**

Step 3. **`i=0, s=0, avg=0`**

Step 4. **`if i<n`**

```
        i=i+1
        s = s + i
```

Step 5. **`Repeat step 4`**

Step 6. **`Display s`**

Step 7. **`avg=s/10`**

Step 8. **`Display avg`**

Step 9. **`Stop`**

Flowchart

Figure 3.6 illustrates the program in the form of a flowchart:

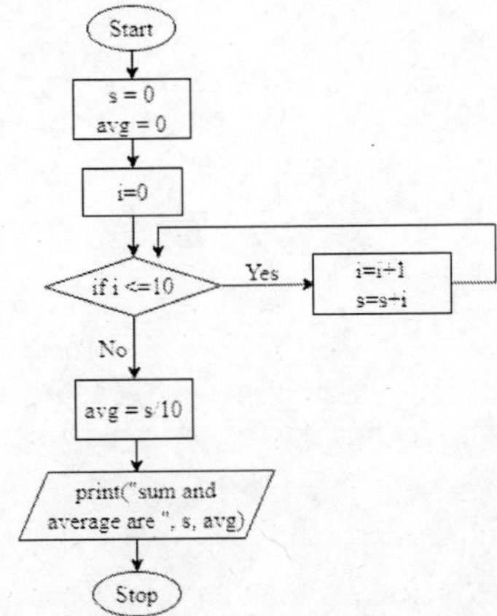

Figure 3.6: *Flowchart illustrating the program 3.6*

Python code

Python code for the program is as follows:

```
i=0
s=0
avg=0
while ( i<10):
      i=i+1
      s = s + i
avg=s/10

print("Sum and Average are ", s, avg)
```

Python code explanation

This code calculates the sum and average of the first 10 natural numbers and then prints the result. Here, a variable **`i`** is initialized with the value **`0`**. This variable will be used as a loop counter. The variables s and avg are used to store the sum and average of the numbers, respectively. Both are initialized with a value of **`0`**, indicating that the initial sum and average are zero. Inside the loop, increment the value of **`i`** by **`1`** to count the loop iterations from **`1`** to **`10`**. Also, the current value of **`i`** is added to s to continuously accumulate the sum of the numbers from **`1`** to **`10`**. Once the sum of 10 numbers is calculated in the while-loop, the sum, **`s`**, is divided by **`10`** to get the average and stored in **`avg`**.

Note: The same problem statement can also be solved without using loops. Use the formula s=n(n+1)/2 and avg=s/n.

C code

C code for the program is as follows:

```
#include<stdio.h>
void main()
{
int i, s=0;
float avg=0.0;
i=0;
while(i<10)
{
```

```
i=i+1;
s=s+i;
}
avg=s/10.0;
printf("The sum and average of first 10 natural numbers are : %d and %f", s, avg);
}
```

C code explanation

This code calculates the sum and average of the first 10 natural numbers and then prints the result. Here, a variable **i** is initialized with the value **0**. This variable will be used as a loop counter. The variables **s** and **avg** are used to store the sum and average of the numbers, respectively. Since the sum of numbers can be an integer value, and the average can be a decimal value, **s** is declared int type and **avg** as float type. Both are initialized with a value of **0**, indicating that the initial sum and average are zero. Inside the loop, increment the value of **i** by **1** to count the loop iterations from **1** to **10**. Also, the current value of **i** is added to **s** to continuously accumulate the sum of the numbers from **1** to **10**. Once the sum of 10 numbers is calculated in the while-loop, the sum, **s**, is divided by **10.0** to get the average and stored in **avg**.

Note: The same problem statement can also be solved without using loops. Use the formula s=n(n+1)/2 and avg=s/n.

Program 3.7: Find sum of sqaure

Display the sum of the square of the first n natural numbers.

Sample input output

Test case #1:

Input: `Enter a number: 10`

Output: **`Sum is 385`**

Test case #2:

Input: `Enter a number: 18`

Output: **`Sum is 2109`**

Algorithm

To run the above program, the following steps are needed to be followed:

Step 1. **`Start`**

Step 2. **`Input n`**

Step 3. **`i=0, s=0`**

Step 4. **`Repeat if i< n:`**

```
i=i+1
s = s+i*i
```

Step 5. **`Display s`**

Step 6. **`Stop`**

Flowchart

Figure 3.7 illustrates the program in the form of a flowchart:

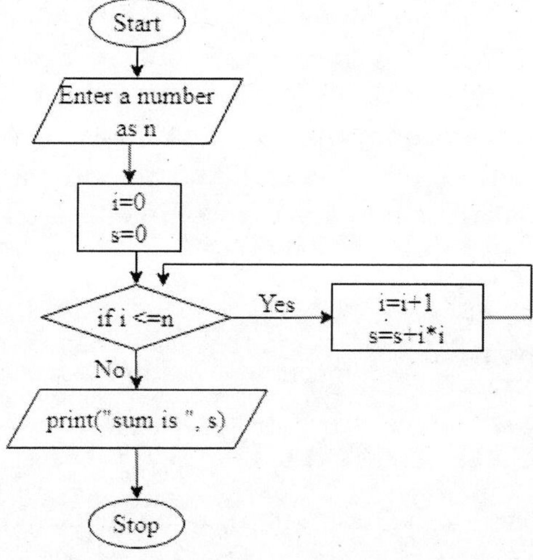

***Figure 3.7**: Flowchart illustrating the program 3.7*

Python code

Python code for the *program 3.7* is as follows:

```
n=int(input("Enter a number: "))
i=0
s=0
while ( i<n):
    i=i+1
    s = s + i*i
print("Sum is ",s)
```

Python code explanation

This code calculates the sum of squares of the first **n** natural numbers and then prints the result. First, it prompts the user to enter a number and reads the input as an integer. Store it in the variable **n**. Then, it initializes a variable **i** with the value **0**. This variable will be used as a loop counter. Variable **s**is initialized with the value **0**. This variable will be used to store the sum of squares. While-loop starts with the condition **(i< n)**. The loop will continue if the value of **i** is less than **n**. Inside the loop, the value of **i** is incremented by **1**. Also, the square of the current value of **i** (**i*i**) is calculated and added to the variable **s**. This will continuously accumulate the sum of squares of the numbers from **1** to **n**.

C code

C code for the program is as follows:

```
#include<stdio.h>
void main()
{
int i, n;
int s=0;
printf("Enter a numbers: " );
scanf("%d", &n);
i=0;
while(i<n)
{
i=i+1;
s=s+i*i;
}
printf("The sum of square of first %d natural numbers is %d", n, s);
}
```

C code explanation

This code calculates the sum of squares of the first **n** natural numbers and then prints the result. First, it prompts the user to enter a number and reads the input as an integer. Store it in the variable **n**. Then, it initializes a variable **i** with the value **0**. This variable will be used as a loop counter. Variable **s** is declared as an integer and initialized with the value **0**. This variable will be used to store the sum of squares. While-loop starts with the condition **(i< n)**. The loop will continue as long as the value of **i** is less than **n**. Inside the loop, the value of **i** is incremented by **1**. Also, the square of the current value of **i**(**i*i**) is calculated and added to the variable **s**. This will continuously accumulate the sum of squares of the numbers from **1** to **n**.

Program 3.8: Find factorial

Display the product of the first n natural numbers (factorial of **n**).

Sample input output

Test case #1:

Input: `Enter a number: 5`

Output: **`Product is 120`**

Test case #2:

Input: `Enter a number: 10`

Output: **`Product is 3628800`**

Algorithm

To run the above program, the following steps are needed to be followed:

Step 1. **Start**

Step 2. **Input n**

Step 3. **i=0, p=1**

Step 4. **Repeat if i< = n:**

```
i=i+1
p = p*i
```

Step 5. **Display p**

Step 6. **Stop**

Flowchart

Figure 3.8 illustrates the program in the form of a flowchart:

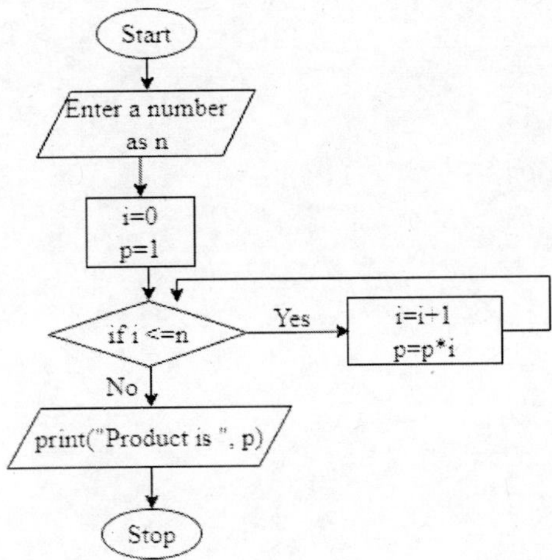

Figure 3.8: Flowchart illustrating the program 3.8

Python code

Python code for the program is as follows:

```
n=int(input("Enter a number: "))
i=0
p=1
while ( i<n):
     i=i+1
     p = p * i
print("Product is ",p)
```

Python code explanation

The code prints the product of first n natural numbers. It is also called the factorial of a number. Here, **i** is used to count the loop repetition. Variable **p** is used to store the accumulated product of n numbers. It is initialized with a value of **1** as something multiplied by a number results in that number itself. While-loop starts with **0** and goes till the value of **i** is less than **n**. Finally, the value of **p** is displayed.

C code

C code for the program is as follows:

```
#include<stdio.h>
void main()
```

```
{
int i, n;
int p=1;
printf("Enter a numbers: " );
scanf("%d", &n);
i=0;
while(i<n)
{
i=i+1;
p=p*i;
}
printf("The factorial of %d is %d", n, p);
}
```

C code explanation

The code prints the product of first n natural numbers. It is also called the factorial of a number. Here, `i` is used to count the loop repetition. Variable `p` is used to store the accumulated product of n numbers. It is initialized with a value of `1` as something multiplied by a number results in that number itself. While-loop starts with `0` and goes till the value of `i` is less than `n`. Finally, the value of `p` is displayed.

Program 3.9: Find 2 raise to the power n

Take **n** as input and compute **2^n** (**2** raised to the power **n**).

Sample input output

Test case #1:

Input: `Enter n:3`

Output: **2^3 =8**

Test case #2:

Input: `Enter n:6`

Output:2^6 = 64**

Algorithm

To run the above program, the following steps are needed to be:

Step 1. **Start**

Step 2. **Read n**

Step 3. **p=1, i=1**

Step 4. **Repeat if i<=n**

```
p=p*2
i=i+1
```

Step 5. **Print("2^",n," = ",p)**

Step 6. **Stop**

Flowchart

Figure 3.9 illustrates the program in the form of a flowchart:

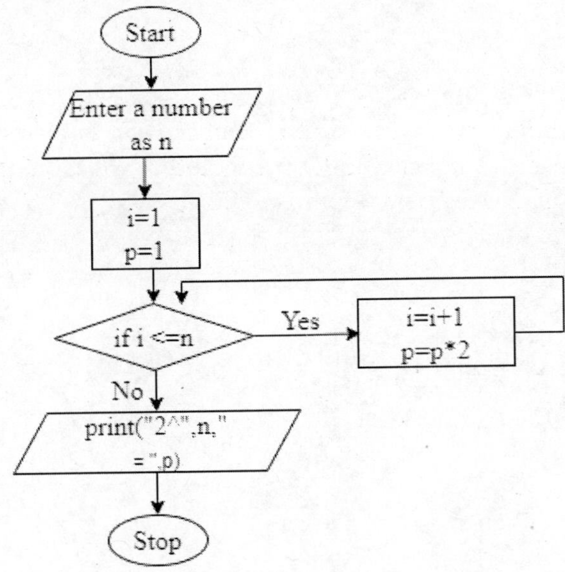

***Figure 3.9**: Flowchart illustrating the program 3.9*

Python code

Python code for the program is as follows:

```
n=int(input("Enter n: "))
p=1
```

```
for i in range(1,n+1):
    p=p*2
print("2^",n," = ",p)
```

Python code explanation

To calculate **2** raised to the power **n**, we need to multiply **2** to itself n times. The same logic is implemented using Python code. In this program, instead of while-loop, for-loop is used, although while-loop can also be used. After taking input from the user, variable **p** is initialized to **1**. This variable calculates and stores the result of **2** raised to the power **n**. In the for-loop, it starts with a keyword **for** that iterates over the values in the range from **1** ton (inclusive). The variable **i** takes the values *1, 2, 3, ..., n* during each iteration represented using range(**1**,**n+1**). The range function includes the first parameter, **1**, and excludes the last parameter. Hence, it will generate the values from **1** to **n**. Then, the current value of **p** is multiplied by **2** (**2** is the base for the exponentiation). This step is performed for each value of **i** in the loop, effectively calculating *2^1, 2^2, 2^3, ..., 2^n*. Finally, the calculated value of **p**, representing **2** raised to the power **n**, is displayed.

C code

C code for the program is as follows:

```
#include<stdio.h>
void main()
{
int i, n;
int p=1;
printf("Enter a numbers: " );
scanf("%d", &n);
i=1;
while(i<=n)
{
p=p*2;
i=i+1;
}
printf("The 2^%d is %d", n, p);
}
```

C code explanation

To calculate **2** raised to the power **n**, we need to multiply **2** to itself n times. The same logic is implemented using this C code. Here, after taking input from the user, variable **p** is initialized to **1**. This variable calculates and stores the result of **2** raised to the power **n**. The while-loop iterates from **1** to **n**. Then, the current value of **p** is multiplied by **2** (**2** is the base for the exponentiation). This step is performed for each value of **i** in the loop, effectively calculating *2^1, 2^2, 2^3, ..., 2^n*. The value of **i** is incremented after every iteration. Finally, the calculated value of **p**, representing **2** raised to the power **n**, is displayed.

Program 3.10: Find x raise to the power n

Take **x** and **n** as input and compute **x^n** (**x** raised to the power **n**).

Sample input output

Test case #1:

Input:

```
Enter n: 3
Enter x: 4
```

Output: 4 ^ 3 = 64

Test case #2:

Input:

```
Enter n: 2
Enter x: 6
```

Output: 6 ^ 2 = 36

Algorithm

To run the above program, the following steps are needed:

Step 1. **Start**

Step 2. **Read n**

Step 3. **Read x**

Step 4. **p=1, i=1**

Step 5. **Repeat if i<=n**

```
p=p*x
i=i+1
```

Step 6. **Print(x, "^",n," = ",p)**

Step 7. **Stop**

Flowchart

Figure 3.10 illustrates the program in the form of a flowchart:

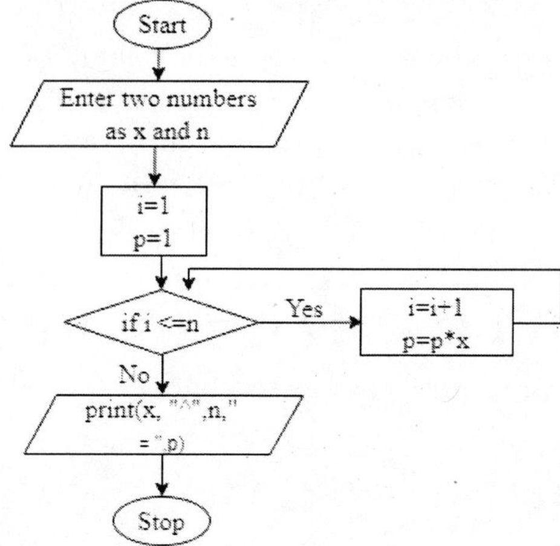

***Figure 3.10**: Flowchart illustrating the program 3.10*

Python code

Python code for the *program 3.10* is as follows:

```
n=int(input("Enter n: "))
x=int(input("Enter x: "))
p=1
for i in range(1,n+1):
    p=p*x
print(x,"^",n," = ",p)
```

Python code explanation

To calculate **x** raised to the power **n**, we need to multiply **x** by itself **n** times. The same logic is implemented using Python code. The remaining part is the same as *program 3.9*.

C code

C code for the program is as follows:

```
#include<stdio.h>
void main()
{
```

```
int i, n, x;
int p=1;
printf("Enter two numbers: " );
scanf("%d%d", &n, &x);
i=1;
while(i<=n)
{
p=p*x;
i=i+1;
}
printf("The %d^%d is %d",x, n, p);
}
```

C code explanation

To calculate `x` raised to the power `n`, we need to multiply `x` by itself n times. The same logic is implemented using this code. The remaining part is the same as *program 3.9*.

Program 3.11: Display the multiplication table

Display the multiplication table of a number taken as input from the user.

Sample input output

Test case #1:

Input: `Enter a number: 11`

Output:

```
11 x 1 = 11
11 x 2 = 22
11 x 3 = 33
11 x 4 = 44
11 x 5 = 55
11 x 6 = 66
11 x 7 = 77
11 x 8 = 88
```

```
11x 9 = 99
11 x 10 = 110
```

Test case #2:

Input: `Enter a number: 4`

Output:

```
4 x 1 = 4
4 x 2 = 8
4 x 3 = 12
4 x 4 = 16
4 x 5 = 20
4 x 6 = 24
4 x 7 = 28
4 x 8 = 32
4 x 9 = 36
4 x 10 = 40
```

Algorithm

To run the above program, the following steps are needed to be followed:

Step 1. **Start**

Step 2. **Accept a number as input from the user and store it in a variable 'num'.**

Step 3. **Loop from 1 to 10:**

Multiply 'num' with the loop variable and store it in a variable 'result'.

Print 'num', '*', loop variable, '=', 'result'.

Step 4. **End of loop.**

Step 5. **Stop**

Flowchart

Figure 3.11 illustrates the program in the form of a flowchart:

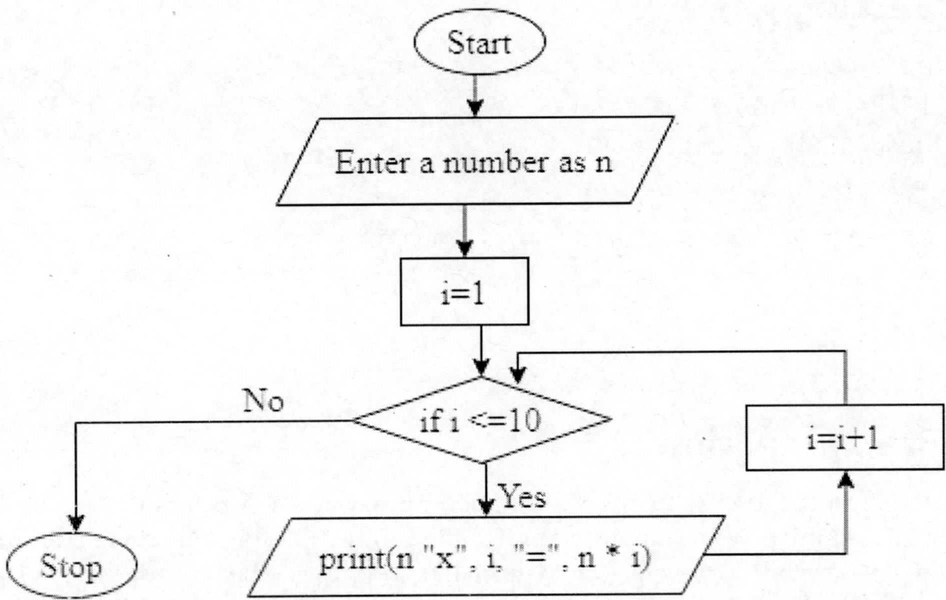

***Figure 3.11**: Flowchart illustrating the program 3.11*

Python code

Python code for the *program 3.11* is as follows:

```
num = int(input("Enter a number: "))

for i in range(1, 11):
    print(num, "x", i, "=", num*i)
```

Python code explanation

The code prompts the user to enter a number and then prints the multiplication table for that number from **1** to **10** using for-loop. Since the **range()** function includes the first parameter and excludes the second parameter, range**(1,11)** is written to iterate the for-loop from **1** to **10**. It displays the multiplication equation with the number and multiples on each line.

C code

C code for the program is as follows:

```
#include <stdio.h>
int main() {
```

```
int num;

printf("Enter a number: ");
scanf("%d", &num);
for (int i = 1; i <= 10; i++) {
printf("%d * %d = %d\n", num, i, num*i);
}
return 0;
}
```

C code explanation

The code prompts the user to enter a number, num, and then prints the multiplication table for that number from **`1`** to **`10`** using for-loop. In C, the for-loop contains three sub-statements separated by a semi-colon: initialization (**`i=1`**), then condition (**`i<10`**), and finally increment (**`i++`**). According to the for-loop statement, the variable **`i`** is used to count the loop iterations. It starts with a value of **`1`**. The value of **`i`** is incremented by **`1`** after every iteration. The loop stops when the value of **`i`** becomes greater than **`10`**. It displays the multiplication equation with the number and multiples on each line.

Program 3.12: Find sum of series 1

Find the sum of the series: *1+ 3 + 5+........+ (2*n-1).*

Sample input output

Test case #1:

Input: `Enter n: 4`

Output: 16

Test case #2:

Input: `Enter n: 7`

Output: 49

Algorithm

To run the above program, the following steps are needed to be followed:

Step 1. **`Start`**

Step 2. **`Read n`**

Step 3. **i=1**

Step 4. **s=0**

Step 5. **Repeat if i<=n**

s=s+2*i-1

Step 6. **Print s**

Step 7. **Stop**

Flowchart

Figure 3.12 illustrates the program in the form of a flowchart:

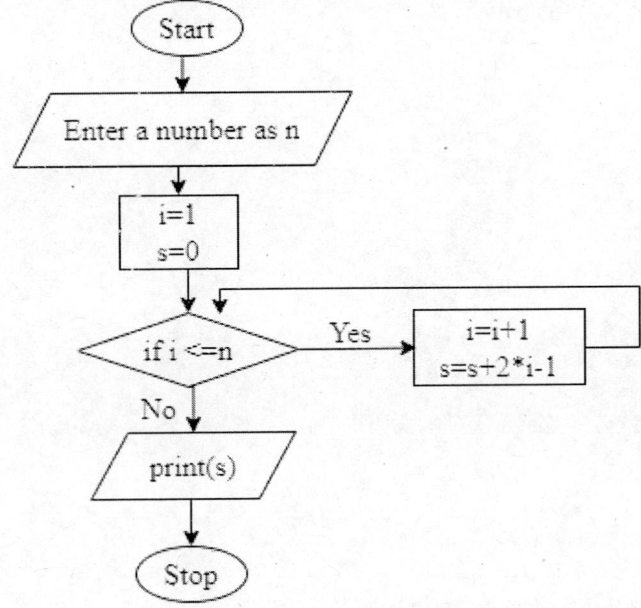

***Figure 3.12**: Flowchart illustrating the program 3.12*

Python code

Python code for the *program 3.12* is as follows:

```
n=int(input("Enter n: "))
s=0

for i in range(1, n+1):
    s=s+2*i-1
print(s)
```

Python code explanation

To print the sum of series: _1+ 3 + 5+........+ (2*n-1)_, any n^{th} number can be generated by substituting the value of **`n`** in (**`2*n-1`**). The same concept is used in the code. After taking input from the user, the variable *s* is initialized with a value of **`0`** and is used to store the sum of the series. Inside the **`for`** loop, the current value of **`i`** is used to calculate the **`i`**-th odd number (**`2*i-1`**), which is added to the variable **`s`**. This step is performed for each value of **`i`** in the loop, effectively calculating the sum of the first **`n`** odd numbers. After the loop, the code prints the calculated sum of the first **`n`** odd numbers.

C code

C code for the program is as follows:

```
#include<stdio.h>
void main()
{
int i, n;
int s=0;
printf("Enter a numbers: " );
scanf("%d", &n);

for(i =1; i<=n; i++)
 {
        s=s+2*i-1;
 }
printf("The sum of the series is %d", s);
}
```

C code explanation

To print the sum of series: _1+ 3 + 5+........+ (2*n-1)_, any n^{th} number can be generated by substituting the value of **`n`** in (**`2*n-1`**). The same concept is used in the code. After taking input from the user, the variable s is initialized with a value of 0 and is used to store the sum of the series. Inside the **`for`** loop, the current value of **`i`** is used to calculate the **`i`**-th odd number (**`2*i-1`**), which is added to the variable **`s`**. This step is performed for each value of **`i`** in the loop, effectively calculating the sum of the first **`n`** odd numbers. After the loop, the code prints the calculated sum of the first **`n`** odd numbers.

Program 3.13: Find sum of series 2

Find the sum of series: *1/2!+2/3!+3/4!..........*

Sample input output

Test case #1:

Input: `Enter the number of terms: 4`

Output: **`Sum of the series is: 1.4833333333333332`**

Test case #2:

Input: `Enter the number of terms: 8`

Output: **`Sum of the series is: 1.4999944885361551`**

Algorithm

To run the above program, the following steps are needed to be followed:

Step 1. **Start**

Step 2. **Initialize a variable n to the number of terms to be added in the series.**

Step 3. **Initialize two variables, sum and fact, to 0 and 1 respectively.**

Step 4. **Using a loop ranging from 1 to n, perform the following steps:**

update fact as fact * (i+1).

sum=sum+i/f

Step 5. **Print the final value of sum.**

Step 6. **Stop**

Flowchart

Figure 3.13 illustrates the program in the form of a flowchart:

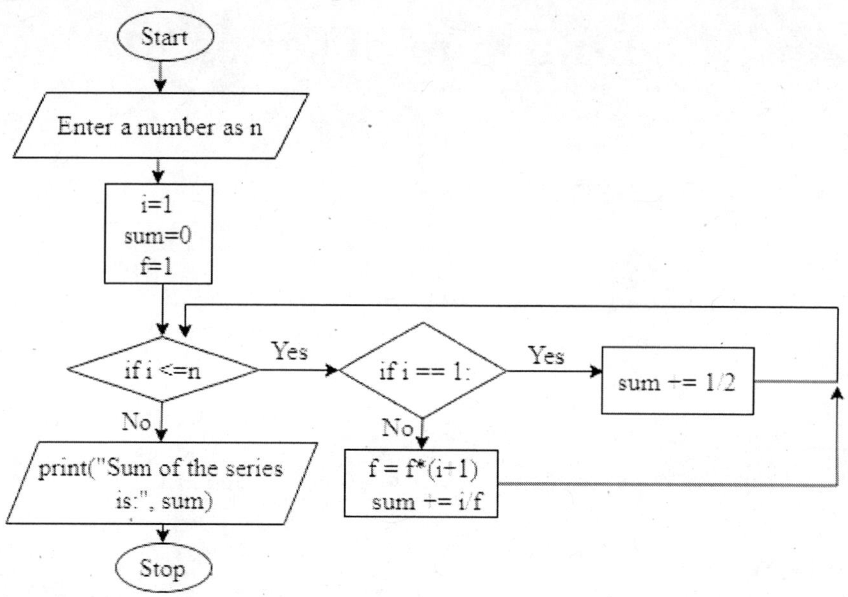

Figure 3.13: Flowchart illustrating the program 3.13

Python code

Python code for the *program 3.13* is as follows:

```
n = int(input("Enter the number of terms: "))
sum = 0
f=1

for i in range(1, n+1):
    if i == 1:
        sum += 1/2
    else:
        f = f*(i+1)
        sum =sum + i/f

print("Sum of the series is:", sum)
```

Python code explanation

The code prompts the user to enter the number of terms (**n**) and then calculates the sum of a series using a for-loop. It considers a special case for the first term (**1/2**) and computes subsequent terms based on the factorial. Finally, it prints the sum of the series. The series formula is *1/2 + 1/2! + 2/3! + 3/4! + ... + (n-1)/n!*.

C code

C code for the program is as follows:

```
#include <stdio.h>

int main() {
int n;
double sum = 0, factorial = 1;
printf("Enter the value of n: ");
scanf("%d", &n);

for(int i = 1; i <= n; i++) {
factorial *= i+1;
sum += i / factorial;
}
printf("Sum of the series is: %lf", sum);
return 0;
}
```

C code explanation

The code prompts the user to enter the number of terms (`n`) and then calculates the sum of a series using a for-loop. Here, the variables, sum and factorial, are declared of type double as the value of these variables will be very high for the high value of `i`. The code considers a special case for the first term (`1/2`) and computes subsequent terms based on the factorial. Finally, it prints the sum of the series. The series formula is *1/2 + 1/2! + 2/3! + 3/4! + ... + (n-1)/n!*.

Program 3.14: Find sum of series 3

Find the sum of the series [*9 + 99 + 999 + 9999 ...*]

Sample input output

Test case #1:

Input: `Enter n: 4`

Output:`11106`

Test case # 2:

Input: `Enter n: 8`

Output:`111111102`

Algorithm

To run the above program, the following steps are needed to be followed:

Step 1. **`Start`**

Step 2. **`Declare the var as i,n,sum,t`**

Step 3. **`Read value of n`**

Step 4. **`i=1,s=0,t=9`**

Step 5. **`Repeat if i<=n`**

```
s =s+t
t=t*10+9
i=i+1
```

Step 6. **`Display sum`**

Step 7. **`Stop`**

Flowchart

Figure 3.14 illustrates the program in the form of a flowchart:

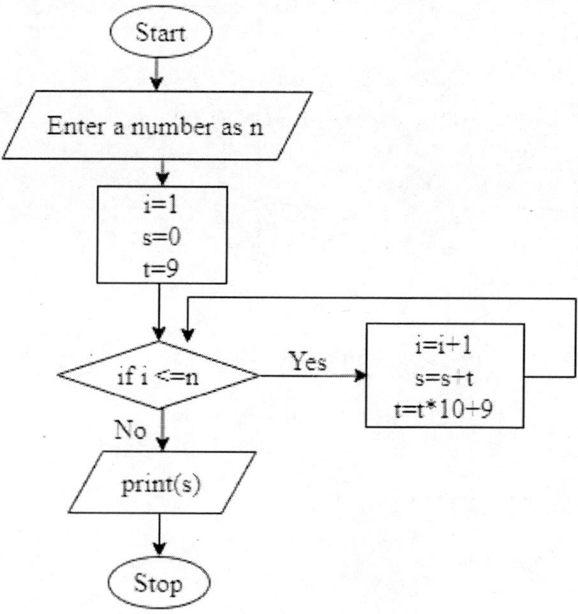

***Figure 3.14**: Flowchart illustrating the program 3.14*

Python code

Python code for the *program 3.14* is as follows:

```
n=int(input("Enter n: "))
s=0
t=9
for i in range(1, n+1):
    s=s+t
    t=t*10+9
print(s)
```

Python code explanation

This code prompts the user to enter a number (**n**) and then calculates and prints the sum of a series based on the pattern of repeating digit **9**. To generate the next value of the series, the current value of **t** is updated by multiplying it by **10** and then adding **9**. This step generates the next term of the series based on the pattern of repeating digit **9**. After the loop, the variable **s** will contain the sum of the series.

C code

C code for the program is as follows:

```
#include<stdio.h>
void main()
{
int i, n, t=9;
float s=0;
printf("Enter a numbers: " );
scanf("%d", &n);
for(i =1; i<=n; i++)
{
s=s+t;
t=t*10+9;
```

```
}

printf("The sum of the series is %f", s);

}
```

C code explanation

This code prompts the user to enter a number (`n`) and then calculates and prints the sum of a series based on the pattern of repeating digit **`9`**. To generate the next value of the series, the current value of `t`is updated by multiplying it by **`10`** and then adding **`9`**. This step generates the next term of the series based on the pattern of repeating digit **`9`**. After the loop, the variable `s` will contain the sum of the series.

Program 3.15: Find sum of n elements

Find the sum of n elements entered by the user.

Sample input output

Test case #1:

Input:

```
Enter n: 5
Enter x: 2
Enter x: 1
Enter x: 6
Enter x: 5
Enter x: 3
```

Output: **`The sum is 17`**

Test case #2:

Input:

```
Enter n: 3
Enter x: 8
Enter x: 7
Enter x: 9
```

Output: **`The sum is 24`**

Algorithm

To run the above program, the following steps are needed to be followed:

Step 1. **Start**

Step 2. **Declare the variables as x**

Step 3. **Read value of n**

Step 4. **i=1, s=0**

Step 5. **Repeat if i<=n**

```
x=read("Enter number", i)
s=s+ x
i=i+1
```

Step 6. **Print("The sum is ", s)**

Step 7. **Stop**

Flowchart

Figure 3.15 illustrates the program in the form of a flowchart:

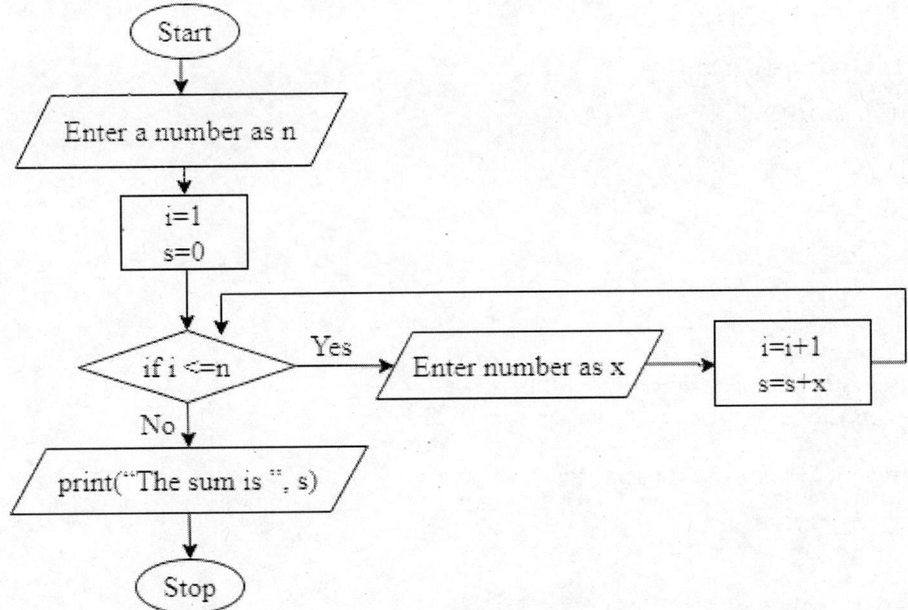

***Figure 3.15**: Flowchart illustrating the program 3.15*

Python code

Python code for the *program3.15* is as follows:

```
s=0
n=int(input("Enter n: "))
for i in range(1, n+1):
    x=int(input("Enter x: "))
    s =s+ x
print("The sum is ", s)
```

Python code explanation

This code prompts the user to enter a number **n**, then it iteratively asks the user to enter **n** values (**x**) inside the loop and calculates the sum of those values. Finally, it prints the calculated sum.

C code

C code for the program is as follows:

```
#include<stdio.h>
void main()
{
int i;
int s=0;
int x,n;
printf("Enter a numbers: " );
scanf("%d", &n);
printf("Enter %d numbers: ",n );
for(i =1; i<=n; i++)
{
scanf("%d", &x);
s=s+x;
}
printf("The sum is %d", s);
```

```

}
```

C code explanation

This code prompts the user to enter a number **n**, then it iteratively asks the user to enter **n** values (**x**) inside the loop and calculates the sum of those values. Finally, it prints the calculated sum.

Program 3.16: Display Fibonacci series

Display the n terms of the Fibonacci series. For example, if **n=6**, the output should be **1 1 2 3 5 8**.

Sample input output

Test case #1:

Input: `Enter n: 5`

Output: **1 1 2 3 5**

Test case #2:

Input: `Enter n: 10`

Output: **1 1 2 3 5 8 13 21 34 55**

Algorithm

To run the above program, the following steps are needed:

Step 1. **Start**

Step 2. **Declare variables n,x,y,z**

Step 3. **Read n**

Step 4. **x=1**

Step 5. **y=1**

Step 6. **print(x)**

Step 7. **print(y)**

Step 8. **Repeat for i=(3, n+1):**

```
z=x+y
print(z)
x=y
y=z
```

Step 1. **Stop**

Flowchart

Figure 3.16 illustrates the program in the form of a flowchart:

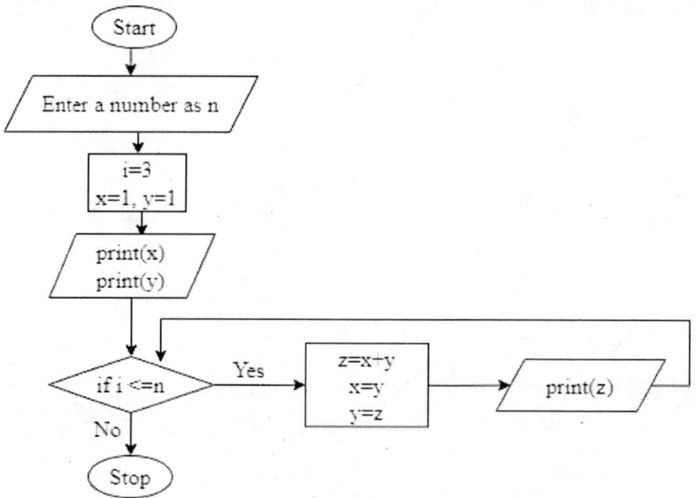

***Figure 3.16**: Flowchart illustrating the program 3.16*

Python code

Python code for the *program 3.16* is as follows:

```
n=int(input("Enter n: "))
x=1
y=1
print(x, end=" ")
print(y, end=" ")
for i in range(3, n+1):
    z=x+y
    print(z, end=" ")
    x=y
    y=z
```

Python code explanation

The Fibonacci sequence is where the next number is found by adding up the two numbers before it. The first two numbers are fixed as 1, 1. This code prompts the user to enter a number **n**, then generates and prints the first **n** numbers of the Fibonacci sequence using a **for** loop. Here, the **x** and **y** variables store the previous two numbers. In the loop, the next number, **z**, in the Fibonacci sequence is calculated by adding the current values of **x** and **y**. Then, the value of **x** is replaced by **y**, and the value of **y** is replaced by the value of **z** for the next iteration. The loop stops after printing n terms.

C code

C code for the program is as follows:

```
#include<stdio.h>
void main()
{
int n,x,y,z;
printf("Enter n:");
scanf("%d", &n);
x=1;
y=1;
printf("%d", x);
printf(" %d", y);
for (int i=3; i<=n; i++)
{
z=x+y;
printf(" %d", z);
x=y;
y=z;
}}
```

C code explanation

The Fibonacci sequence is where the next number is found by adding up the two numbers before it. The first two numbers are fixed as 1, 1. This code prompts the user to enter a number **n**, then generates and prints the first **n** numbers of the Fibonacci sequence using a **for** loop. Here, the **x** and **y** variables store the previous two numbers. In the loop, the next number, **z**, in the Fibonacci sequence is calculated by adding the current values of **x** and **y**. Then, the value of **x** is replaced by **y**, and the value of **y** is replaced by the value of **z** for the next iteration. The loop stops after printing n terms.

Conclusion

The chapter has discussed simple control statements (while-loop and for-loop) in the form of flowcharts, algorithms, and coding. With the help of several examples, the different flavors of loop statements are presented.

In the next chapter, complex control flow statements (loops) will be discussed with the help of a good number of solved programs.

Points to remember

- If some statements are supposed to be repeated in a code, write them once inside a loop statement instead of writing the same statements repeatedly. It makes the code more efficient.
- For the while-loop, the loop counter, generally **`i`**, is initialized before the loop and is incremented inside the loop.
- In the for-loop, initialization, condition check, and increment, all three operations are mentioned in one statement at the beginning.
- In Python code, the loop block should be indented toward the right side.
- In C code, the loop block should be enclosed within curly brackets **`{}`**.
- Loop counter value should be assigned carefully. For instance, we want to execute a loop 5 times. Then either assign **`i=0`** and check the condition as **`i<n`** or assign **`i=1`** and check the condition as **`i<=n`**.

Questions

1. Display first n whole numbers. For example:*0,1,2,3,4…*
2. Find the sum of every fifth number in the range *0-500*
3. Display all the numbers between 1 to 10, incrementing each time by 2.
4. Accept a number as input from the user. If the number is less than 0, change it to zero, print **`Negative change to zero`**, and ask the user to enter again until the number is **`≥ 0`**, and print the number.
5. Display a cube of first n natural numbers.
6. Display the sum of the first n natural numbers.
7. Display the sum of the cube of the first n natural numbers.
8. Find the sum of the series: *2+ 5 + 8+........+ (3*n-1).*
9. Find the sum of the series: *5+ 9 + 13+........+ (4*n + 1).*
10. Find the sum of the series: *1/2 + 1/5 + 1/8+........+ 1/(3*n-1).*
11. Find the sum of the series:*1+1/1!+1/2!+....+ 1/n!*

Chapter 4
Complex Loops

Introduction

In this chapter, the complex usage of loop statements, while-loop and for-loop are discussed. In programming, a loop is a fundamental control structure that allows you to execute a block of code repeatedly as long as a certain condition is met. The loops can be used along with multiple conditional statements to solve complex problems. Moreover, some of the problems require the use of multiple loops, one after the other, or nested loops. All these variants of problems are discussed in this chapter.

Structure

In this chapter, there are a total of 20 programs, and five sub-sections complement each program:

- Understand the program objective with sample test cases consisting of inputs and outputs. It will give the user an understanding of what kind of user input is expected and what result will be projected for a particular program.
- Understand the program with an algorithm. This will help the user to understand the logic and methodology behind writing the sequence of steps required to solve a program.

- Visualize the program flow with flowcharts. Program objectives can be understood easily with the flowchart representation. Users will get an understanding of which symbols to be used in which context throughout different program's flowchart representations.
- Python source code of each program. Each program's source code in Python programming language is provided to the user so the user can understand the basic operations of the language. An explanation of each code is also provided.
- C implementation of each program. Users can learn the basic concepts of C language with the provided C language code and its explanation for every program.

Objectives

In this chapter, the reader will learn the complex control statements and their significance in program development. Additionally, the chapter imparts knowledge required for designing algorithms to perform decisions using while-loop and for-loop in combination with nested loops or conditional statements. Further, it focuses on the skills of creating visual representations of complex control statements in program flow using flowcharts. Moreover, it will develop the ability to use complex control statements while writing code in Python and C programming languages. With the sample codes, users can gain hands-on experience.

Program 4.1: Find sum and check if even

Display **EVEN** if the sum of the first n natural numbers is even; otherwise, display **ODD**.

Sample input output

Test case #1:

Input: `Enter a number: 7`

Output: **EVEN**

Test case #2:

Input: `Enter a number: 5`

Output: **ODD**

Algorithm

To run the above program, the following steps are needed to be followed:

1. **Start**
2. **Read n**

```
i=1
s=0
Repeat if i<=n
s=s+i
i=i+1
if s%2==0
print "EVEN"
else
print "ODD"
Stop
```

Flowchart

Figure 4.1 illustrates the program in the form of a flowchart:

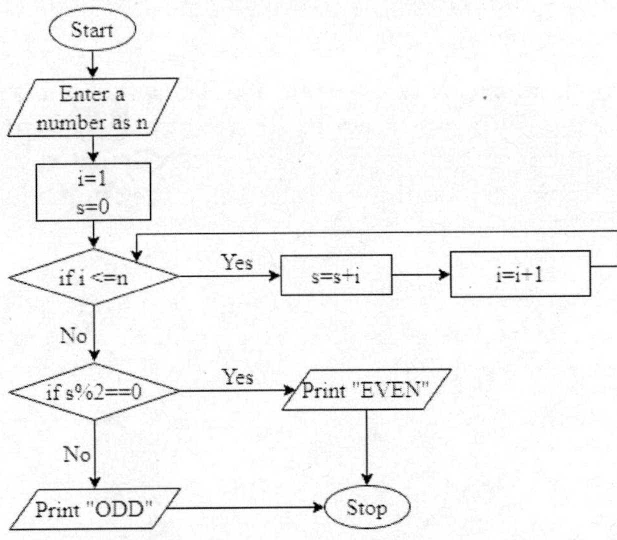

***Figure 4.1**: Flowchart illustrating the program 4.1*

Python code

Python code for the program is as follows:

```
n=int(input("Enter a number "))
i=1
```

```
s=0
while(i<=n):
    s=s+i
    i=i+1
#end of while loop
print("The sum is ",s)
if(s%2==0):
    print("EVEN");
else:
    print("ODD");
```

Python code explanation

The Python code takes an input number **n**, calculates the sum of numbers from **1** to **n**, and then determines whether the sum is even or odd.

After inputting a number, variable **i** is initialized with the value **0** to control the loop iterations. Then, variable **s** is initialized with the value **0**. This variable will be used to keep track of the sum of the numbers.

The while-loop will run until **i** reaches the value of **n**. The value of **i** is incremented by **1** in each iteration. The current value of **i** is added to the variable **s**, accumulating the sum of the numbers. After completing the loop, it prints out the calculated sum and checks if the sum **s** is even or odd using the modulus operator (**%**). If the remainder when **s** is divided by **2** is **0**, then the sum is even otherwise odd.

C code

The C code for the program is as follows:

```
#include<stdio.h>
void main()
{
int i, n;
int s=0;
printf("Enter a numbers: " );
scanf("%d", &n);
i=1;
while(i<=n)
```

```
{
s=s+i;
i=i+1;
}
if (s%2==0)
    {printf("EVEN");}
else
    {printf("ODD");}
}
```

C code explanation

The C code takes an input number `n`, calculates the sum of numbers from `1` to `n`, and then determines whether the sum is even or odd.

Inside the main function, the local variables are declared and initialized. The variable **`i`** is initialized with **`0`** to control the loop iterations. Then, variable **`s`** is initialized with the value **`0`**. This variable will be used to keep track of the sum of numbers. Then, it reads an integer input from the user and stores it in the variable **`n`**.

The while-loop will run until **`i`** reaches the value of **`n`**. The value of **`i`** is incremented by **`1`** in each iteration. The current value of **`i`** is added to the variable **`s`**, accumulating the sum of the numbers. This calculates the sum of numbers from **`1`** to **`n`**. After the loop completes, it prints out the calculated sum. And check if the sum **`s`** is even or odd using the modulus operator (**`%`**). If the remainder when **`s`** is divided by **`2`** is **`0`**, then the sum is even otherwise odd.

Program 4.2: Display odd numbers

Display odd numbers between the range **`n`** and **`m`** where **`n`** and **`m`** are inclusive.

Sample input output

Test case #1:

Input: `Enter two numbers: 2 6`

Output: **`3 5`**

Test case #2:

Input: `Enter two numbers: 2 19`

Output: **`3 5 7 9 11 13 15 17 19`**

Algorithm

To run the above program, the following steps are needed to be followed:

1. `Start`
2. `Read n,m`
3. `i=n`
4. `Repeat if i<=m`
5. `if i%2 !=0`
6. `print i`
7. `i=i+1`
8. `Stop`

Flowchart

Figure 4.2 illustrates the program in the form of a flowchart:

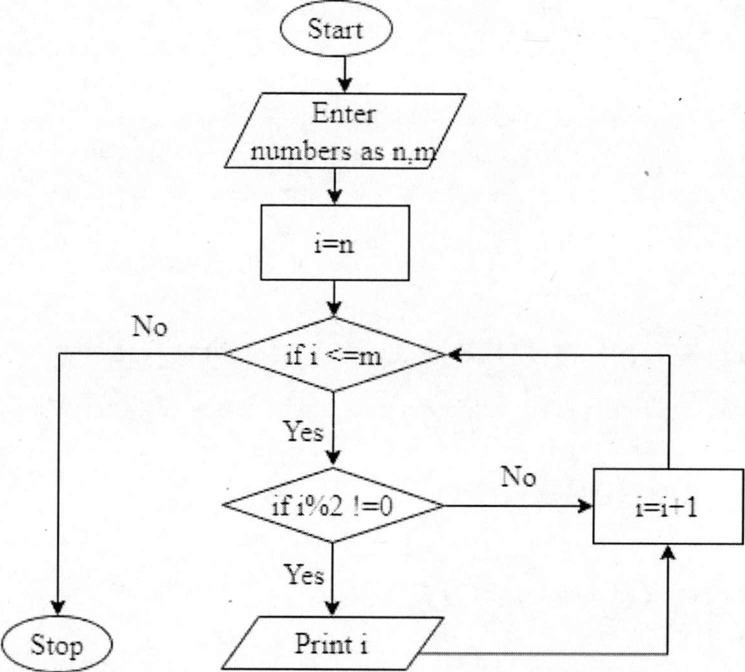

***Figure 4.2**: Flowchart illustrating the program 4.2*

Python code

Python code for the program is as follows:

```
n=int(input("Enter n: "))
m=int(input("Enter m: "))
for i in range(n,m+1):
    if(i%2 !=0):
        print(i)
```

Python code explanation

This Python code takes two input integers, `n` and `m`, then iterates through the range of numbers from `n` to `m`, printing each odd number in that range. Here is what each part of the code does:

First, it takes two numbers, `n` and `m`, as input to set the range. In the for-loop, it iterates through the range of numbers from `n` to `m` (inclusive of `m`). The **`range()`** function returns a sequence of numbers starting from `n` till `m`, incrementing by `1`. The variable `i` takes each value in this range during each iteration and is checked if the current value of `i` is not divisible by `2` (odd) using the modulus operator `%`. If the remainder is not `0`, that means `i` is odd, and it prints the value of `i` if odd. The loop continues until the range is exhausted, and the program displays all odd numbers between `n` and `m`.

C code

C code for the program is as follows:

```
#include<stdio.h>
void main()
{
int i, n, m;
printf("Enter two numbers: " );
scanf("%d%d", &n, &m);
i=n;
while(i<=m)
{
if (i%2 !=0)
{ printf("%d ", i); }
i=i+1;
```

```
}
}
```

C code explanation

This C code prompts the user for two input numbers, **n** and **m**. Variable **I** is the loop invariant, which is initialized with **n**. It then uses a while loop to iterate through the range of numbers from **n** to **m**. Within the loop, it checks if each number is odd using the condition **i% 2 != 0**. If the number is odd, it is printed. The loop continues until the range is exhausted, and the program displays all odd numbers between **n** and **m**.

Program 4.3: Count number of even numbers

Ask the user to enter n numbers and count how many are even.

Sample input output

Test case #1:

Input: `Enter a number: 6`

`Enter six numbers: 3 4 8 7 6 5`

Output: **`There are 3 even numbers`**

Test case #2:

Input: `Enter a number: 5`

`Enter five numbers:2 2 2 2 2`

Output: **`There are 5 even numbers`**

Algorithm

To run the above program, the following steps are needed to be followed:

1. **`Start`**
2. **`declare the variables as n, x`**
3. **`read value of n`**
4. **`c=0,i=1`**
5. **`if i<=n`**
6. **`x=read("Enter number")`**
7. **`if (x%2==0)`**

8. `c=c+1`
9. `i=i+1`
10. `repeat step 5`
11. `print("There are ", c , " even numbers")`
12. `Stop`

Flowchart

Figure 4.3 illustrates the program in the form of a flowchart:

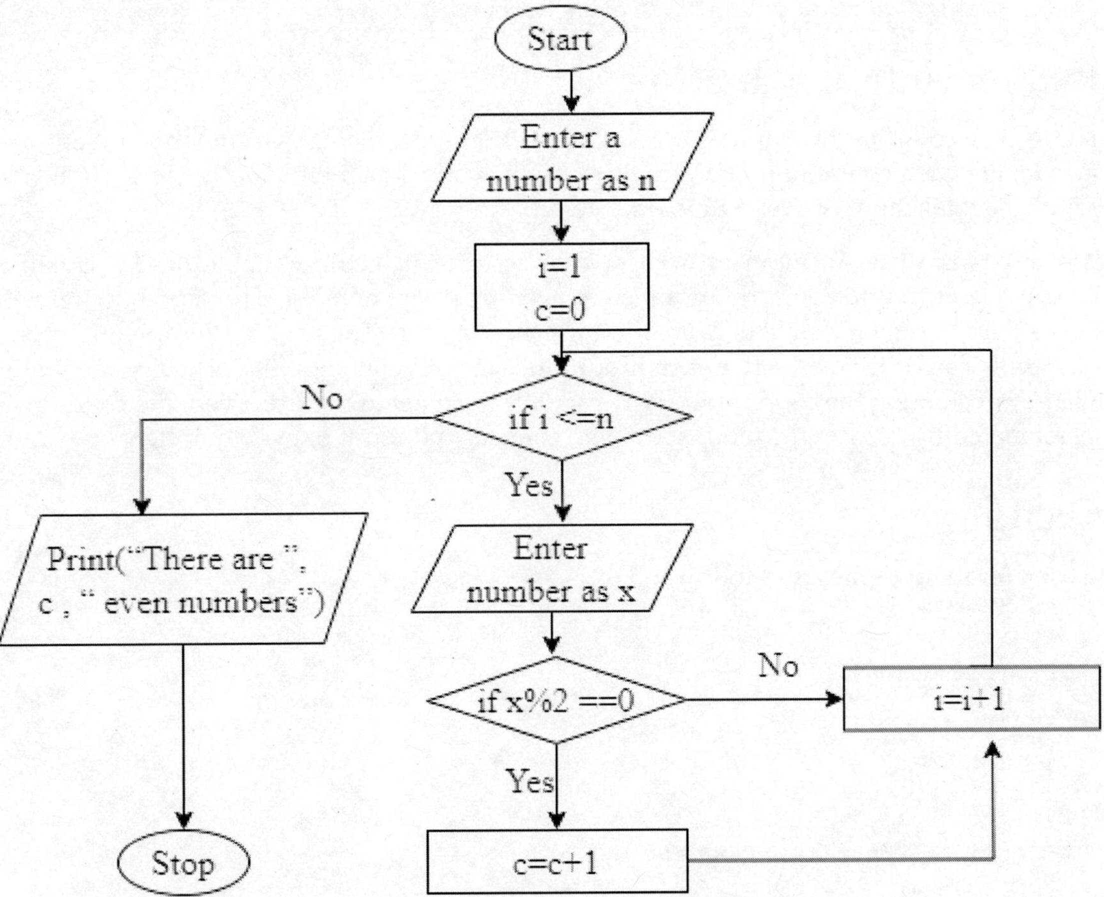

***Figure 4.3**: Flowchart illustrating the program 4.3*

Python code

Python code for the program is as follows:

```
n=int(input("Enter n: "))
c=0
for i in range(1, n+1):
    x=int(input("Enter x:"))
    if(x%2 == 0):
        c=c+1
print("There are ", c , " even numbers")
```

Python code explanation

The Python code takes an input integer **n**. Then, it prompts the user to enter **n** numbers one by one. For each entered number, if it is even, the code increments the count **c**. Finally, it prints the total count of even numbers entered.

It prompts the user to input an integer **n** and stores it in the variable **n**. The variable **c**is initialized to **0** to count the number of even numbers entered. The **for** loop iterates through the range of numbers from **1** to **n** (inclusive of **n**). The user is prompted to input the number **x** for n times. After each input, the current value of **x** is checked to see if it is even by evaluating the condition **x % 2 == 0**. If the entered value is even, the count **c** is incremented by **1**. After the loop completes, it prints the count of even numbers.

C code

C code for the program is as follows:

```
#include<stdio.h>
void main()
{
int i, n, x;
int c=0;
printf("Enter a numbers: " );
scanf("%d", &n);
printf("Enter %d numbers:", n);
for(i =1; i<=n; i++)
{
scanf("%d", &x);
```

```
if(x%2==0)
c=c+1;
}

printf("There are %d even numbers", c);

}
```

C code explanation

The C code takes an input integer **n**, then it prompts the user to enter **n** numbers one by one. For each entered number, if it is even, the code increments the count **c**. Finally, it prints the total count of even numbers entered.

The variable **c** is initialized to **0** to count the number of even numbers entered. It prompts the user to input an integer **n** and stores it in the variable **n**. The **for** loop iterates through the range of numbers from **1** to **n** (inclusive of **n**). The user is prompted to input the number **x** for n times. After each input, the current value of **x** is checked to see if it is even by evaluating the condition **x % 2 == 0**. If the entered value is even, the count **c** is incremented by **1**. After the loop completes, it prints the count of even numbers.

Program 4.4: Find sum of even numbers

Display the sum of the first ten even terms of natural numbers.

Sample input output

Test case #1:

Output: `The sum is 110`

Algorithm

To run the above program, the following steps are needed to be followed:

1. `Start`
2. `Declare the variable as i,n,s`
3. `i=1,s=0,n=20`
4. `Repeat if i<=n`
5. `If i%2==0`
6. `s = s + i`

7. **i=i+1**
8. **Display s**
9. **Stop**

Flowchart

Figure 4.4 illustrates the program in the form of a flowchart:

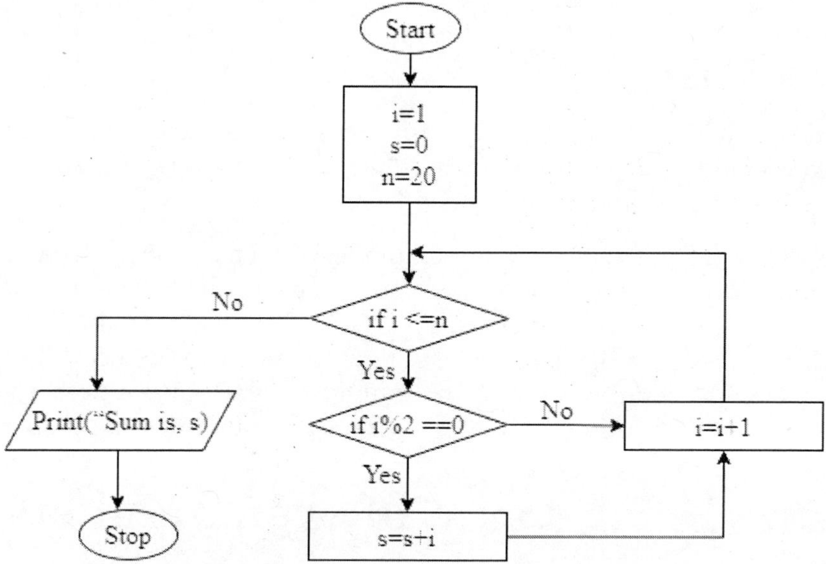

***Figure 4.4**: Flowchart illustrating the program 4.4*

Python code

Python code for the program is as follows:

```
s=0
for i in range(1,21):
    if(i%2==0):
        s = s+ i
print("sum is ",s)
```

Python code explanation

The Python code calculates the sum of even numbers from 1 to 20 and then prints the sum. The loop iterates through the numbers and the condition **`i % 2 == 0`** is used to select even numbers for summation.

C code

C code for the program is as follows:

```
#include<stdio.h>
void main()
{
int i, n;
int s=0;
n=20;
i=1;
while(i<=n)
{
if (i%2==0)
{ s=s+i; }
i=i+1;
}
printf("The sum is %d", s);
}
```

C code explanation

The C code calculates the sum of even numbers from 1 to 20 using a `while` loop and then prints the sum. The loop iterates through the numbers and the condition `i % 2 == 0` is used to select even numbers for summation.

Program 4.5: Find sum of numbers divisble by 9

Display the sum of all integers between 100 and 200,divisible by 9.

Sample input output

Test case #1:

Output: `Sum is 1683`

Algorithm

To run the above program, the following steps are needed to be followed:

1. **Start**
2. **Declare the variable as i,n,s**
3. **i=100,s=0,n=200**
4. **Repeat if i<=n**
5. **If i%9==0**
6. **s = s + i**
7. **i=i+1**
8. **Display s**
9. **Stop**

Flowchart

Figure 4.5 illustrates the program in the form of a flowchart:

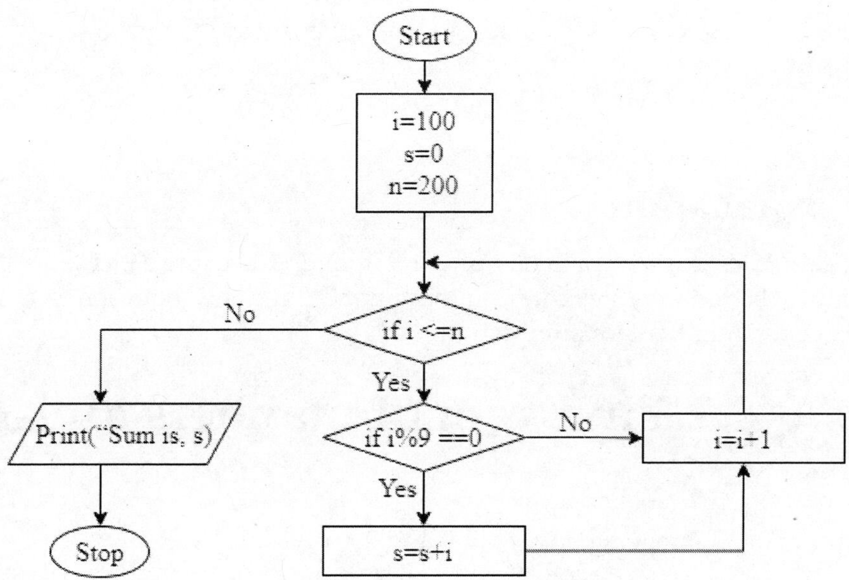

***Figure 4.5**: Flowchart illustrating the program 4.5*

Python code

Python code for the program is as follows:

```
s=0
for i in range(100,201):
```

```
    if(i%9==0):
        s = s+ i
print("sum is ",s)
```

Python code explanation

The Python code calculates the sum of numbers between 100 and 200 divisible by 9 and then prints the sum. The loop iterates through the range and the condition **`i % 9 == 0`** is used to select numbers for summation. The variable **`s`** is used to accumulate the sum of numbers. Inside the loop, in every iteration, if the number **`i`** is divisible by 9, the value of **`s`** is updated by adding the value of **`i`** to it. After the loop completes, it prints the accumulated sum of numbers.

C code

C code for the program is as follows:

```
#include<stdio.h>
void main()
{
int i=100;
int s=0;

while(i <=200)
{
if (i%9 ==0)
{s=s+i;}
i=i+1;
}
printf("Sum is %d", s);
}
```

C code explanation

The C code calculates the sum of numbers between 100 and 200 divisible by 9 and then prints the sum. The loop iterates through the range, and the condition **`i % 9 == 0`** is used to select numbers for summation. The variable **`s`** is used to accumulate the sum of numbers. Inside the loop, in every iteration, if the number **`i`** is divisible by **`9`**, the value of **`s`** is updated by adding the value of **`i`** to it. After the loop completes, it prints the accumulated sum of numbers.

Program 4.6: Difference of sum of even and odd numbers

Find the difference between the sum of all even and odd numbers in the first 50 natural numbers.

Sample input output

Test case #1:

Output: `Difference is 25`

Algorithm

To run the above program, the following steps are needed to be followed:

1. `Start`
2. `n=50`
3. `i=1`
4. `sumE=0, sumO=0`
5. `repeat if i<=n`
6. `if i%2==0`
7. `sumE=sumE+i`
8. `else`
9. `sumO=sumO+i`
10. `i=i+1`
11. `d = sumE-sumO`
12. `Display d`
13. `Stop`

Flowchart

Figure 4.6 illustrates the program in the form of a flowchart:

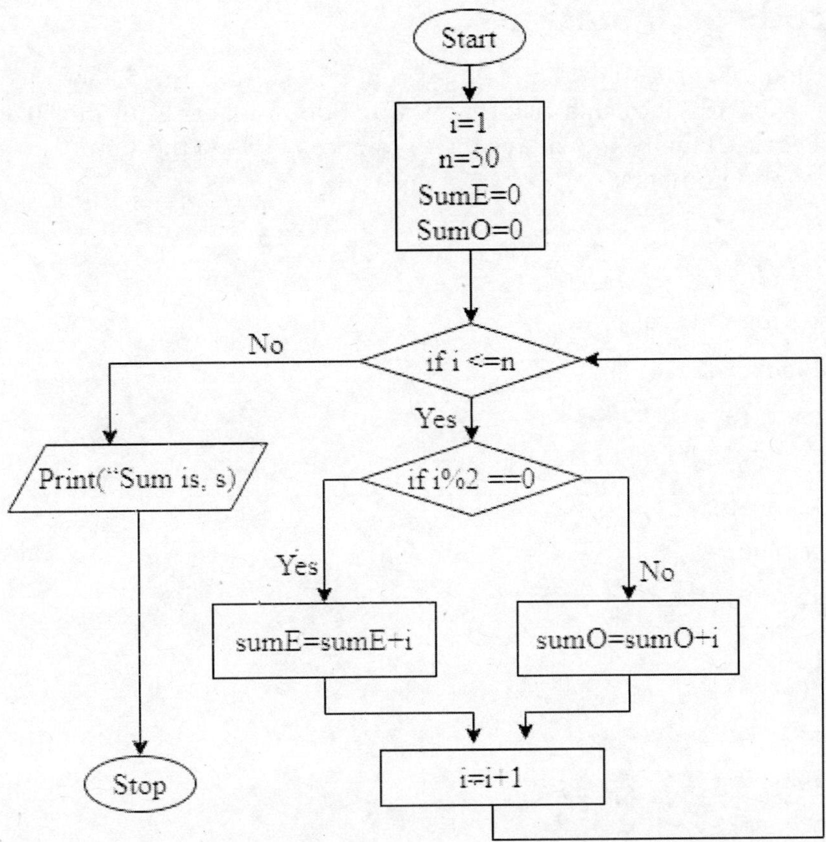

Figure 4.6: Flowchart illustrating the program 4.6

Python code

Python code for the program is as follows:

```
sumE=0
sumO=0
n=50
for i in range(1,n+1):
    if(i%2==0):
        sumE = sumE + i
    else:
        sumO = sumO + i
print("Difference is ",sumE-sumO)
```

Python code explanation

The Python code calculates the sum of all even numbers from 1 to 50 and stores it in the variable **sumE**. Similarly, it calculates the sum of all odd numbers from 1 to 50 and stores it in the variable **sumO**. Finally, it displays the difference between the sum of even numbers and the sum of odd numbers.

C code

C code for the program is as follows:

```
#include<stdio.h>
void main()
{
int i, n=50;
int sumE=0;
int sumO=0;
i=1;
while(i<=n)
{
if (i%2==0)
{ sumE=sumE+i; }
else
{ sumO=sumO+i; }
i=i+1;
}
printf("Difference is %d ", sumE-sumO);
}
```

C code explanation

The C code calculates the sum of all even numbers from 1 to 50 and stores it in the variable **sumE**. Similarly, it calculates the sum of all odd numbers from 1 to 50 and stores it in the variable **sumO**. Finally, it displays the difference between the sum of even numbers and the sum of odd numbers.

Program 4.7: Display list of divisor

Ask the user for a number and then display a list of all the factors of that number in increasing order.

Hint: Factor means the number that can divide another number completely.

Sample input output

Test case #1:

Input: `Enter a number 10`

Output: **`1 2 5 10`**

Test case #2:

Input: `Enter a number 254`

Output: **`1 2 127 254`**

Algorithm

To run the above program, the following steps are needed to be followed:

1. **`Start`**
2. **`Declare variables i, n`**
3. **`Read n`**
4. **`i=1`**
5. **`while i<=n:`**
6. **`if n%i==0`**
7. **`print i`**
8. **`Stop`**

Flowchart

Figure 4.7 illustrates the program in the form of a flowchart:

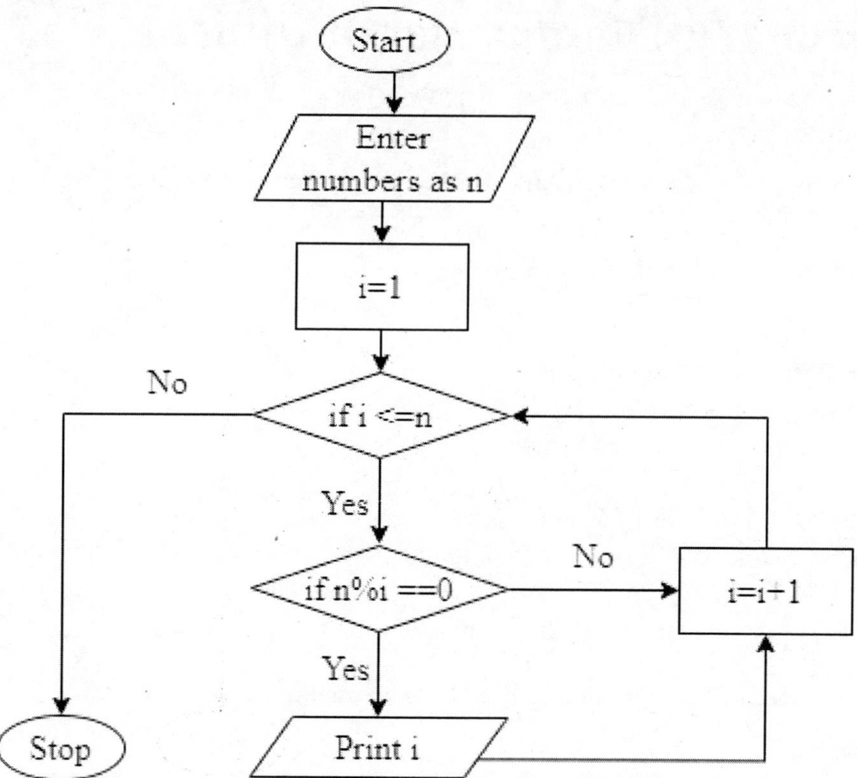

Figure 4.7: Flowchart illustrating the program 4.7

Python code

Python code for the program is as follows:

```
n=int(input("Enter a number "))
for i in range(1,n+1):
    if n%i==0:
        print(i)
```

Python code explanation

The Python code takes an input number **n**, then prints all the positive divisors (factors) of **n** by iterating through the numbers from **1** to **n** and checking if they divide **n**.

First, it prompts the user to input a number and stores it in the variable **n**. Then, it checks if the current value of **n** is divisible by the value of **i**, by evaluating the condition **n % i == 0**. If the condition is true (meaning **n** is divisible by **i** and **i** is a factor of **n**), it prints the value **i**.

C code

C code for the program is as follows:

```
#include<stdio.h>
void  main()
{
int n, i;
printf("Enter a number ");
scanf("%d", &n);
for (i=1; i<=n;i++)
{
if( n%i==0)
printf("%d ", i) ;
}}
```

C code explanation

The C code takes an input number `n`, then prints all the positive divisors (factors) of `n` by iterating through the numbers from `1` to `n` and checking if they divide `n`.

First, it prompts the user to input a number and stores it in the variable `n`. Then, it checks if the current value of `n` is divisible by the value of `i`, by evaluating the condition `n % i == 0`. If the condition is true (meaning `n` is divisible by `i` and `i` is a factor of `n`), it prints the value `i`.

Program 4.8: Find max 1

Find the max of the given five numbers.

Sample input output

Test case #1:

Input: `Enter 5 numbers: 98 78 990 65 32`

Output: **`The maximum number is 990`**

Test case #2:

Input: `Enter 5 numbers: 23 34 45 56 78`

Output: **`The maximum number is 78`**

Algorithm

To run the above program, the following steps are needed to be followed:

1. `Start`
2. `declare the variables as  x`
3. `n =5`
4. `i=1, max_no=0`
5. `if i<=n`
    a. `x=read("Enter number", i)`
    b. `if (x >max_no)`
    c. `max_no = x`
    d. `i=i+1`
    e. `repeat step 5`
6. `print("The maximum number is ", max_no)`
7. `Stop`

Flowchart

Figure 4.8 illustrates the program in the form of a flowchart:

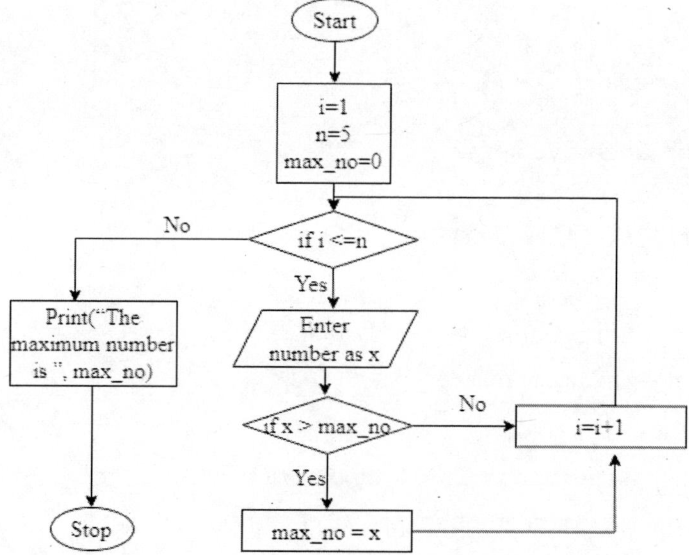

***Figure 4.8**: Flowchart illustrating the program 4.8*

Python code

Python code for the program is as follows:

```
max_no=0
n=5
for i in range(1, n+1):
    x=int(input("Enter x:"))
    if (x > max_no):
        max_no = x
print("The maximum number is ", max_no)
```

Python code explanation

The Python code prompts the user to input 5 numbers one by one. Initially, a variable **max_no** is initialized to **0**. This variable will keep track of the maximum number entered.

For each entered number, if it is greater than the current maximum (**max_no**), the code updates the maximum number. Finally, it prints the maximum number among the input numbers.

C code

C code for the program is as follows:

```
#include<stdio.h>
void main()
{
int i, x;
int max_no=0;
int n=5;
printf("Enter 5 numbers: ");
for(i =1; i<=n; i++)
{
scanf("%d", &x);
if (x > max_no)
max_no = x;
}
printf("The maximum number is %d", max_no );
}
```

C code explanation

The C code prompts the user to input 5 numbers one by one. Initially, a variable **max_no** is initialized to **0**. This variable will keep track of the maximum number entered.

For each entered number, if it is greater than the current maximum (**max_no**), the code updates the maximum number. Finally, it prints the maximum number among the input numbers.

Program 4.9: Find max 2

Find the max of **n** numbers as entered by the user.

Sample input output

Test case #1:

Input: `Enter a number: 8`

`Enter 8 numbers: 3 2 1 7 6 5 4 3`

Output: **`The maximum number is 7`**

Algorithm

To run the above program, the following steps are needed to be followed:

1. **Start**
2. **declare the variables as x**
3. **read value of n**
4. **i=1, max_no=0**
5. **if i<=n**
   a. **x=read("Enter number", i)**
   b. **if (x >max_no)**
   c. **max_no = x**
   d. **i=i+1**
   e. **repeat step 5**
6. **print("The maximum number is ", max_no)**
7. **Stop**

Flowchart

Figure 4.9 illustrates the program in the form of a flowchart:

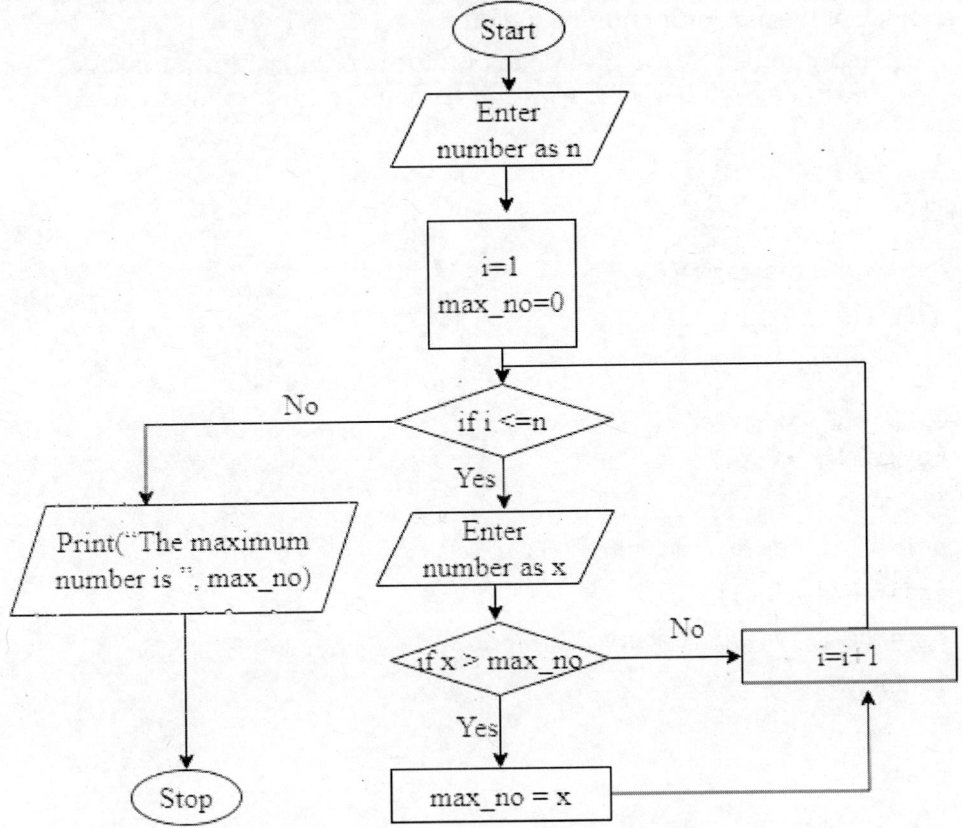

***Figure 4.9**: Flowchart illustrating the program 4.9*

Python code

Python code for the program is as follows:

```
max_no=0
n=int(input("Enter n:"))
for i in range(1, n+1):
    x=int(input("Enter x:"))
    if (x > max_no):
        max_no = x
print("The maximum number is ", max_no)
```

Python code explanation

This program is an extended version of the previous one. Here, it prompts the user to input **n** numbers one by one. Initially, a variable **max_no** is initialized to **0**. This variable will keep track of the maximum number entered.

For each entered number, if it is greater than the current maximum (**max_no**), the code updates the maximum number. Finally, it prints the maximum number among the input numbers.

C code

C code for the program is as follows:

```
#include<stdio.h>
void main()
{
int i, n, x;
int max_no=0;
printf("Enter a numbers: " );
scanf("%d", &n);
printf("Enter %d numbers: ", n );
for(i =1; i<=n; i++)
{
scanf("%d", &x);
if (x > max_no)
max_no = x;
}
printf("The maximum number is %d", max_no );

}
```

C code explanation

This program is an extended version of the previous one. Here, it prompts the user to input **n** numbers one by one. Initially, a variable **max_no** is initialized to **0**. This variable will keep track of the maximum number entered.

For each entered number, if it is greater than the current maximum (**max_no**), the code updates the maximum number. Finally, it prints the maximum number among the input numbers.

Program 4.10: Count number of consonants

Count the number of consonants in a string. If the consonant appears twice, the count is 2.

Hint: In the English alphabet, there are five vowels: a, e, i, o, u, and all others are consonants.

Sample input output

Test case #1:

Input: `Enter a string: codefactory`

Output: **`There are 7 consonants in the string.`**

Test case #2:

Input: `Enter a string: programming`

Output: **`There are 8 consonants in the string.`**

Algorithm

To run the above program, the following steps are needed to be followed:

1. **`Start`**
2. **`Declare the variables as s, i, v`**
3. **`Read a string as s`**
4. **`i=0, v=0`**
5. **`if s[i] != "\0" and (ord(s[i]) in range(65,91) or ord(s[i]) in range(97, 123))`**
    a. **`if s[i] != 'a' AND s[i] != 'e' AND s[i] != 'i' AND s[i] != 'o' AND s[i] != 'u'`**
        i. **`v=v+1`**
    b. **`i=i+1`**
    c. **`repeat Step 5`**
6. **`Print ("There are ", v, " consonants in the string.")`**
7. **`Stop`**

Flowchart

Figure 4.10 illustrates the program in the form of a flowchart:

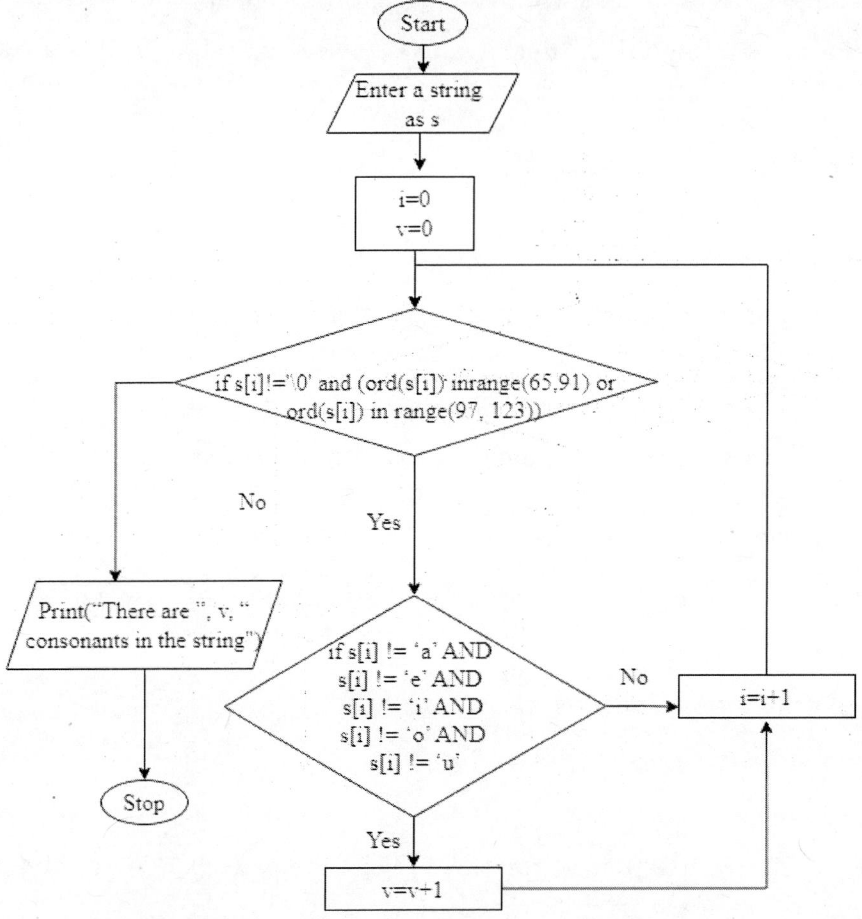

***Figure 4.10**: Flowchart illustrating the program 4.10*

Python code

Python code for the program is as follows:

```
s= input("Enter a string: ")
v=0
for i in s:
        if ord(i) in range(65,91) or ord(i) in range(97,123):
        if(i != 'a' and i != 'e' and i != 'i' and i != 'o' and i != 'u')
:
```

```
        v=v+1
    else:
        print("Special character encountered. ")
        break
print ("There are ", v, "consonants in the string.")
```

Python code explanation

The main logic behind counting the number of consonants is to count the number of characters that are not vowels. First, it prompts the user to input a string and stores the input in the variable **s**. It initializes a variable **v** to **0**. This variable will count the number of consonants in the input string. The for-loop iterates through each character in the string **s**. First, it checks if the entered characters are valid English characters using the **ASCII** value of each character using the **ord()** function. The **ACSII** value of uppercase characters lies between [**65** and **90**] and [**97** and **122**] for lowercase characters. Then, it checks if the current character **i** is not equal to any vowels **a**, **e**, **i**, **o**, and **u**. If the condition is true (**i** is a consonant), the count **v** is incremented by **1**. After the loop completes, this line prints the count of consonants in the input string.

C code

C code for the program is as follows:

```
#include<stdio.h>
void main()
{
int i, v=0;
char s[30];
printf("Enter a string: ");
gets(s);
i=0;
while(s[i] != ‘\0’){
if ((((int)(s[i]) >=65) && ((int)(s[i]) <=90)) || (((int)(s[i]) >=97) && ((int)(s[i]) <=122)))
{
if (s[i] != ‘a’ && s[i] != ‘e’ && s[i] != ‘i’ && s[i] != ‘o’ && s[i] != ‘u’)
    {v=v+1;}
i=i+1;
}
```

```
}
else{
printf("Special character encountered.\n");
    break;
}
printf("There are %d consonants in the string.", v);
}
```

C code explanation

This code is a simple C program that counts the number of consonants in a given input string.

An array, **`s[30]`** of character type, is declared to store the input string provided by the user. Then, it reads the text (string) from the user using the **`gets()`** function and stores it in the **`s`** array. It initializes a variable **`v`** to **`0`**. This variable will count the number of consonants in the input string. The while-loop iterates through each character in the string **`s`**. The loop will continue if the current character in the string **`s`** is not the null character (**`\0`**), which marks the end of a C-style string. First, it checks if the entered characters are valid English characters using the **`ASCII`** value of each character. The **`ACSII`** value of uppercase characters lies between [**`65`** and **`90`**] and [**`97`** and **`122`**] for lowercase characters. Then, it checks if the current character, **`s[i]`**, at index **`i`** is not equal to any vowels **`a`**, **`e`**, **`i`**, **`o`**, and **`u`**. If the condition is true (**`s[i]`** is a consonant), the count **`v`** is incremented by **`1`**. After the loop completes, this line prints the count of consonants in the input string.

Program 4.11: Check if a number is prime

Check whether a given number is a prime number or not.

Hint: A prime number is a natural number greater than 1 that has no positive divisors other than 1 and itself.

Sample input output

Test case #1:

Input: `Enter a number: 6`

Output: **`6 is not a prime number`**

Test case #2:

Input: `Enter a number: 127`

Output: **`127 is a prime number`**

Algorithm

To run the above program, the following are **s** are needed to be followed:

1. **Start**
2. **Declare the variable n, i, flag**
3. **Read n**
4. **flag =0**
5. **i=2**
6. **if n==1**
    a. **print("it is neither prime or composite.")**
    b. **exit**
7. **Repeat till i<n**
    a. **if(n%i==0):**
        i. **flag =1**
        ii. **print(n, "is not a prime number")**
        iii. **break**
    b. **i=i+1**
8. **if flag==0:**
    a. **print(n, "is a prime number")**
9. **Stop**

Flowchart

Figure 4.11 illustrates the program in the form of a flowchart:

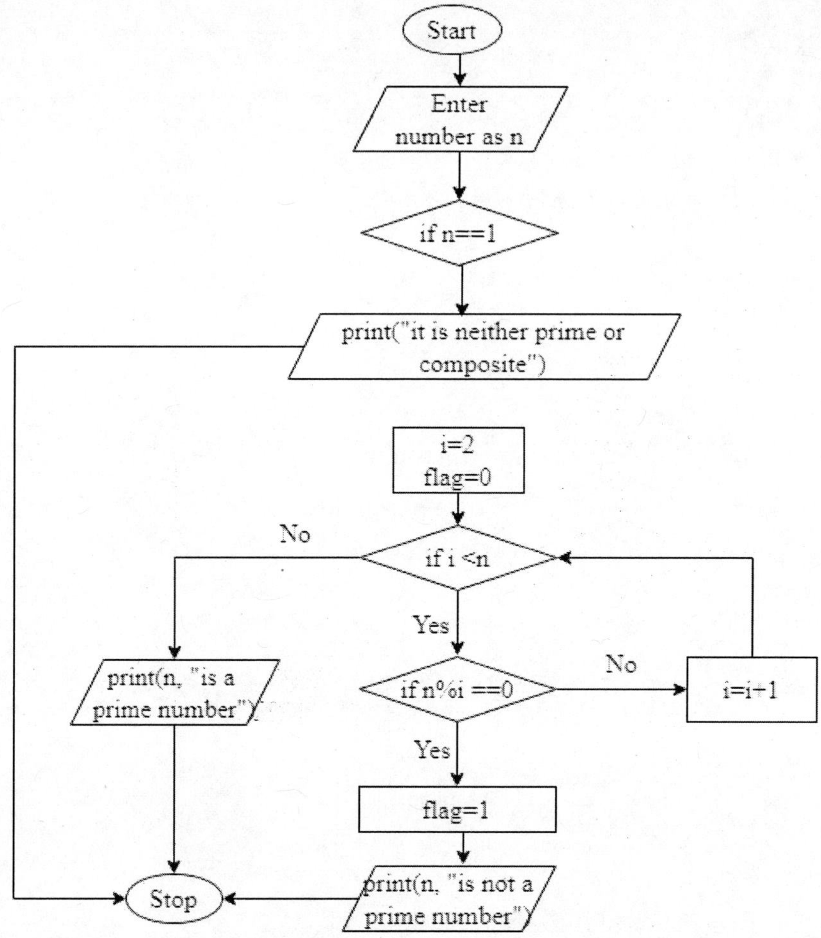

Figure 4.11: Flowchart illustrating the program 4.11

Python code

Python code for the program is as follows:

```
n=int(input("Enter a number: "))
if n==1:
    print("it is neither prime or composite")
    exit(1)
flag =0
for i in range(2,n):
    if(n%i==0):
        flag =1
```

```
            break
    if flag==0:
        print(n, "is a prime number")
    else:
        print(n, "is not a prime number")
```

Python code explanation

This code is a Python program that checks whether a given input number is prime. It prompts the user to input a number and stores it as an integer in the variable **n**. The variable **flag** is initialized to **0**. This variable indicates whether the input number is prime or not. The for-loop iterates through the numbers from **2** to **n-1**. The loop variable **i** takes on values from **2** to the input number **n**. Then, it checks if the input number **n** is divisible evenly by the current value of **i**. If the condition is satisfied (**n** is divisible by **i** and has a factor), the **flag** variable is set to **1**, indicating that the number is not prime. **break** statement is used to terminate the loop if **n** is found to be divisible by any value of **i**, then it is already not a prime number. There is no need to continue checking further. If, after the loop, the value of the **flag** is still **0**, it means the loop is completed without finding any divisors for **n**, indicating that the number is prime. So, it prints that **n is a prime number**. If the flag value is **1**,**n** is divisible by at least one number other than **1** and the number itself. Hence, it prints that **n is not a prime number**).

C code

C code for the program is as follows:

```
#include<stdio.h>
void main()
{
int n, flag,i;
printf("Enter a number: ");
scanf("%d", &n);
if (n==1)
{
printf("it is neither prime or composite");
exit(1);
}
flag =0;
for (i=2; i<n;i++)
```

```
{
if(n%i==0)
{
flag =1;
break;
}
}
if (flag==0)
printf( "%d is a prime number", n);
else
printf("%d is not a prime number", n);
}
```

C code explanation

This code is a Python program that checks whether a given input number is prime. It prompts the user to input a number and stores it as an integer in the variable **n**. The variable **flag** is initialized to **0**. This variable indicates whether the input number is prime or not. The for-loop iterates through the numbers from **2** to **n-1**. The loop variable **i** takes on values from **2** to the input number **n**. Then, it checks if the input number **n** is divisible evenly by the current value of **i**. If the condition is satisfied (**n** is divisible by **i** and has a factor), the **flag** variable is set to **1**, indicating that the number is not prime. **break** statement is used to terminate the loop if **n** is found to be divisible by any value of **i**, then it is already not a prime number. There is no need to continue checking further. If, after the loop, the value of flag is still **0**, it means the loop is completed without finding any divisors for **n**, indicating that the number is prime. So, it prints that **n is a prime number**. If the flag value is **1** that means **n** is divisible by at least one number other than **1** and the number itself. Hence, it prints that **n is not a prime number**).

Program 4.12: Find LCM

Find the LCM of given numbers X and Y.

Sample input output

Test case #1:

Input: `Enter 2 numbers: 45 100`

Output: **`LCM is 900`**

Test case #2:

Input: `Enter 2 numbers: 76 33`

Output: `LCM is 2508`

Algorithm

To run the above program, the following steps are needed to be followed:

1. `Start`
2. `Declare variables as n,m, lcm,i`
3. `Read n, m`
4. `lcm=1`
5. `for i = min(n,m) to 1:`
    a. `if n>=i and m >=i:`
        i. `if n%i ==0 and m%i == 0:`
            1. `n=n/i`
            2. `m=m/i`
            3. `lcm=lcm*i`
    b. `else:`
        i. `break`
6. `if n!=0:`
    a. `lcm = lcm*n`
7. `if m!=0:`
    a. `lcm = lcm*m`
8. `print(lcm)`
9. `Stop`

Flowchart

Figure 4.12 illustrates the program in the form of a flowchart:

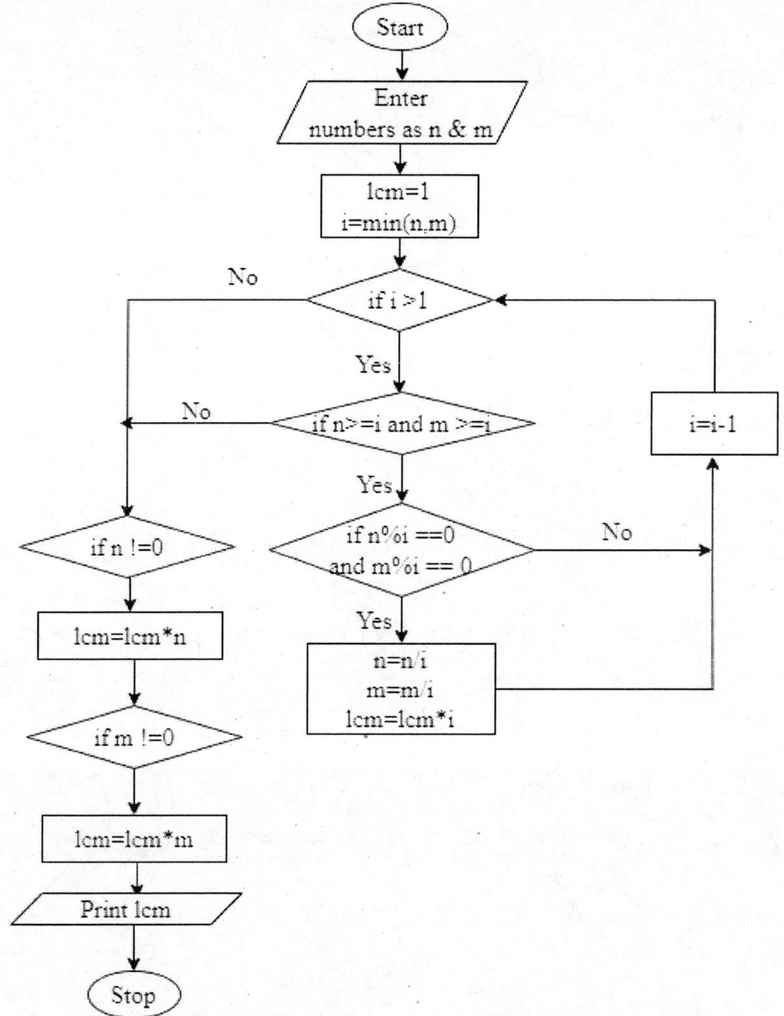

***Figure 4.12**: Flowchart illustrating the program 4.12*

Python code

Python code for the program is as follows:

```
n=int(input("Enter 1st number: "))
m=int(input("Enter 2nd number: "))
lcm=1
for i in range(min(n,m),1, -1):
    if n>=i and m >=i:
        if n%i ==0 and m%i == 0:
```

```
            n=n/i
            m=m/i
            lcm=lcm*i
    else:
        break
if n!=0:
    lcm = lcm*n
if m!=0:
    lcm = lcm*m
print(lcm)
```

Python code explanation

The logic behind finding LCM is to find the common factors of both the numbers: `n`, `m`. Divide `n` and `m` by the common factor and then multiply the common factor with the remaining values of `n` and `m` to obtain LCM.

It prompts the user to input two numbers and store them in the variables n and m. It initializes a variable **`lcm`** to **`1`** to store the **least common multiple** (**LCM**) of the two input numbers. The for-loop iterates backward from the minimum of `n` and `m` down to **`1.min()`** if a function in Python returns a minimum of two. Keyword and is used to ensure the true value for both conditions. It checks if both `n` and `m` are greater than or equal to **`i`**. If yes, it checks if the current **`i`** is a common factor of `n` and `m`. If this condition is also true, then update the value of `n` by **`n/i`** and `m` by **`m/i`**. It updates the **`lcm`** by multiplying it with **`i`**, which is a common factor. As **`i`** becomes greater than `n` or `m`, it indicates that no more common factors can be obtained, so a break statement is used to come out of the loop. Then, it multiplies **`lcm`** by the remaining value of `n` and `m`. Finally, it prints the calculated least common multiple (**`lcm`**) of the two.

C code

C code for the program is as follows:

```
#include<stdio.h>
#include<math.h>
#define min(n,m) n<m?n:m
void main()
{
int n,m,lcm,i;
printf("Enter 2 numbers: ");
```

```
scanf("%d%d", &n, &m);
lcm=1;
for (i=min(n,m); i>1; i--)
{
if (n>=i  && m >=i)
{
if (n%i ==0 && m%i == 0)
{n=n/i;
m=m/i;
lcm=lcm*i;
}
}
else
break;
}
if (n!=0)
lcm = lcm*n;
if (m!=0)
lcm = lcm*m;
printf("LCM is %d", lcm);
}
```

C code explanation

The logic behind finding LCM is to find the common factors of both the numbers: `n`, `m`. Divide `n` and `m` by the common factor and then multiply the common factor with the remaining values of `n` and `m` to obtain LCM.

It prompts the user to input two numbers and store them in the variables `n` and `m`. It initializes a variable **`lcm`** to **`1`** to store the LCM of the two input numbers. The for-loop iterates backward from the minimum of `n` and `m` down to **`1`**. In C, **`min`** is not a predefined function. So, a preprocessor directive, **`#define`**, is used to define the function. **`#define min(n,m) n<m?n:m`**: This line defines a macro named min that takes two arguments: n and m. It uses the ternary conditional operator **`(? :)`** to create a shorthand if-else statement. The purpose of this macro is to find the minimum of the two values `n` and `m`. The ternary conditional expression **`(n<m?n:m)`** checks if the condition `n < m` is true. If it is true, the expression evaluates to n. Otherwise, it evaluates to `m`.

Further, **&&** is used to ensure the true value for both conditions. It checks if both `n` and `m` are greater than or equal to `i`. If yes, it checks if the current `i` is a common factor of `n` and `m`. If this condition is also true, then update the value of `n` by `n/i` and m by `m/i`. It updates the `lcm` by multiplying it with `i`, which is a common factor. As `i` becomes greater than `n` or `m`, it indicates that no more common factors can be obtained, so a **`break`** statement is used to come out of the loop. Then, it multiplies `lcm` by the remaining value of `n` and `m`. Finally, it prints the calculated least common multiple (`lcm`) of the two.

Program 4.13: Find HCF

Find the HCF of given numbers X and Y.

Sample input output

Test case #1:

Input: `Enter 2 numbers: 15 3`

Output: `HCF is 3`

Test case #2:

Input: `Enter 2 numbers: 65 52`

Output: `HCF is 13`

Algorithm

To run the above program, the following steps are needed to be followed:

1. `Start`
2. `Declare variables as n, m, hcf,i`
3. `Read n, m`
4. `hcf=1`
5. `for i = min(n,m) to 2:`
   a. `if n>=i and m >=i:`
      i. `if n%i ==0 and m%i == 0:`
         1. `n=n/i`
         2. `m=m/i`
         3. `hcf=hcf*i`
   b. `else:`
      i. `break`

6. **Print(hcf)**
7. **Stop**

Flowchart

Figure 4.13 illustrates the program in the form of a flowchart:

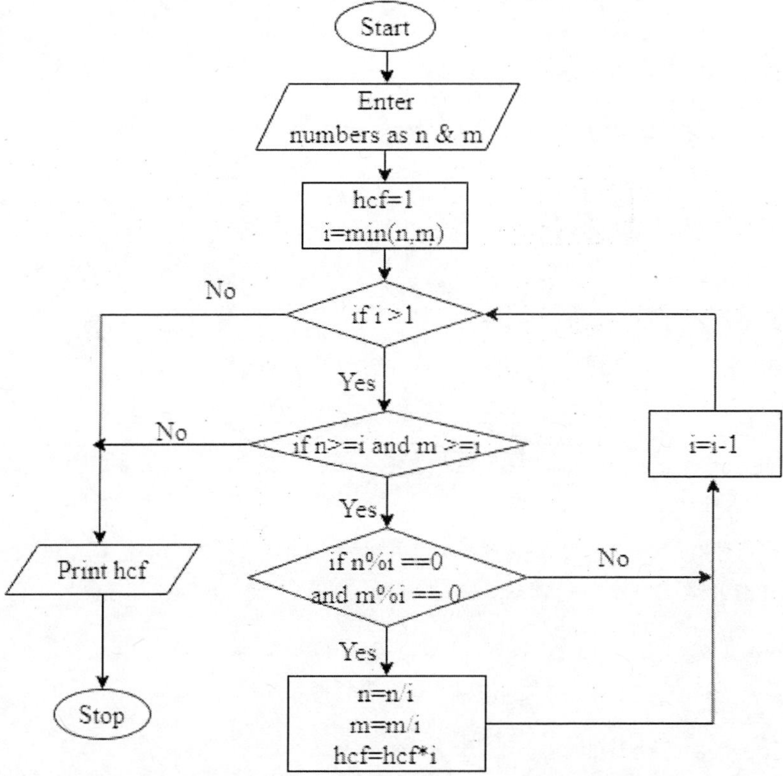

***Figure 4.13**: Flowchart illustrating the program 4.13*

Python code

Python code for the program is as follows:

```
n=int(input("Enter 1st number: "))
m=int(input("Enter 2nd number: "))
hcf=1
for i in range(min(n,m), 1, -1):
    if n>=i and m >=i:
        if n%i ==0 and m%i == 0:
```

```
            n=n/i
            m=m/i
            hcf=hcf*i
    else:
        break
print(hcf)
```

Python code explanation

The Python program calculates the **highest common factor** (HCF), also known as the **greatest common divisor** (GCD), of two given input numbers `n` and `m`. The logic and program are the same as those used in the previous program for finding LCM.

C code

C code for the program is as follows:

```
#include<stdio.h>
#define min(n,m) n<m?n:m

void main()
{
int n,m,hcf,i;
printf("Enter 2 numbers: ");
scanf("%d%d", &n, &m);
hcf=1;
for (i=min(n,m); i>1; i--)
{
if (n>=i  && m >=i)
{
if (n%i ==0 && m%i == 0)
{
n=n/i;
m=m/i;
hcf=hcf*i;
}
}
else
```

```
break;
}
printf("HCF is %d", hcf);
}
```

C code explanation

The C program calculates the HCF, also known as GCD, of two given input numbers `n` and `m`. The logic and program are the same as those used in the previous program for finding LCM.

Program 4.14: Search a number

Search for an element in a list.

Sample input output

Test case #1:

Input: `Enter the size of the list: 10`

`Enter the elements of the list:1 2 3 4 5 6 7 8 9 8`

`Enter the element to be searched: 10`

Output: `10 is not present in the list.`

Test case #2:

Input: `Enter the size of the list: 5`

`Enter the elements of the list:`

`23 45 21 87 44`

`Enter the element to be searched: 87`

Output: `87 is present at position 4 in the list.`

Algorithm

To run the above program, the following steps are needed to be followed:

1. **`Start`**
2. **`Declare n, a, flag, x, el`**
3. **`Read the size of the list as n`**
4. **`Initialize a as empty, a=[]`**
5. **`flag=0`**

6. **for i =0 to n-1**
    a. **Read element as el**
    b. **Append el to a**
7. **Read the element to be searched as x**
8. **for i = 0 to n-1**
    a. **if (a[i] == x)**
        i. **flag = 1**
        ii. **break**
9. **if (flag == 1)**
    a. **Display number to be searched is present**
10. **else**
    a. **Display number to be searched is not present**
11. **Stop**

Flowchart

Figure 4.14 illustrates the program in the form of a flowchart:

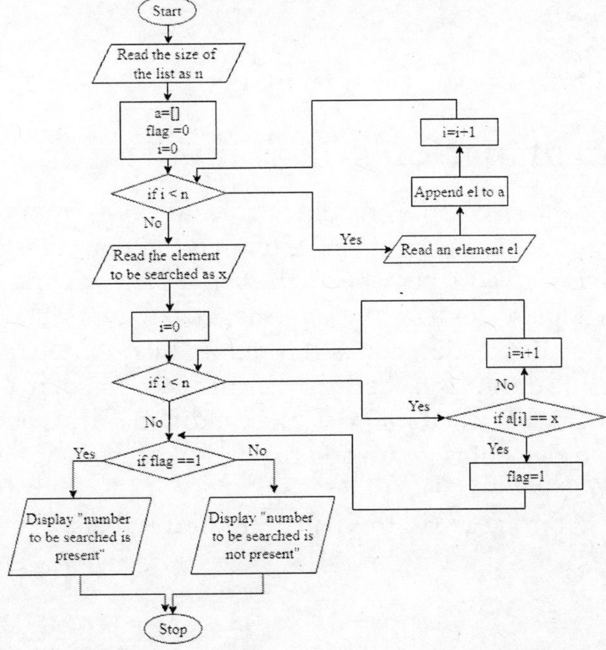

***Figure 4.14**: Flowchart illustrating the program 4.14*

Python code

Python code for the program is as follows:

```
n=int(input("Enter the size of the list: "))
print("Enter the elements of the list:\n");
a=[]
flag=0
for i in range(0, n):
    el=int(input("Enter :"))
    a.append(el)
x=int(input("Enter the element to be searched: "))
for i in range(0, n):
    if (a[i] == x):
        flag = 1
        break
if (flag == 1):
    print(a[i]," is present at position ",i+1, " in the list")
else:
    print(a[i]," is not present in the list")
```

Python code explanation

The Python code takes the size and elements of a list as input from the user. Here, a is a list that can store **n** number of elements in it. Initially, an empty list is created **(a=[]). append()** function is used to add elements to the list. It then prompts the user to input an element to search for. It initializes a flag variable **flag** to **0** to indicate whether the searched element is found or not. The code iterates through the list to determine if the searched element is present. Inside the loop, it checks if the current element in the list **a** at index **i** is equal to the element being searched for (**x**). If the condition is true, it sets the **flag** variable to **1**, indicating that the element is found and breaks out of the loop since there is no need to continue searching. Outside the loop, if a flag is equal to **1**, it prints the found element **a[i]** and its position in the list **i+1**. Otherwise, it indicates that it is not present in the list.

C code

C code for the program is as follows:

```c
#include <stdio.h>
int main() {
int n, i, x, flag = 0;
printf("Enter the size of the list: ");
scanf("%d", &n);
int a[n];
printf("Enter the elements of the list:\n");
for (i = 0; i < n; i++) {
scanf("%d", &a[i]);
}
printf("Enter the element to be searched: ");
scanf("%d", &x);
for (i = 0; i < n; i++) {
if (a[i] == x) {
flag = 1;
break;
}
}
if (flag == 1) {
printf("%d is present at position %d in the list.\n", x, i+1);
}
else {
printf("%d is not present in the list.\n", x);
}
return 0;
}
```

C code explanation

In this program, the user first inputs the size of the list and then enters the elements of the list. Here, a is an integer-type array used to store **n** elements. The user also inputs the element to be searched. The program then uses a for-loop to search for the element in the list. If the element is found, the program sets a **flag** variable to **1** and breaks out of the loop. If the element is not found, the **flag** variable remains **0**. Finally, the program checks the value of the **flag** variable and prints the appropriate message.

Program 4.15: Handling list/ arrays

Given two integer lists, create a third list such that it has only odd numbers from the first list and even numbers from the second list.

Sample input output

Test case #1:

Input: `List 1: 1 2 3 5 70 11 13`

`List 2: 21 42 63 82 10`

Output: **`List 3: 1 3 5 11 13 42 82 10`**

Test Case #1:

Input: `List 1: 11 12 13 14 15`

`List2 = 16 17 18 19 20`

Output: **`List 3 = 11 13 15 16 18 20`**

Algorithm

To run the above program, the following steps are needed to be followed:

1. **`Start`**
2. **`Initialize list1 = [1, 3, 5, 7, 9]`**
3. **`Initialize list2 = [2, 4, 6, 8, 10]`**
4. **`Create empty list, result_list = []`**
5. **`for each element (num) of the list1:`**
   a. **`if num % 2 != 0:`**
   b. **`append to result_list`**
6. **`for each element (num) of the list2:`**
   a. **`if num % 2 == 0:`**
   b. **`append to result_list`**
7. **`Display result_list`**
8. **`Stop`**

Flowchart

Figure 4.15 illustrates the program in the form of a flowchart:

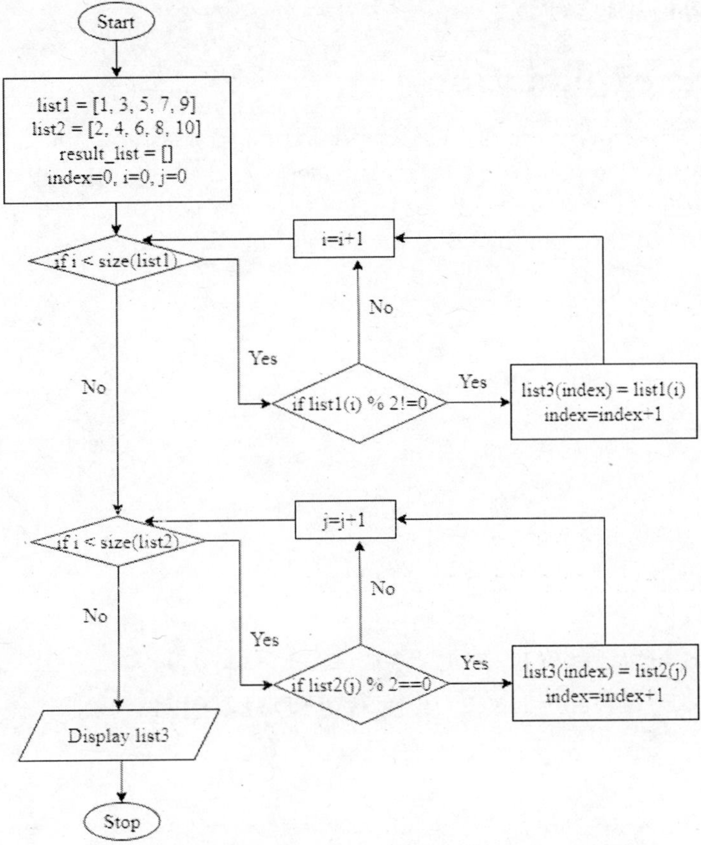

***Figure 4.15**: Flowchart illustrating the program 4.15*

Python code

Python code for the program is as follows:

```
list1 = [1, 3, 5, 7, 9]
list2 = [2, 4, 6, 8, 10]
result_list = []
for num in list1:
    if num % 2 != 0:
        result_list.append(num)

```

```
for num in list2:
    if num % 2 == 0:
        result_list.append(num)
print(result_list)
```

Python code explanation

The Python code creates two lists **list1** and **list2**, containing some numbers. It then initializes an empty list **result_list** and uses loops to iterate through both **list1** and **list2**, appending odd numbers from **list1** and even numbers from **list2** to the **result_list**. Finally, it prints the combined result list.

C code

C code for the program is as follows:

```
#include <stdio.h>
int main()
{
int list1[] = {1, 2, 3, 5, 70,11,13};
int list2[] = {21, 42, 63, 82, 10};
int size1 = sizeof(list1) / sizeof(list1[0]);
int size2 = sizeof(list2) / sizeof(list2[0]);
int list3[size1 + size2];
int index = 0;

for(int i = 0; i < size1; i++)
{
if(list1[i] % 2 != 0)
{
list3[index] = list1[i];
index++;
}
}

for(int j = 0; j < size2; j++)
{
```

```
if(list2[j] % 2 == 0)
{
list3[index] = list2[j];
index++;
}
}
printf("List 1: ");
for(int i = 0; i < size1; i++)
{
printf("%d ", list1[i]);
}
printf("\nList 2: ");
for(int i = 0; i < size2; i++)
{
printf("%d ", list2[i]);
}
printf("\nList 3: ");
for(int i = 0; i < index; i++)
{
printf("%d ", list3[i]);
}

return 0;
}
```

C code explanation

The C code creates and initializes two arrays **`list1`** and **`list2`**, containing some numbers. It then initializes an empty array, **`list3`**, and uses loops to iterate through both **`list1`** and **`list2`**, appending odd numbers from **`list1`** and even numbers from **`list2`** to **`list3`**. Finally, it prints the combined result array. Here, the **`sizeof()`** function is used to find the arrays **`list1`**and**`list2`**.

Program 4.16: Frequency of occurrence of elements

Count the frequency of occurrence of each element entered by the user.

Sample input output

Test case #1:

Input: `Enter the size of list: 6`

`7 8 7 3 1 8`

Output: **`Frequency of 7 is 2`**

`Frequency of 8 is 2`

`Frequency of 3 is 1`

`Frequency of 1 is 1`

Test case #2:

Input: `Enter the size of list: 5`

`1 2 1 2 1`

Output: **`Frequency of 1 is 3`**

`Frequency of 2 is 2`

Algorithm

To run the above program, the following steps are needed to be followed:

1. **`Start`**
2. **`Declare variables n, x, a, f, count, i, j`**
3. **`Read the size of list as n`**
4. **`a=[]`**
5. **`f=[]`**
6. **`for i =0 to n-1`**
   a. **`read a number as x`**
   b. **`append x to a`**
   c. **`append -1 to f`**
7. **`for i = 0 to n-1`**
   a. **`count=0`**

b. `if f[i] == 1:`

   i. `continue`

c. `for j =0 to n-1`

   i. `if a[i]==a[j]:`

      1. `f[j]=1`

      2. `count=count+1`

d. `print("Frequency of ", a[i] , " is ", count)`

8. **`Stop`**

Flowchart

Figure 4.16 illustrates the program in the form of a flowchart:

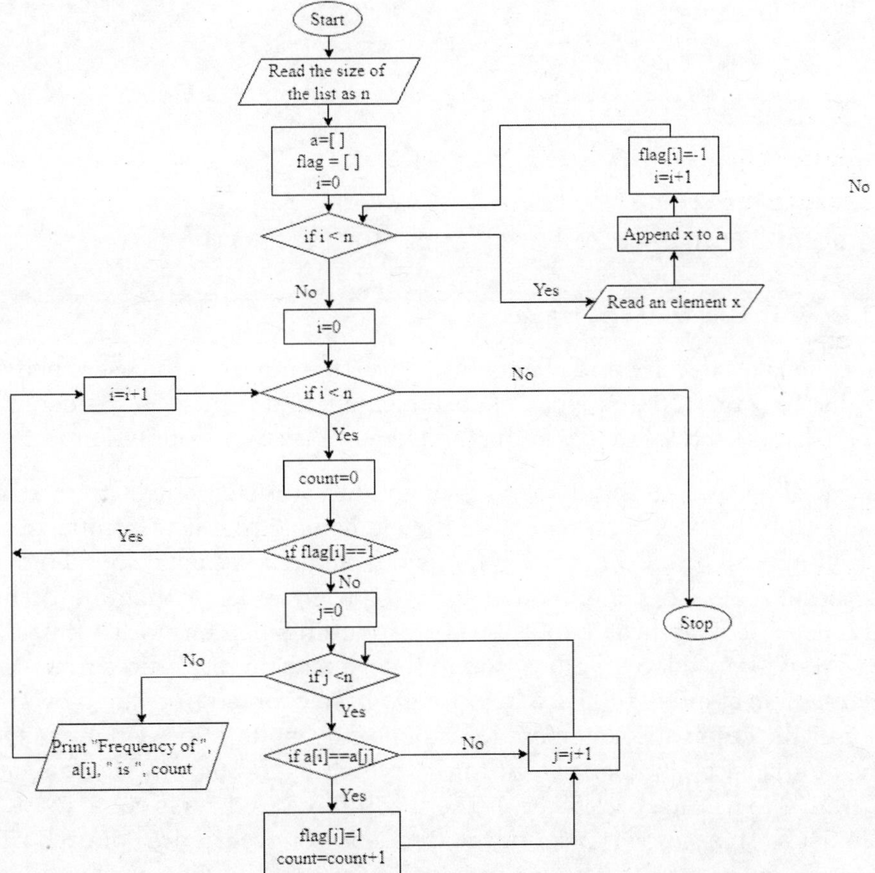

***Figure 4.16**: Flowchart illustrating the program 4.16*

Python code

Python code for the program is as follows:

```
n=int(input("Enter the size of list: "))
a=[]
f=[]
for i in range(0,n):
    x=int(input("Enter the number: "))
    a.append(x)
    f.append(-1)
for i in range(0, n):
    count=0
    if f[i] == 1:
        continue
    for j in range(0,n):
        if a[i]==a[j]:
            f[j]=1
            count=count+1
    print("Frequency of ", a[i] , " is ", count)
```

Python code explanation

The Python code takes the size and elements of a list as input from the user, then it iterates through the list to count the frequency of each element and prints the frequency for each element. The `f` list is used to track whether an element has been counted or not.

First, it prompts the user to input the size of the list and stores it in the variable **`n`**. It initializes an empty list **`a`** which will store the elements of the list. It initializes another empty list `f` which will be used to track whether an element has been counted or not. The for-loop iterates **`n`** times. It reads n values from the user, appends them in the list a, and sets **`-1`** to the list `f`. This indicates that the corresponding element in list **`a`** has not been counted yet. Another for-loop iterates through the list **`a`** using the indices from **`0`** to **`n-1`**. It checks if the element at index **`i`** in list **`a`** has already been counted (indicated by **`f[i]`** being **`1`**). If yes, it uses the **`continue`** statement to skip the current iteration and move to the next element. Inside the loop, another nested for-loop iterates through the list **`a`** again, using the indices from **`0`** to **`n-1`** to check if the element at index **`i`** in list **`a`** is equal to the element at index **`j`** in list **`a`**. This is done to count the frequency of occurrences of each element. If the condition is true, it sets the value at index **`j`** in list **`f`** to **`1`**, indicating that this element has been counted. Also, the **count** variable value is incremented by **1**. Finally, it prints the frequency of the element at index **i** in list **a**.

C code

C code for the program is as follows:

```
#include<stdio.h>
void main()
{
int a[50], f[50], n,count, i, j;

printf("Enter the size of list: ");
scanf("%d", &n);
for( i =0; i<n; i++)
{
scanf("%d", &a[i]);
f[i]= -1;
}
for( i =0; i<n; i++)
{
count=0;
if (f[i] == 1)
continue;
for( j =0; j<n; j++)
{
if (a[i]==a[j])
{
f[j]=1;
count=count+1;
}
}
printf("\nFrequency of %d is %d ", a[i], count);
}
}
```

C code explanation

The C code takes the size and elements of a list as input from the user. Then, it iterates through the array to count the frequency of each element and prints the frequency for each element. The `f` array is used to track whether an element has been counted or not.

First, it prompts the user to input the size of the array and stores it in the variable **`n`**. It declares an empty array **`a`**, which will store the elements of the array. It initializes another empty array **`f`**, which will be used to track whether an element has been counted or not. The for-loop iterates **`n`** times. It reads **`n`** values from the user, appends them in the array **`a`**, and sets **`-1`** to the array **`f`**. This indicates that the corresponding element in array **`a`** has not been counted yet. Another for-loop iterates through the array **`a`** using the indices from **`0`** to **`n-1`**. It checks if the element at index **`i`** in array **`a`** has already been counted (indicated by **`f[i]`** being **`1`**). If yes, it uses the **`continue`** statement to skip the current iteration and move to the next element. Inside the loop, another nested for-loop iterates through the array **`a`** again, using the indices from **`0`** to **`n-1`** to check if the element at index **`i`** in array **`a`** is equal to the element at index **`j`** in array **`a`**. This is done to count the frequency of occurrences of each element. If the condition is true, it sets the value at index **`j`** in array **`f`** to **`1`**, indicating that this element has been counted. Also, the **`count`** variable value is incremented by **`1`**. Finally, it prints the frequency of the element at index **`i`** in array **`a`**.

Program 4.17: Find length of a string

Find the length of a string (without using library functions).

Sample input output

Test case #1:

Input: `Enter a String: codefactory`

Output: **`The length of the string is 11`**

Test case #2:

Input: `Enter a String: bookforprogramming`

Output: **`The length of the string is 18`**

Algorithm

To run the above program, the following steps need to be followed:

1. **`Start`**
2. **`s=input("Enter a String: ")`**
3. **`l=0`**

4. **`for i in s:`**
    a. **`l=l+1`**
5. **`print("The length of the string is ", l)`**
6. **`Stop`**

Flowchart

Figure 4.17 illustrates the program in the form of a flowchart:

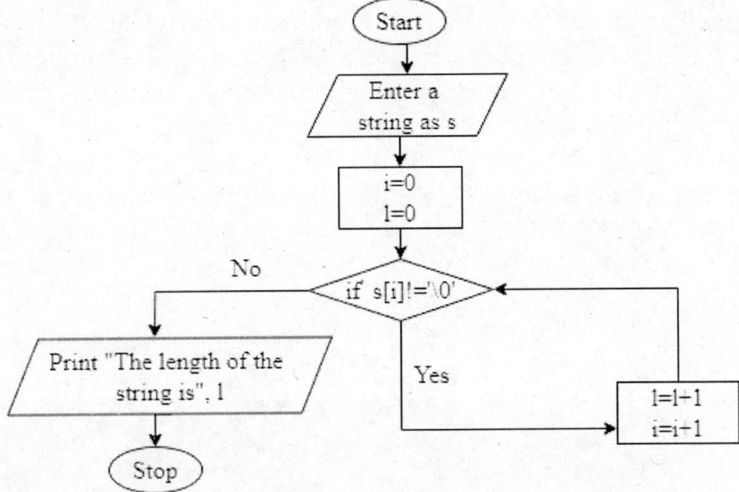

***Figure 4.17**: Flowchart illustrating the program 4.17*

Python code

Python code for the program is as follows:

```
s=input("Enter a String: ")
l=0
for i in s:
    l=l+1
print("The length of the string is ", l)
```

Python code explanation

The Python code prompts the user to input a string, counts the number of characters in the string using a loop that iterates through all characters of the string, and then prints the length of the string.

It reads a string input from the user and stores it in **s**. The variable l is set to **0**and is used to store the length of the string. The for-loop iterates through each character of the string **s**. Inside the loop, it increments the **l** variable for each character encountered, effectively counting the length of the string. After the loop completes, it prints the calculated length of the string.

C code

C code for the program is as follows:

```
#include<stdio.h>
void main()
{
char  s[30];
int l,i;
printf("Enter a String: ");
scanf("%s",s);
l=0;
for (i=0; s[i]!=’\0’; i++)
l=l+1;
printf("The length of the string is  %d", l);
}
```

C code explanation

The C code prompts the user to input a string, counts the number of characters in the string using a loop that iterates until the null character is encountered, and then prints the length of the string using the **printf** function.

First, it declares a character array **s** that can hold up to 30 characters. It reads a string input from the user and stores it in array **s**. The variable l is set to **0**and is used to store the length of the string. The **for** loop iterates through each character of the string **s** until the null character (**\0**) is encountered, which indicates the end of the string. Inside the loop, it increments the **l** variable for each character encountered, effectively counting the length of the string. After the loop completes, it prints the calculated length of the string.

Program 4.18: Check if string is a palindrome

Check whether a given string is palindrome or not (without using library functions).

Hint: Palindrome means a sequence of characters that reads the same forwards as it does backward.

Sample input output

Test case #1:

Input: `Enter a String: madam`

Output: **`The string is a palindrome`**

Test case #2:

Input: `Enter a String: codefactory`

Output: **`The string is not palindrome`**

Algorithm

To run the above program, the following steps are needed to be followed:

1. **`Start`**
2. **`Declare the variables i, l, s`**
3. **`Read s`**
4. **`l=0`**
5. **`for i in s:`**
    a. **`l=l+1`**
6. **`for i = 0 to l`**
    a. **`if s[i] !=s[l-i-1]`**
        i. **`print("The string is not palindrome")`**
        ii. **`break`**
7. **`else //this else belongs to the loop statement`**
    a. **`print("The string is a palindrome")`**
8. **`Stop`**

Flowchart

Figure 4.18 illustrates the program in the form of a flowchart:

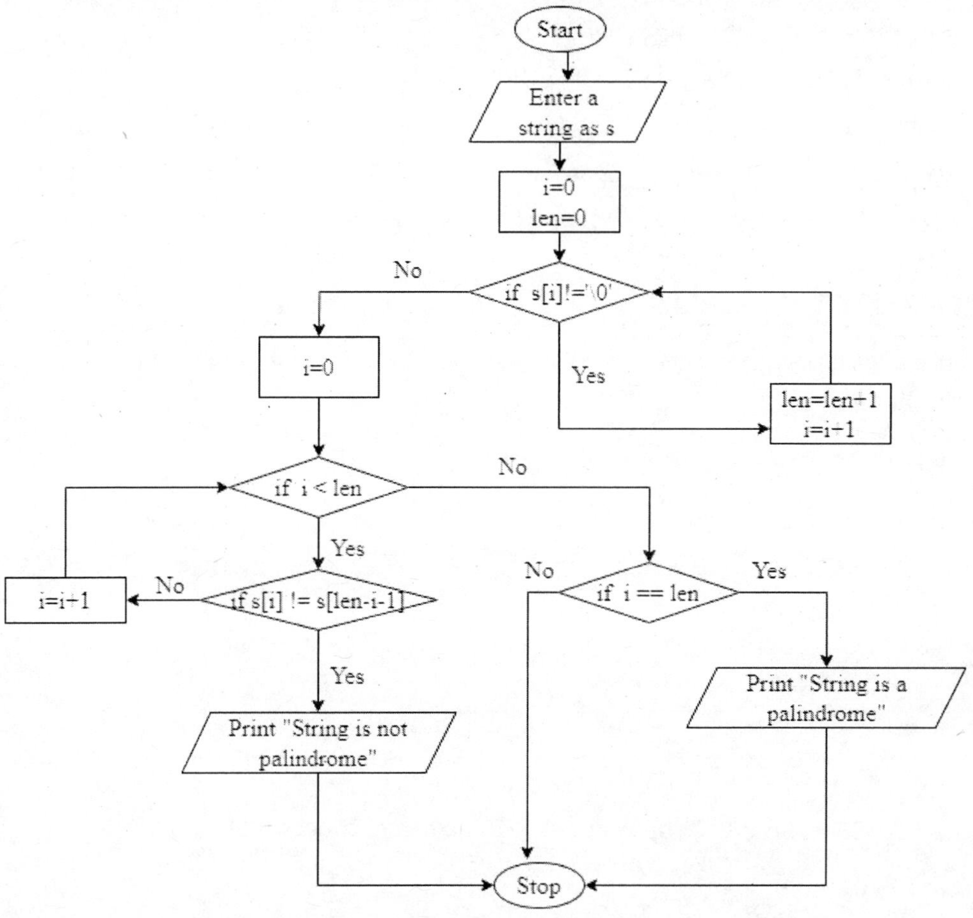

***Figure 4.18**: Flowchart illustrating the program 4.18*

Python code

Python code for the program is as follows:

```
s=input("Enter a String: ")
l=0
for i in s:
    l=l+1
for i in range(0, l):
    if s[i] !=s[l-i-1]:
```

```
        print("The string is not palindrome")
        break
else:  //else of for-loop
    print("The string is a palindrome")

```

Python code explanation

This Python code checks whether a given input string is a palindrome or not. The user is prompted to enter a string. It initializes a variable **`l`** to store the length of the string. Then, it iterate through each character in the string using a loop to count the length of the string. It starts another loop that runs from **`0`** to **`l-1`**. Within the loop, it compares characters at positions **`i`** and **`l-i-1`** to check if the string is a palindrome. If a character pair is found that does not match, print **`The string is not a palindrome`** and exit the loop using break. Otherwise, if the loop completes without finding a mismatched character pair, print **`The string is a palindrome`**.

C code

C code for the program is as follows:

```
#include<stdio.h>
void main()
{
char s[30];
int l,i;
printf("Enter a String: ");
scanf("%s",s);
l=0;
for(i=0; s[i]!= '\0'; i++)
l=l+1;
for( i=0;i<l;i++)
{
if (s[i] !=s[l-i-1])
{
printf("The string is not palindrome");
break;
}
```

```
}
if (i==l)
printf("The string is a palindrome");
}
```

C code explanation

This C code checks whether a given input string is a palindrome or not. The user is prompted to enter a string. It initializes a variable `l` to store the length of the string. Then, it iterate through each character in the string using a loop to count the length of the string. It starts another loop that runs from `0` to `l-1`.Within the loop, it compares characters at positions `i` and `l-i-1` to check if the string is a palindrome. If a character pair is found that does not match, print **`The string is not a palindrome`** and exit the loop using **`break`**. Otherwise, if the loop completes without finding a mismatched character pair, print **`The string is a palindrome`**.

Program 4.19: Display even indexed characters

Read a string from the user and display only those characters that are present at an even index. For example, **`str ='python'`**, so you should display **p,t,o**.

Sample input output

Test case #1:

Input: `Enter a String: codefactory`

Output: **`c d f c o y`**

Test case #2:

Input: `Enter a String: programming`

Output: **`p o r m i g`**

Algorithm

To run the above program, the following steps are needed to be followed:

1. **`Start`**
2. **`Declare the variables l, i`**
3. **`Read s`**
4. **`l=0`**

5. **for i in s:**
   a. **if (l%2==0)**
      i. **print i**
   b. **l=l+1**
6. **Stop**

Flowchart

Figure 4.19 illustrates the program in the form of a flowchart:

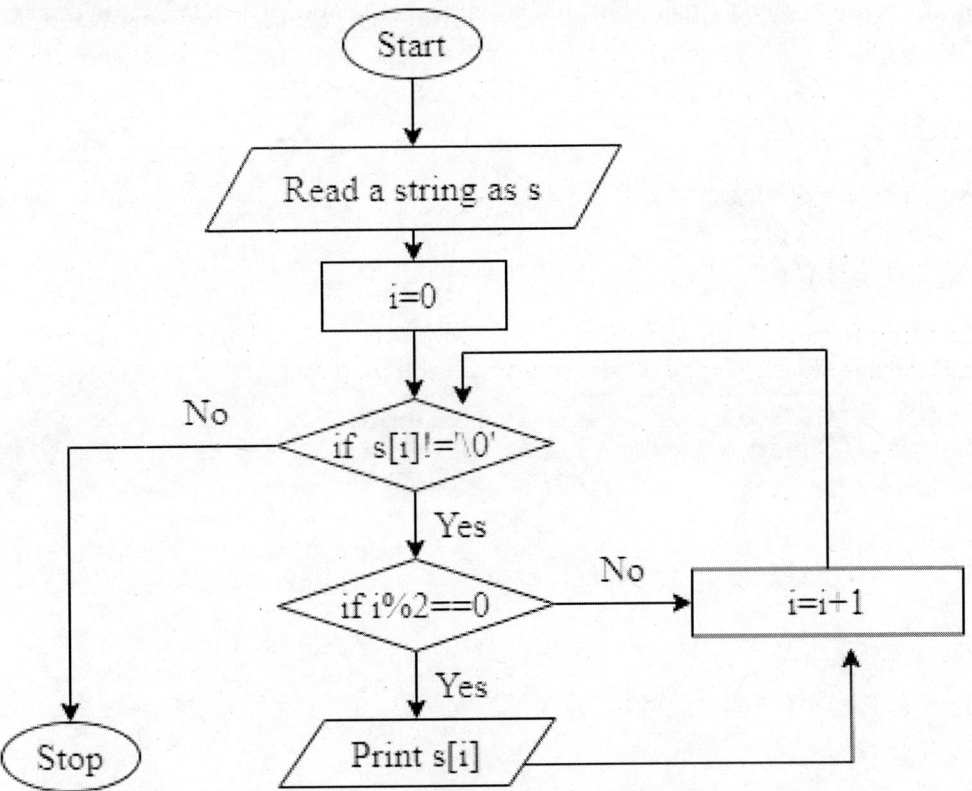

***Figure 4.19**: Flowchart illustrating the program 4.19*

Python code

Python code for the program is as follows:

```
1. s=input("Enter a String: ")
2. l=0
```

```
for i in s:
    if l%2==0:
        print(i)
    l=l+1
```

Python code explanation

The Python code takes a string as input and then prints out every other character of the string (starting from the first character) using a loop. The variable **l** is used to determine whether the current character should be printed based on its position. For that, it checks if the current value of **l** (the position of the character being considered) is even. If the condition is true, the code inside this block will execute and print the character at index **i** in the string **s**.

C code

C code for the program is as follows:

```
#include<stdio.h>
void main()
{
char s[30];
int l,i;
printf("Enter a String: ");
scanf("%s",s);
l=0;
for(i=0; s[i]!= '\0'; i++)
{
if (l%2==0)
    {printf("%c ", s[i]);}
l=l+1;
}}
```

C code explanation

The C code takes a string as input and then prints out every other character of the string (starting from the first character) using a loop. The variable **l** is used to determine whether the current character should be printed based on its position. For that, it checks if the current value of **l** (the position of the character being considered) is even. If the condition is true, the code inside this block will execute and print the character at index **i** in the string **s**.

Program 4.20: Concatenate two strings

Concatenate two strings (without using library functions).

Sample input output

Test case #1:

Input: `Enter a string: code`

`Enter second string: factory`

Output: Concatenated string is codefactory

Test case #2:

Input: `Enter a string: programming`

`Enter second string: book`

Output: **Concatenated string is programmingbook**

Algorithm

To run the above program, the following steps are needed to be followed:

1. **Start**
2. **Declare variables as s1, s2, s3**
3. **Read a string s1, s2**
4. **i=0**
5. **while(s1[i]!= '\0')**
   a. **s3[i]=s1[i]**
   b. **i=i+1**
6. **while(s2[i]!= '\0')**
   a. **s3[i]=s2[i]**
   b. **i=i+1**
7. **print(s3)**
8. **Stop**

Flowchart

Figure 4.20 illustrates the program in the form of a flowchart:

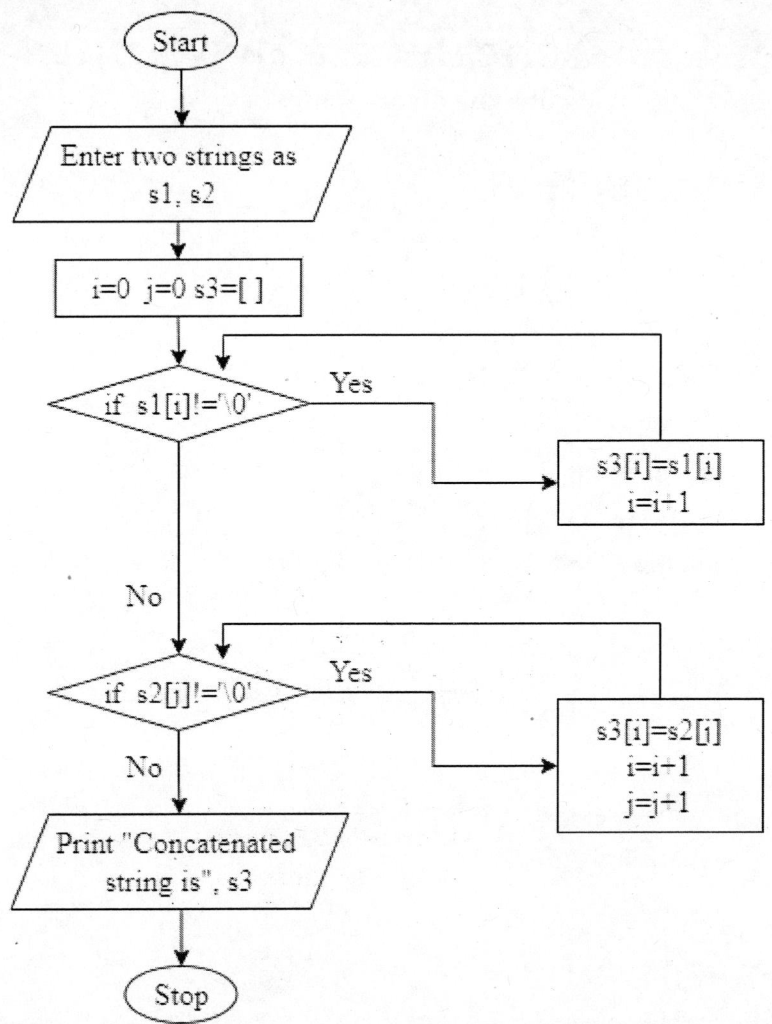

***Figure 4.20**: Flowchart illustrating the program 4.20*

Python code

Python code for the program is as follows:

```
s1=input("Enter a String: ")
s2=input("Enter second String: ")
s3=s1+s2
print(s3)
```

Python code explanation

This Python code takes two input strings from the user, concatenates them together, and then prints the resulting concatenated string. In Python, the **+** operator can be used with string as a concatenation operator.

C code

C code for the program is as follows:

```
#include<stdio.h>
void main()
{
char s1[20], s2[20], s3[20];
int i=0, j=0;
printf("Enter a string: ");
scanf("%s", s1);
printf("Enter a string: ");
scanf("%s", s2);
while(s1[i]!= ‘\0’)
{
s3[i]=s1[i];
i=i+1;
}
while(s2[j]!= ‘\0’)
{
s3[i]=s2[j];
i=i+1;
j=j+1;
}
printf("Concatenated string is %s", s3);
}
```

C code explanation

The C code declares three character arrays,`s1`, `s2`, and `s3`, that can hold up to `20` characters each. These arrays will be used to store the input strings and the concatenated string. It reads two strings input from the user and stores them in the character arrays`s1` and `s2`.

The **while** loop iterates through each character of the string **s1** until the null character (**\0**) is encountered, which indicates the end of the string and copies the character at index **i** from string **s1** to the corresponding index **i** in the string **s3**. Similarly, another **while** loop iterates through each character of the string **s2** until the null character (**\0**) and copies the character at index **j** from string **s2** to the current index **i** in the string **s3**. Finally, it prints the concatenated string stored in **s3** using the **printf** function.

Conclusion

The chapter has discussed complex control statements (while-loop and for-loop) with conditional statements in the form of flowcharts, algorithms, and coding. With the help of several examples, the different flavors of loop statements are presented.

In the next chapter, more complex programs will be discussed with the help of a good number of solved examples.

Points to remember

- Range() function in Python **generates** the sequence from a lower value to one less than the upper value. For example, **range(1,4)** generates **1**,**2**,**3**.
- The append () function in Python is used to add elements to the list.
- In C, **#define** can be used to define macro, an inline function.
- In C, **?:** operator is used to check condition and assign value.
- Double equal, ==, is used for comparing the values, whereas single equal, =, is used to assign the value.
- In the for-loop, the value of the induction variable is incremented/ decremented automatically. Meanwhile, in the while-loop, it is to be done in the loop deliberately.
- In Python code, the loop block should be indented towards the right side.
- In C code, the loop block should be enclosed within curly brackets **{}**.

Questions

1. Display even numbers between the range **n** and **m** where **n** and **m** are inclusive.
2. Display *** (three stars) if the number is divisible by 5. Numbers are between the range **n** and **m**, where **n** and **m** are inclusive.
3. Display *** (three stars) if the number is divisible by 5. Otherwise, display **x** (one cross). Numbers are between the range **n** and **m**, where **n** and **m** are inclusive.

4. Display the numbers divisible by three between the range `n` and `m` where `n` and `m` are inclusive.
5. Display the sum of all the numbers that are divisible by 11 between the range `n` and `m` where `n` and `m` are inclusive.
6. Find the smallest of n numbers as entered by the user.
7. Count the number of consonants in a string.
8. Copy one string into another (without using library functions).
9. Print all the prime numbers between 0 and 50
10. Print all the prime numbers between the values X and Y. For example, if X=1 and Y=10, then the output should display**1, 2, 3, 5, 7**.

Join our book's Discord space

Join the book's Discord Workspace for Latest updates, Offers, Tech happenings around the world, New Release and Sessions with the Authors:

https://discord.bpbonline.com

Chapter 5
Complex Problem Solving

Introduction

This chapter discusses the complex logic building using various programming constructs (as discussed in previous chapters). The chapter's main focus is solving difficult problems by thinking of some logic. The chapter presents the problems or challenges that require creative and intricate solutions. These problems often go beyond simple algorithmic steps and may involve multiple steps, conditional logic, loops, lists, and matrices. The chapter discusses creating a logical flow for solving complex problems, including algorithms and flowcharts, to plan solutions before writing code.

Structure

In this chapter, there are a total of 20 programs, and five sub-sections complement each program:

- Understand the program objective with sample test cases consisting of inputs and outputs. It will give the user an understanding of what kind of user input is expected and what result will be projected for a particular program.
- Understand the program with an algorithm. This will help the user to understand the logical flow for solving complex problems.
- Visualize the program flow with flowcharts. Program objectives can be understood

easily with the flowchart representation. Users will understand which symbols to use in which context throughout different program's flowchart representations.

- Python source code of each program. Each program's source code in Python programming language is provided to the user so the user can understand the basic operations of the language. An explanation of each code is also provided.
- C implementation of each program. Users can learn the basic concepts of C language with the provided C language code and its explanation for every program.

Objectives

In this chapter, readers will explore techniques for solving intricate problems that often involve multiple sequential steps, intricate combinations of conditional statements and nested loops, and manipulation of data structures like lists and matrices. The readers will also explore constructing a coherent problem-solving strategy, incorporating algorithm design and flowcharts to chart solutions before coding implementation.

Furthermore, the chapter strongly emphasizes practical application, demonstrating how to implement these logical approaches using Python and C programming languages. Sample codes are provided to offer hands-on experience, allowing readers to practice and gain confidence in effectively utilizing various programming constructs in different coding scenarios.

Program 5.1: Find sum of digits of a number

Find the sum of the digits of a number. For example, if number is 2134, then sum = 10.

Sample input output

Test case #1:

Input: `Enter a number: 78`

Output: **`The sum of the digits of the number is 15`**

Test case #2:

Input: `Enter a number: 204874`

Output: **`The sum of the digits of the number is 25`**

Algorithm

To run the above program, the following steps are needed to be followed:

1. **`Start`**
2. **`Variable declaration: m, s, r`**

3. `Read m`
4. `s=0`
5. `Iterate  till m>0`
6. `r=m%10`
7. `s=s+r`
8. `m=m/10`
9. `Print ("Sum of digits of the number is:",s)`
10. `Stop`

Flowchart

Figure 5.1 illustrates the program in the form of a flowchart:

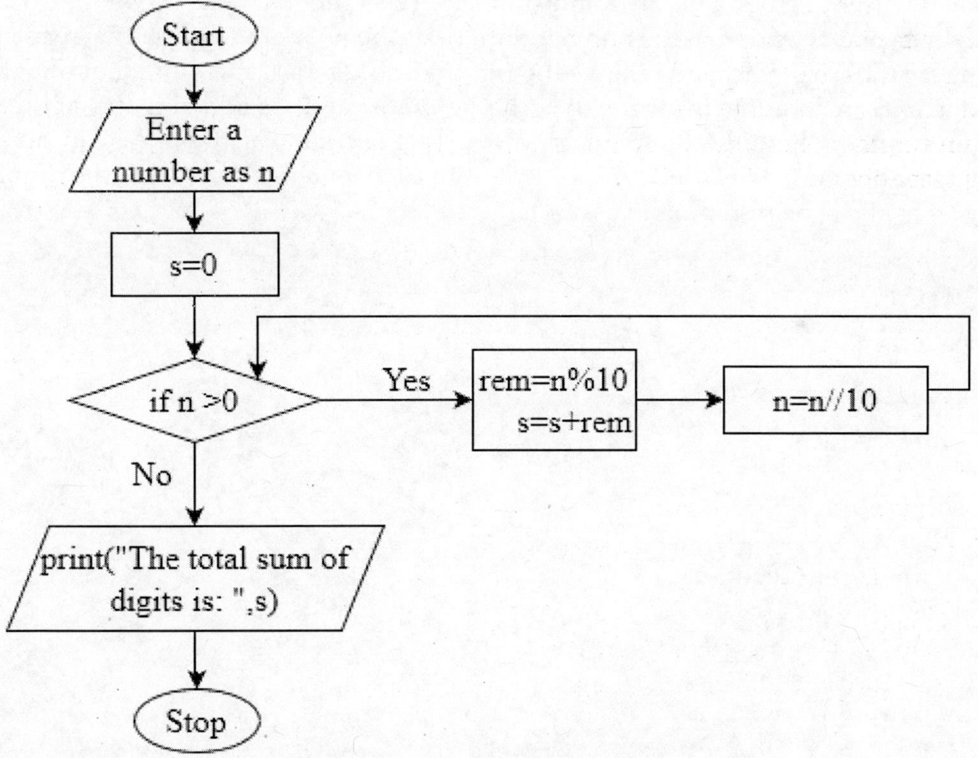

***Figure 5.1**: Flowchart illustrating the program 5.1*

Python code

Python code for the program is as follows:

```
m=int(input("Enter a number:"))
s=0
while(m>0):
        r=m%10
        m=m//10
        s=s+r
print("Sum of digits of the number is: ",s)
```

Python code explanation

This Python program calculates the sum of the digits of a number the user enters. It prompts the user to enter a number and stores it in the variable `m`. `while` loop is used to extract digits one by one from the number until there are no more digits left by repeatedly dividing `m` by `10` to extract and remove the rightmost digit of `m`, and storing quotient and reminder. In each iteration, the value of `r` (the rightmost digit) is added to the cumulative value of `s`. This is how the program keeps track of the sum of the digits. To obtain a quotient, the operator `//` is used. This operator gives the integer division of the numbers. Finally, it displays the result to the user.

C code

The C code for the program is as follows:

```
#include<stdio.h>
void main()
{
int m, s, r;
printf("Enter n: ");
scanf("%d",&m);
s=0 ;
while(m>0)
{
  r=m%10 ;
  s=s+r ;
 m=m/10 ;
```

```
}
printf("Sum of digits of the number is : %d",s);
}
```

C code explanation

The C code takes a number as input from the user. It initializes a variable `s` to `0` to store the sum. It enters a loop where it repeatedly extracts the rightmost digit of `m` using the `%` operator, adds it to the sum `s`, and then removes that digit from `m` using the division operator. Unlike Python, `/` operator is used for integer division. The loop continues until there are no more digits left in `m`. Finally, it prints the total sum of the digits to the user.

Program 5.2: Reverse the number

Reverse an n digit number. For example, if the number is 2134, the reverse number is 4312.

Sample input output

Test case #1:

Input: `Enter a number: 1234`

Output: `The reversed number is: 4321`

Test case #2:

Input: `Enter a number: 8720`

Output: `The reversed number is: 278`

Algorithm

To run the above program, the following steps need to be followed:

1. `Start`
2. `Variables declaration: n, s, r`
3. `Read n`
4. `s=0`
5. `Iterate while(n>0)`

   `rem=n%10`

   `s=s*10+rem`

   `n=n/10`

6. **Print("The reversed number is: ",s)**
7. **Stop**

Flowchart

Figure 5.2 illustrates the program in the form of a flowchart:

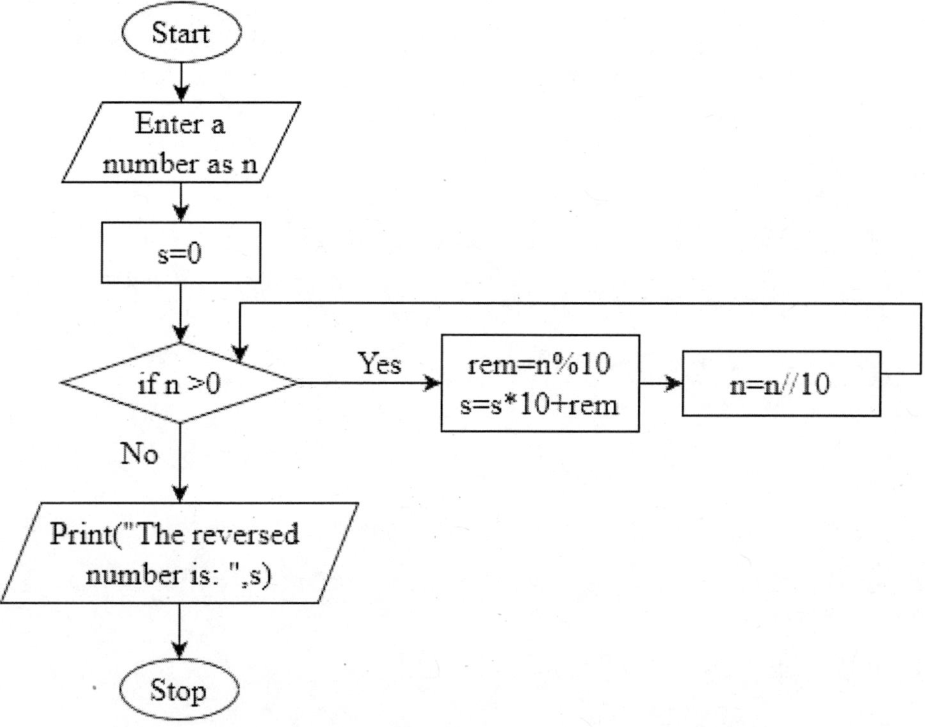

***Figure 5.2**: Flowchart illustrating the program 5.2*

Python code

Python code for the program is as follows:

```
n=int(input("Enter a number:"))
s=0
while(n>0):
          rem=n%10
          s=s*10+rem
          n=n//10
print("The reversed number is:",s)
```

Python code explanation

This Python program is a continuation of the previous program. It prompts the user to enter a number and stores it in the variable **n**. **while** loop is used to extract digits one by one from the number until there are no more digits left by repeatedly dividing **n** by **10** to extract and remove the rightmost digit of **n**, and storing quotient and reminder both. Here, to reverse the number, the current value of **s** is multiplied by **10** (which shifts all digits one position to the left), and then **rem** (rightmost digit) is added to it. This effectively builds the reversed number digit by digit. Finally, it displays the result to the user.

C code

C code for the program is as follows:

```
#include<stdio.h>
void main()
{
int n, s, rem;
printf("Enter n: ");
scanf("%d",&n);
s=0 ;
while(n>0)
{
   rem=n%10 ;
   s=s*10+rem ;
   n=n/10 ;
}
printf("The total sum of digits is: %d",s);
}
```

C code explanation

The C code takes a number as input from the user. It initializes a variable **s** to **0** to store the reversed number. It enters a loop where it repeatedly extracts the rightmost digit of **n**, multiplies the current value of **s** by **10** (which shifts all digits from one position to the left), and then adds **rem** (rightmost digit). Then, it removes that digit from **n**. The loop continues until there are no more digits left in **n**. Finally, it prints the reversed number to the user.

Program 5.3: Find all Armstrong numbers

Find all Armstrong numbers in the range of 0 and 999. [Example: A 3-digit number N is an Armstrong number if *N=A^3+B^3+C^3*, where A, B, and C are individual digits of number N. 371 is an Armstrong).

Sample input output

Test case #1:

Output: `0 1 2 3 4 5 6 7 8 9 153 370 371 407`

Algorithm

To run the above program, the following steps are needed to be followed:

1. `Start`
2. `Variables declaration: n, m, s, rem, i, j, ar, a[]`
3. `m=0`
4. `Iterate while m<=999`

```
n=m, ar=0 , i=0, j=0, a=[]
Iterate  while(n>0)
rem=n%10
a[i]=rem
i=i+1
n=n/10
Iterate  while (j<i)
ar=ar+pow(a[j],i)
j=j+1
if m==ar
Print(m," is an Armstrong Number")
m=m+1
del a
```

5. `Stop`

Flowchart

Figure 5.3 illustrates the program in the form of a flowchart:

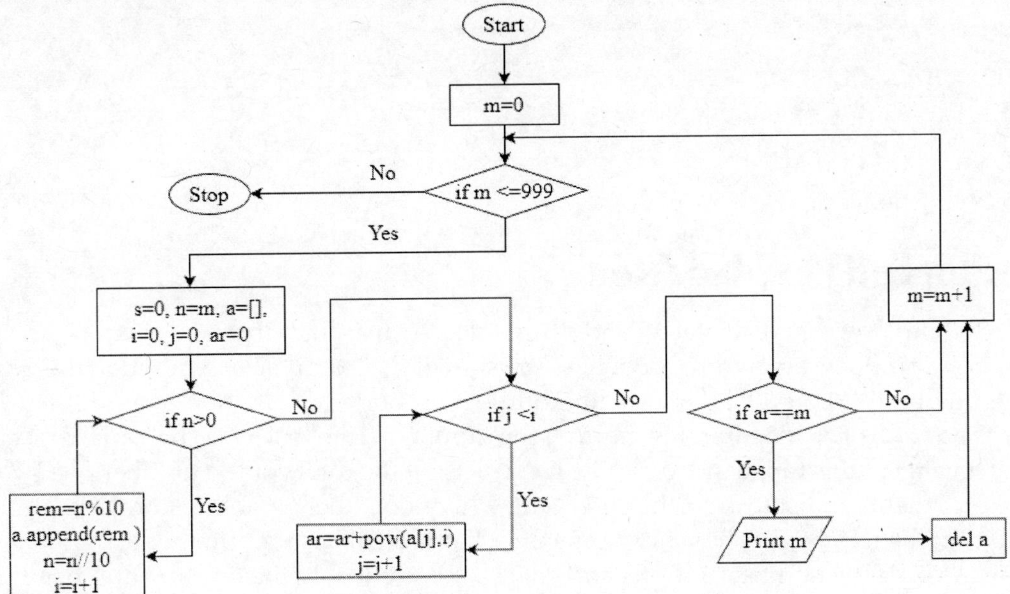

Figure 5.3: Flowchart illustrating the program 5.3

Python code

Python code for the program is as follows:

```
import math
for m in range(0,1000):
    n=m
    a=[]
    i=0
    j=0
    ar=0
    while(n>0):
        rem=n%10
        a.append(rem )
        n=n//10
        i=i+1
```

```
    while (j<i):
        ar=ar+pow(a[j],i)
        j=j+1
    if ar == m:
      print(m)
    del a
```

Python code explanation

This Python program calculates and prints all Armstrong numbers from 0 to 999. Armstrong numbers are numbers equal to the sum of their digits. Each raised to the power of the number of digits. The first **`math`** module is imported to use some math functions, such as **`pow()`**. A **`for`** loop iterates through the numbers from 0 to 999. The variable **`m`** takes on each value in this range individually. It extracts all the digits of the number one by one and stores them in a list **`a[]`**. At the end of the while-loop, the variable **`i`** stores the number of digits of the number **`n`**. Then, next, the while-loop calculates the sum of the digits raised to the power of the number of digits and checks if it is equal to the original number. If it is equal, it prints the Armstrong number.

C code

C code for the program is as follows:

```
#include<stdio.h>
#include<math.h>
void main()
{
int n, ar, m, rem, a[10];
for(m=0;m<=999;m++)
{
n=m;
int i=0;
int j=0;
int ar=0;
while(n>0)
{
```

```
    rem=n%10 ;
    a[i]=rem ;
    n=n/10 ;
    i=i+1;
}
while (j<i)
{
      ar=ar+pow(a[j],i);
      j=j+1;
}
if( ar == m)
    printf("%d ", m);
}
}
```

C code explanation

This C code calculates and prints all Armstrong numbers from 0 to 999. Armstrong numbers are numbers equal to the sum of their digits, and each is raised to the power of the number of digits. Here, the first **`math.h`** library is included to use some **`maths`** functions such as **`pow()`**. A **`for`** loop iterates through the numbers from 0 to 999. The variable **`m`** takes on each value in this range individually. It extracts all the digits of the number one by one and stores it in an array **`a[]`**. At the end of the while-loop, the variable **`i`** stores the number of digits of the number **`n`**. Then, next, the while-loop calculates the sum of the digits raised to the power of the number of digits and checks if it is equal to the original number. If it is equal, it prints the Armstrong number.

Program 5.4: Find n based on a condition

Given a list of numbers, find all its elements greater than their left neighbor and lesser than the right neighbor. For example, for the input **`[2 6 8 5 4]`**, the output is **`[6]`**.

Sample input output

Test case #1:

Input: `l=[2, 6, 8, 5, 4]`

Output: **`6`**

Test case # 2:

Input: `l=[2, 6, 8, 9, 4]`

Output: **`6, 8`**

Algorithm

To run the above program, the following steps are needed to be followed:

1. **`Start`**
2. **`l=[2, 6, 8, 5, 4]`**
3. **`for i = (1, len(l)-1):`**
4. **`if (l[i] >l[i-1] and l[i] < l[i+1]):`**
   `print(l[i])`
5. **`Stop`**

Flowchart

Figure 5.4 illustrates the program in the form of a flowchart:

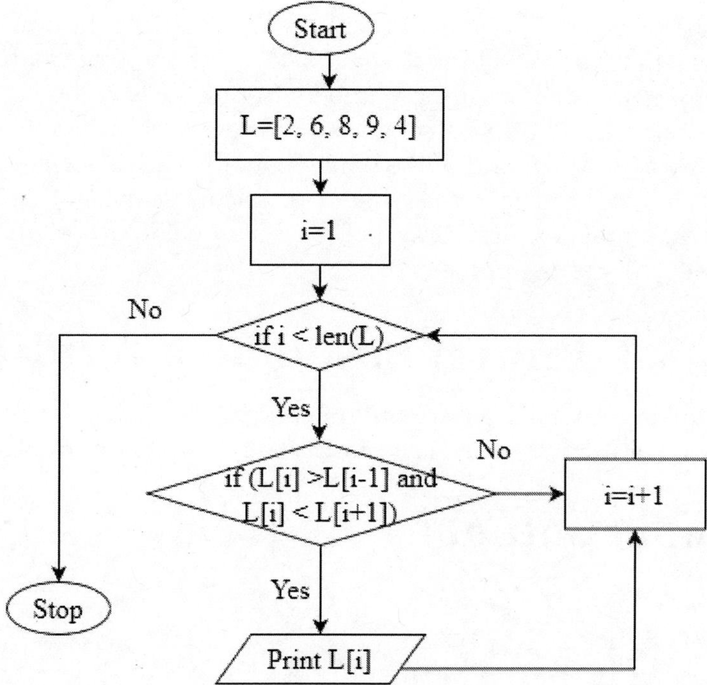

***Figure 5.4**: Flowchart illustrating the program 5.4*

Python code

Python code for the program is as follows:

```
l=[2, 6, 8, 9, 4]
for i in range(1, len(l)-1):
    if (l[i] >l[i-1] and l[i] < l[i+1]):
        print(l[i])
```

Python code explanation

This Python code snippet analyzes a list **`l`** and prints elements greater than the preceding element and less than the succeeding element. First, a list **`l`** is initialized as **`l= [2, 6, 8, 9, 4]`**. Then, a **`for`** loop iterates through the list of **`l`** indices. It starts at index **`1`** and goes up to **`len(l) - 2`**. The reason for excluding the first and last elements is to ensure we do not get an **`out of range`** error when checking elements before and after the current element. Inside the loop, it checks if the element at index **`i`** is greater than the element at index **`i-1`** (the preceding element) and less than the element at index **`i+1`** (the succeeding element). If yes, it prints the element at index **`i`**.

C code

C code for the program is as follows:

```
#include<stdio.h>
void main()
{
int l[]={2, 6, 8, 9, 5, 4};
int i ;
for (i =1; i< 5; i++)
{
    if ((l[i] >l[i-1])&& (l[i] < l[i+1]))
{
        printf("%d ", l[i] );
}
}
}
```

C code explanation

This C code analyzes an array `l` and prints elements greater than the preceding element and less than the succeeding element. First, an array, `l`, is initialized as `l= [2, 6, 8, 9, 4]`. Then, a `for` loop iterates through the list `l` indices. It starts at index `1` and goes up to `4`. The reason for excluding the first and last elements is to ensure we do not get an `out of range` error when checking elements before and after the current element. Inside the loop, it checks if the element at index `i` is greater than the element at index `i-1` (the preceding element) and less than the element at index `i+1` (the succeeding element). If yes, it prints the element at index `i`.

Program 5.5: Obtain list having prime numbers

Create list `L1` from list `L2` such that `L1` has all values that are prime numbers in `L2`.

Sample input output

Test case #1:

Input: `L2 = [15, 17, 20, 25, 11]`

Output: `L1: [17, 11]`

Test case #2:

Input: `L2 = [45,31,17,33,97,118]`

Output: `L1: [31, 17, 97]`

Algorithm

To run the above program, the following steps are needed to be followed:

1. `Start`
2. `Declare L2 = [45,31,17,33,97,118]`
3. `L1 = []`
4. `Iterate while n is in L2:`

   `bl = True`

   `Iterate for i = 2 to n`

   `if n % i == 0:`

   `bl = False`

```
break

if bl == True:

L1.append(n)
```

5. `Print  L1`
6. `Stop`

Flowchart

Figure 5.5 illustrates the program in the form of a flowchart:

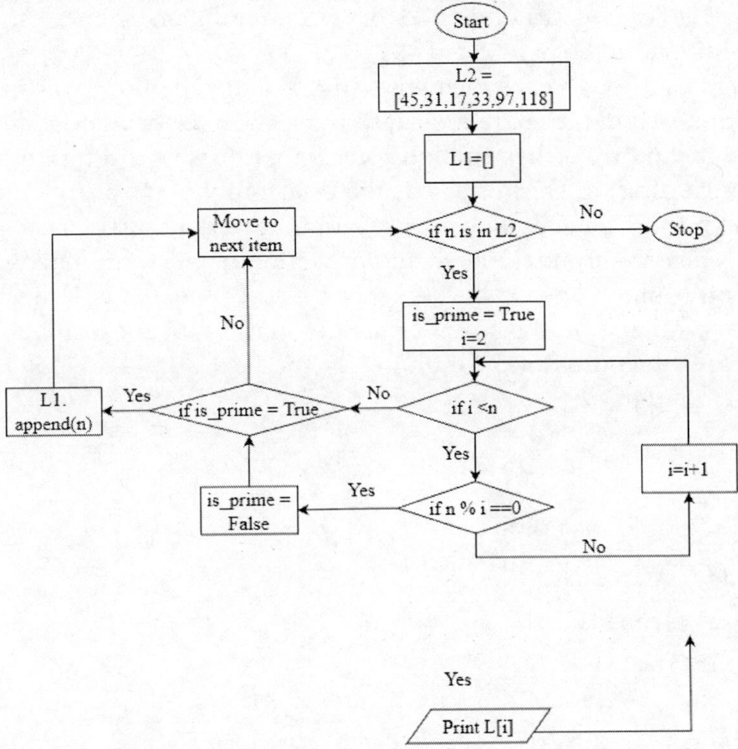

***Figure 5.5:** Flowchart illustrating the program 5.5*

Python code

Python code for the program is as follows:

```
L2 = [45,31,17,33,97,118]
L1 = []
for n in L2:
```

```
    bl = True
    for i in range(2, n):
        if n % i == 0:
            bl = False
            break
    if bl == True:
        L1.append(n)
print("L1:", L1)
```

Python code explanation

The Python code is designed to find and store prime numbers from a list **`L2`** into another list **`L1`**. First, it initializes the list **`L2`** as **`[45, 31, 17, 33, 97, 118]`** and an empty list **`L1`**. **`for`** loop iterates through each element **`n`** in the list **`L2`**. **`bl`** is a boolean variable that is set to **`True`** before each iteration. It is used to track whether or not the current number **`n`** is prime. Inside the loop, another **`for`** loop starts that iterates through numbers **`i`** from **`2`** up to (but not including) **`n`**. This loop tests the divisibility of **`n`** by any number between **`2`** to **`n-1`**. Suppose **`n`** is divisible by any of them. In that case, the **`bl`** variable becomes false, indicating that **`n`** is not a prime number, and the inner loop is terminated using the **`break`** statement. After the inner **`for`** loop, it checks if **`bl`** is still **`True`**. If it is, it means that **`n`** cannot be divided by any number in the specified range, so it is a prime number and appends it to the **`L1`** list. Now, the outer loop continues for the next number. Finally, it displays the prime numbers found in **`L2`**.

C code

C code for the program is as follows:

```
#include <stdio.h>
#include <stdbool.h>
int bl(int nn) {
    if (nn < 2) {
        return 0;
    }
    for (int ii = 2; ii * ii <= nn; i++) {
        if (nn % ii == 0) {
            return 0;
        }
    }
    return 1;
```

```
13. }
14. int main() {
15.     int L2[] = {45,31,17,33,97,118};
16.     int n = sizeof(L2) / sizeof(L2[0]);
17.     int L1[n];
18.     int c = 0;
19.     for (int i = 0; i < n; i++) {
20.         if (bl(L2[i])) {
21.             L1[c++] = L2[i];
22.         }
23.     }
24.     printf("L1 = { ");
25.     for (int i = 0; i < c; i++) {
26.         printf("%d ", L1[i]);
27.     }
28.     printf("}\n");
29.     return 0;
30. }
31.
```

C code explanation

This code declares an array **L2** of integers and uses the **bl()** function to check if each number in the array is prime. If a number is prime, it is added to a new array **L1**. Finally, the program prints out the values in **L1**. Note that the code assumes that the maximum size of **L2** is **9**, the size of the provided list. To handle larger lists, the code would need to be modified accordingly. This program uses the concept of function definition (*Line no 3-13*) and function call (*Line no 20*). Each element of array **L2** is passed to the function **bl()**. The function checks whether the element is prime and returns the value **True** if it is.

Program 5.6: Remove duplicate items

Remove duplicate items from a given list.

Sample input output

Test case #1:

Input: `[78, 89, 78, 65, 89, 89, 65]`

Output: **`[78, 89, 65]`**

Test case #2:

Input: `[19, 24, 19, 19, 19, 19, 24, 24]`

Output: `[19, 24]`

Algorithm

To run the above program, the following steps are needed to be followed:

1. **`Start`**
2. **`Declare my_list = [19, 24, 19, 19, 19, 19, 24, 24]`**
3. **`new_list = []`**
4. **`Iterate for each item in my_list`**

   `if item not in new_list:`

   `append item in new_list`
5. **`Print new_list`**
6. **`Stop`**

Flowchart

Figure 5.6 illustrates the program in the form of a flowchart:

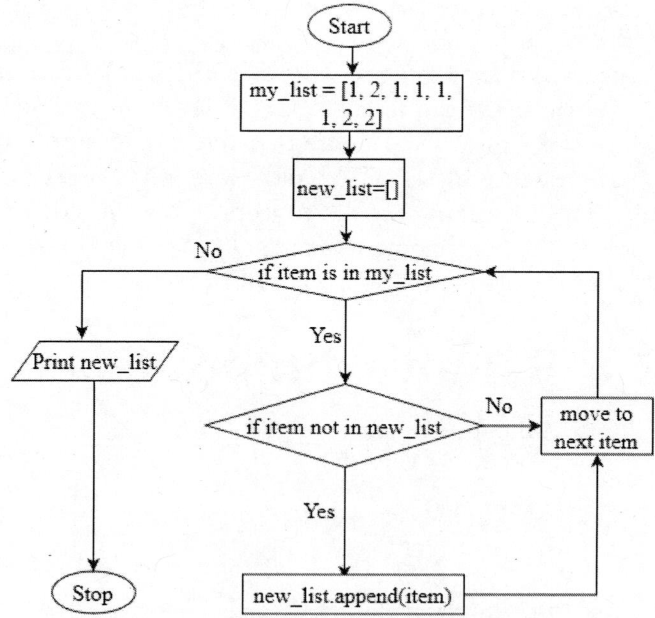

***Figure 5.6**: Flowchart illustrating the program 5.6*

Python code

Python code for the program is as follows:

```
my_list = [19, 24, 19, 19, 19, 19, 24, 24]
new_list = []

for item in my_list:
    if item not in new_list:
        new_list.append(item)

print(new_list)
```

Python code explanation

This Python code first creates a list with some duplicate items and then creates a new list that only includes the unique items from the original list. The for-loop iterates through each item in the original list and checks whether it is already in the new list. If not, it is added to the new list using the **append()** method. Finally, the new list is printed to the console.

C code

C code for the program is as follows:

```
#include <stdio.h>
int main() {
    int my_array[] = {19, 24, 19, 19, 19, 19, 24, 24};
    int new_array[11];
    int i, j, n, exists;
    n = 0;
    for (i = 0; i < 11; i++) {
        exists = 0;
        for (j = 0; j < n; j++) {
            if (my_array[i] == new_array[j]) {
                exists = 1;
                break;
            }
        }
```

```
        if (!exists) {
            new_array[n] = my_array[i];
            n++;
        }
    }
    for (i = 0; i < n; i++) {
        printf("%d ", new_array[i]);
    }
    return 0;
}
```

C code explanation

This code declares an array **`my_array`** with some duplicate items and creates a new array **`new_array`** to hold the unique items. It then uses nested loops to iterate through the **`my_array`** and checks for duplicate items. The outer loop goes through each element in **`my_array`**, and the inner loop iterates through each item in **`new_array`** to check whether the item already exists. If the item does not exist in **`new_array`**, it is added to the array using the **`new_array[n] = my_array[i]`** syntax, where **`n`** is the current length of **`new_array`**. Finally, the **`new_array`** is printed to the console using a loop that iterates through each item in the array.

Program 5.7: Sort the numbers

Arrange all the elements of an array in increasing order.

Sample input output

Test case #1:

Input: `[6, 3, 25, 1, 22, 11, 90]`

Output: **`Sorted List is : [1, 3, 6, 11, 22, 25, 90]`**

Test case #2:

Input: `[21,27,23,97,20,6,93]`

Output: **`[6, 20, 21, 23, 27, 93, 97]`**

Algorithm

To run the above program, the following steps are needed to be followed:

1. `Start`
2. `Declare a_r = [6, 3, 25, 1, 22, 11, 90]`
3. `n = len(a_r)`
4. `Iterate for i =0 to n-1`

   `Iterate for j =0 to n-i`

   `if a_r[j] > a_r[j+1] :`

   `interchange a_r[j], a_r[j+1]`
5. `Print a_r`
6. `Stop`

Flowchart

Figure 5.7 illustrates the program in the form of a flowchart:

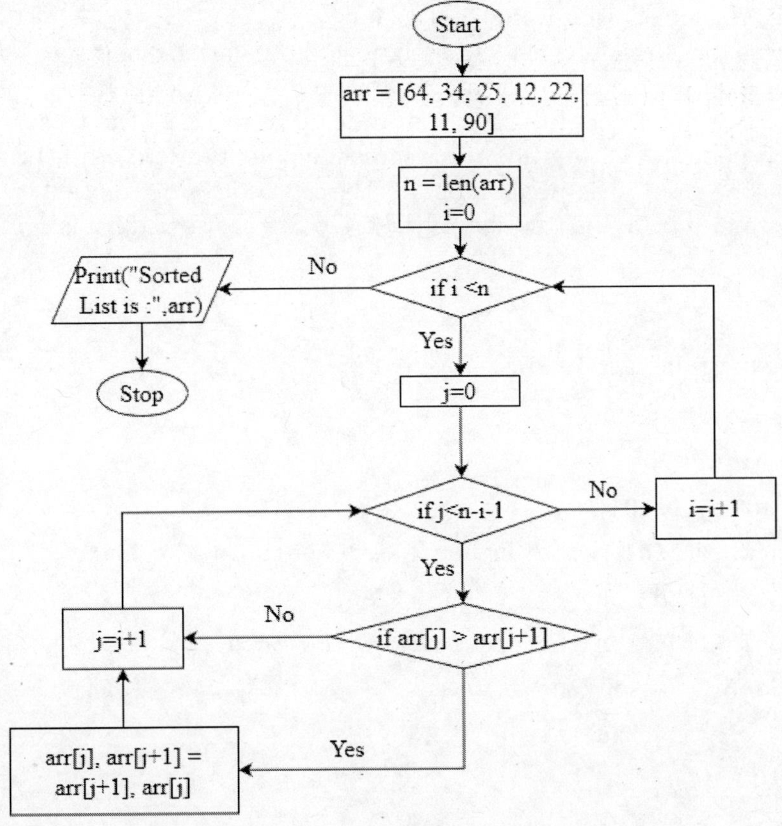

***Figure 5.7**: Flowchart illustrating the program 5.7*

Python code

Python code for the program is as follows:

```
a_r = [6, 3, 25, 1, 22, 11, 90]
n = len(a_r)
for ii in range(n):
    for jj in range(0, n-ii-1):
        if a_r[jj] > a_r[jj+1] :
            a_r[jj], a_r[jj+1] = a_r[jj+1], a_r[jj]
print("Sorted List is :",a_r)
```

Python code explanation

The provided Python code implements the Bubble Sort algorithm to sort a list called **`a_r`** in ascending order. In bubble sort, it repeatedly compares each element with its next element given in the list, and if the elements are not in increasing order, then the elements are interchanged. Here, a list is initialized as **`a_r = [6, 3, 25, 1, 22, 11, 90]`**. **`len()`** function returns the length of a list and assigns it to the variable **`n`**. It starts the outer loop, which iterates over the list of **`a_r`** elements. Inside the outer loop, it starts the inner loop, which iterates over a subset of the list from index **`0`** to **`n-ii-1`**. The reason for the **`-ii`** is that after each pass of the outer loop, the largest element (after sorting) is moved to the end, so there is no need to compare it again. The elements are swapped if the element at index **`jj`** is greater than at the next index **`jj+1`**. Finally, the sorted list is printed.

C code

C code for the program is as follows:

```
#include <stdio.h>
int main() {
    int a_r[100], n, i, j, tt, bl;
    printf("Enter the number of elements in the array: ");
    scanf("%d", &n);
    printf("Enter the elements of the array: ");
    for(i = 0; i < n; i++) {
        scanf("%d", &a_r[i]);
    }
    for(i = 0; i < n - 1; i++) {
        bl = 0;
```

```
        for(j = 0; j < n - i - 1; j++) {
            if(a_r[j] > a_r[j + 1]) {
                tt = a_r[j];
                a_r[j] = a_r[j + 1];
                a_r[j + 1] = tt;
                bl = 1;
            }
        }
        if(bl == 0) {
            break;
        }
    }
    printf("Sorted array in ascending order: «);
    for(i = 0; i < n; i++) {
        printf("%d ", a_r[i]);
    }
    printf("\n");
    return 0;
}
```

C code explanation

The code repeatedly compares each element with its next element given in the list, and if the elements are not in increasing order, they are interchanged. This process continues until no more swaps are needed, indicating that the list is sorted. The result is a sorted list printed to the console.

Program 5.8: Print matrix

Input a matrix of size 3x3 from the user and print the same as the output.

Sample input output

Test case #1:

Input:

```
Enter element at position ({,i,},{,j, }): 6
Enter element at position ({,i,},{,j, }): 5
```

```
Enter element at position ({,i,},{,j, }): 6
Enter element at position ({,i,},{,j, }): 4
Enter element at position ({,i,},{,j, }): 6
Enter element at position ({,i,},{,j, }): 3
Enter element at position ({,i,},{,j, }): 3
Enter element at position ({,i,},{,j, }): 5
Enter element at position ({,i,},{,j, }): 2
```

Output:

```
The matrix is:
6 5 6
4 6 3
3 5 2
```

Test case #2:

Input:

```
Enter element at position ({i},{j}): 1
Enter element at position ({i},{j}): 2
Enter element at position ({i},{j}): 3
Enter element at position ({i},{j}): 4
Enter element at position ({i},{j}): 5
Enter element at position ({i},{j}): 6
Enter element at position ({i},{j}): 7
Enter element at position ({i},{j}): 8
Enter element at position ({i},{j}): 4
```

Output:

```
The matrix is:
1 2 3
4 5 6
7 8 4
```

Algorithm

To run the above program, the following steps are needed to be followed:

1. **Start**
2. **Initialize a 3x3 matrix**

3. **Accept 9 integer inputs from the user and assign them to the matrix elements**
4. **Print the matrix**
5. **Stop**

Flowchart

Figure 5.8 illustrates the program in the form of a flowchart:

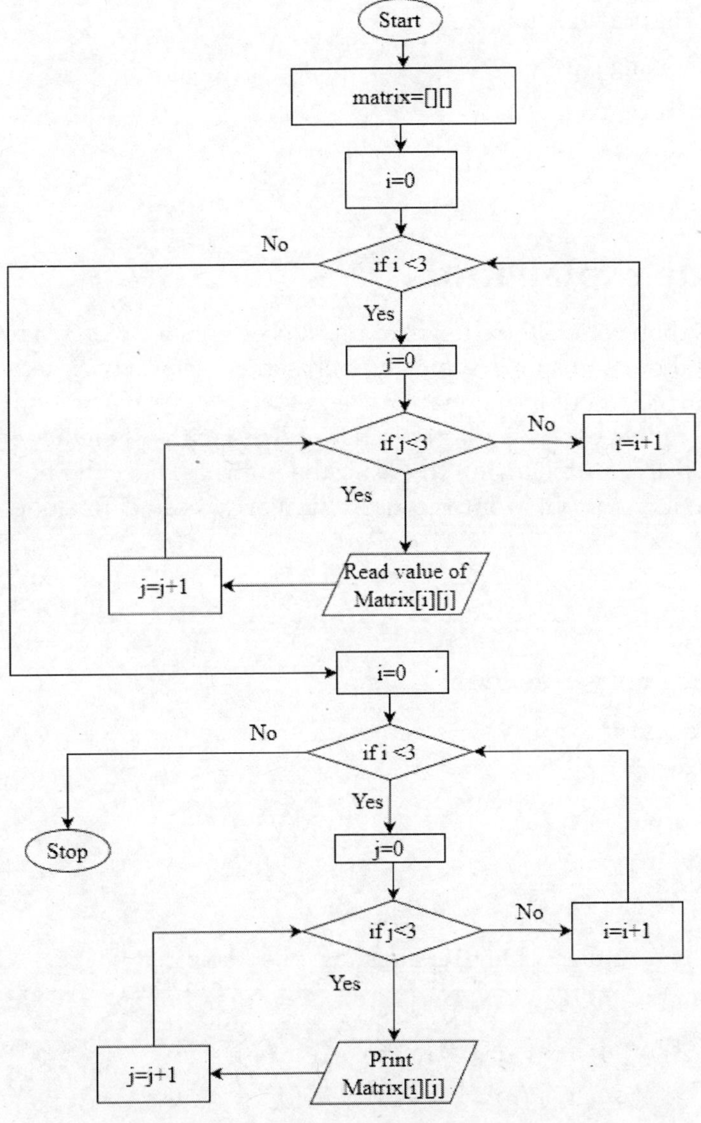

***Figure 5.8**: Flowchart illustrating the program 5.8*

Python code

Python code for the program is as follows:

```
matrix = [[0 for j in range(3)] for i in range(3)]
for i in range(3):
    for j in range(3):
        matrix[i][j] = int(input("Enter element at position ({,i,},{,j, }): "))
print("The matrix is:")
for i in range(3):
    for j in range(3):
        print(matrix[i][j], end=" ")
    print()
```

Python code explanation

The provided Python code allows users to input elements for a 3x3 matrix and then print the matrix. In Python, a matrix is typically represented as a two-dimensional array or list of lists, where each element in the matrix is accessed by specifying both row and column indices. First, it initializes a 3x3 matrix (a list of lists) with all elements initially set to `0`. It uses a nested list comprehension to create the matrix. Then, the nested for-loop takes all matrix elements as input from the user. Similarly, nested for-loop prints all matrix elements to the user.

C code

C code for the program is as follows:

```
#include <stdio.h>
int main() {
    int matrix[3][3];
    int i, j;
    printf("Enter the elements of the matrix:\n");
    for (i = 0; i < 3; i++) {
        for (j = 0; j < 3; j++) {
            scanf("%d", &matrix[i][j]);
        }
```

```
    }
    printf("The matrix you entered is:\n");
    for (i = 0; i < 3; i++) {
        for (j = 0; j < 3; j++) {
            printf("%d ", matrix[i][j]);
        }
        printf("\n");
    }
    return 0;
}
```

C code explanation

This program declares a matrix of size 3x3 to store the input and then uses nested for loops to input and print the matrix elements. In C, a matrix is a 2-D array. A two-dimensional array in C is essentially an array of arrays where each element is identified by row and column indices. A nested for-loop takes the matrix as input and prints the matrix where the outer loop takes care of the rows, and the inner loop handles the columns in each row.

Program 5.9: Add two matrics

Add two matrices. Also, print error message when matrices are not of the same size.

Sample input output

Test case #1:

Input:

```
A=[[1,2,3,4],[3,4,5,7],[5,6,7,1]]
B=[[9,9,8,1],[3,6,5,3],[2,6,8,2]]
```

Output:

```
Matrix C (sum of A and B):
10 11 11 5
6 10 10 10
7 12 15 3
```

Test case #2:

Input:

```
A=[[1,1,2,2],[1,1,1,1],[3,3,3,3]]
```

```
B=[[9,9,8,8],[2,2,2,2],[4,4,8,6]]
```

Output:

```
Matrix C (sum of A and B):
10 10 10 10
3 3 3 3
7 7 11 9
```

Algorithm

Step 1. To run the above program, the following steps are needed to be followed:

Step 2. Take the dimensions (no of rows and no of columns) of two matrices, A and B, as input from the user.

Step 3. If the dimension of A is not the same as that of B, print an error message and terminate the program.

Step 4. Take the matrices A and B elements as input.

Step 5. Create an empty matrix C of the same size as A and B.

Step 6. Perform the element-wise addition of A and B and store the result in C.

Step 7. Print the matrices A, B, and C.

Flowchart

Figure 5.9 illustrates the program in the form of a flowchart:

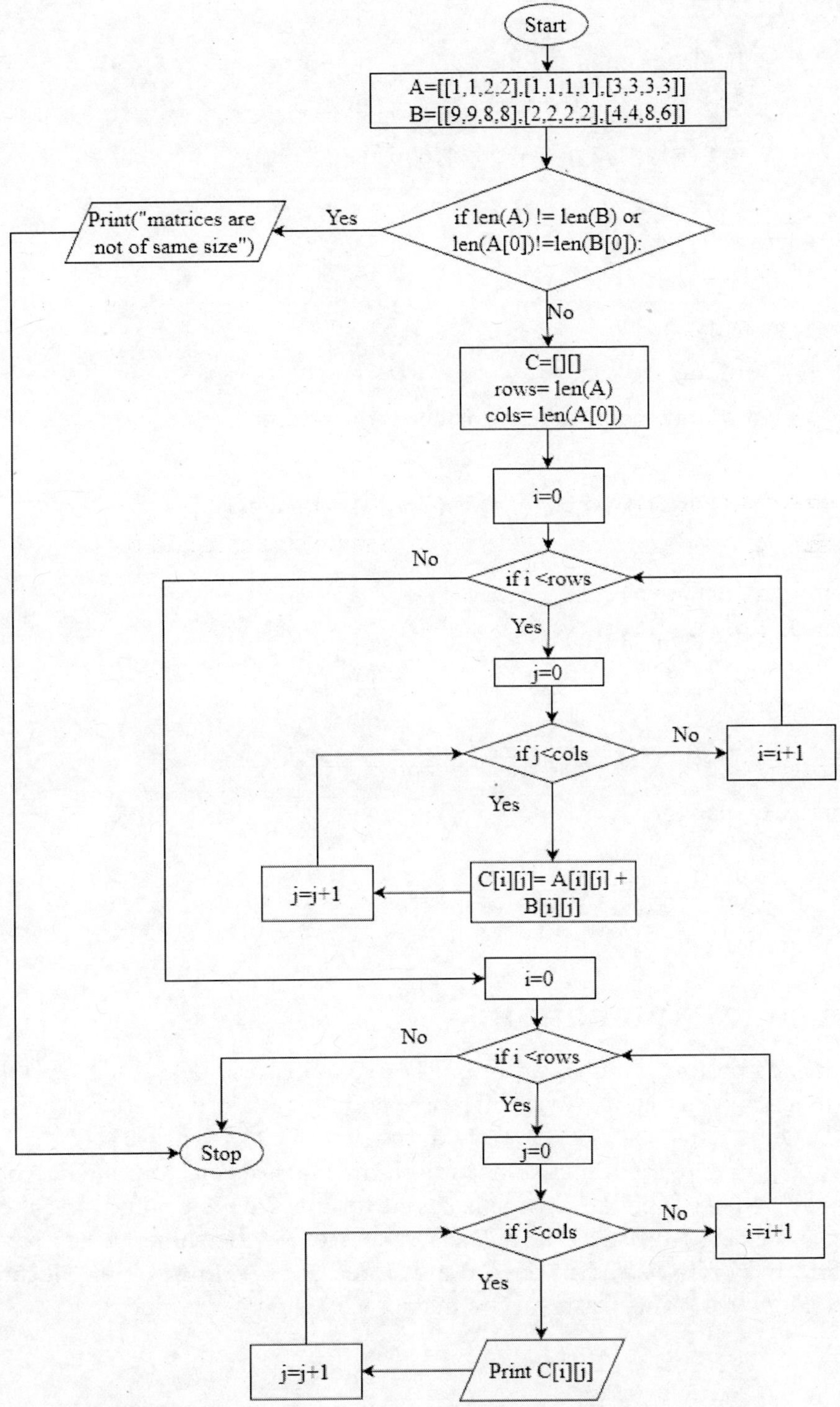

Figure 5.9: Flowchart illustrating the program 5.9

Python code

Python code for the program is as follows:

```
m_a=[[1,1,2,2],[1,1,1,1],[3,3,3,3]]
m_b=[[9,9,8,8],[2,2,2,2],[4,4,8,6]]
r=len(m_a)
c=len(m_a[0])
r1=len(m_b)
c1=len(m_b[0])
if r != r1 or c!=c1:
    print("matrices are different dimensions.")
    exit()
m_c = [[0 for j in range(c)] for i in range(r)]

for i in range(r):
    for j in range(c):
        m_c[i][j] = m_a[i][j] + m_b[i][j]

print("Matrix m_c (sum of m_a and m_b):")
for i in range(r):
    for j in range(c):
        print(m_c[i][j], end=' ‘)
    print()
```

Python code explanation

The Python code performs matrix addition for two matrices **m_a** and **m_b**, and then prints the result in matrix **m_c**. Here, two matrix **m_a** and **m_b** are initialized as **m_a = [[1, 1, 2, 2], [1, 1, 1, 1], [3, 3, 3, 3]]** and **m_b = [[9, 9, 8, 8], [2, 2, 2, 2], [4, 4, 8, 6]]**. Then, the dimensions of both the matrices are compared. Addition can be performed if they are equal. Otherwise, an error message is printed, and the program exits using the **exit()** function. If the size of matrices is the same, nested for-loops are used to perform point-wise addition and are stored at the corresponding location in the **m_c** matrix. Finally, it prints the resulting matrix **m_c** using nested loops.

C code

C code for the program is as follows:

```
#include <stdio.h>
#include <stdlib.h>
int main() {
    int r, c, r1, c1, i, j;
    printf("Matrix 1: no of rows and columns «);
    scanf("%d %d", &r, &c);
    printf("Matrix 2: no of rows and columns ");
    scanf("%d %d", &r1, &c1);
    if ((r != r1) || (c != c1)) {
        printf("\matrices are different dimensions.");
        exit(0);
    }
    int m_a[r][c], m_b[r1][c1], m_c[r][c];

    printf("\nEnter the elements of the first matrix:\n»);
    for (i = 0; i < r; i++) {
        for (j = 0; j < c; j++) {
            printf("Enter element[%d][%d]: ", i, j);
            scanf("%d", &m_a[i][j]);
        }
    }

    printf("\nEnter the elements of the second matrix:\n»);
    for (i = 0; i < r1; i++) {
        for (j = 0; j < c1; j++) {
            printf("Enter element[%d][%d]: ", i, j);
            scanf("%d", &m_b[i][j]);
        }
    }

    for (i = 0; i < r; i++) {
```

```
        for (j = 0; j < c; j++) {
            m_c[i][j] = m_a[i][j] + m_b[i][j];
        }
    }

    printf("\nThe m_c of the matrices is:\n»);
    for (i = 0; i < r; i++) {
        for (j = 0; j < c; j++) {
            printf("%d ", m_c[i][j]);
        }
        printf("\n");
    }
    return 0;
}
```

C code explanation

The C code performs matrix addition for two matrices **m_a** and **m_b** and then prints the result in matrix **m_c**. The library **stdlib.h** is used for the **exit()** function. Here, the user takes two matrices, **m_a** and **m_b**, as input. Then, the dimensions of both the matrices are compared. Addition can be performed if they are equal. Otherwise, an error message is printed, and the program exits using the **exit()** function. If the size of matrices is the same, nested for-loops are used to perform point-wise addition and are stored at the corresponding location in the **m_c** matrix. Finally, it prints the resulting matrix **m_c** using nested loops.

Program 5.10: Check if matrix is upper triangular

Input a matrix and check whether it is upper triangular or not.

Sample input output

Test case #1:

Input: `[[1,1,1],[0,1,1],[0,0,1]]`

Output:

```
Matrix is [[1, 1, 1], [0, 1, 1], [0, 0, 1]]
Matrix is upper triangular
```

Test case #2:

Input: `[[1,1,1],[10,11,12],[0,0,1]]`

Output:

```
Matrix is [[1, 1, 1], [10, 11, 12], [0, 0, 1]]
Matrix is not upper triangular
```

Algorithm

To run the above program, the following steps are needed to be followed:

1. `Start`
2. `Let a be a matrix`
3. `bl= 0`
4. `Iterate for i = 0 to 2`
   ```
   Iterate   for j = 0 to i - 1
   if a[i][j] is not equal to 0
   set bl to 1
   break out of inner loop
   ```
5. `if bl is equal to 0`
   ```
   print "Matrix is upper triangular"
   else
   print "Matrix is not upper triangular"
   ```
6. `Stop`

Flowchart

Figure 5.10 illustrates the program in the form of a flowchart:

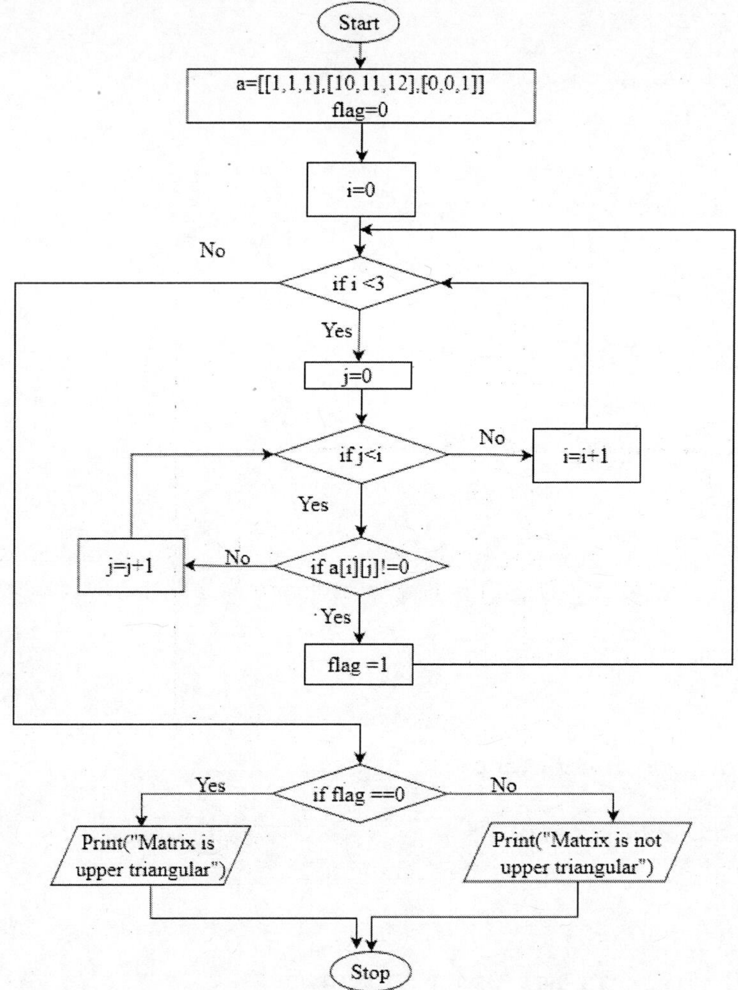

Figure 5.10: Flowchart illustrating the program 5.10

Python code

Python code for the program is as follows:

```
a=[[1,1,1],[10,11,12],[0,0,1]]

bl=0
for i in range(0, 3):
    for j in range(0, i):
        if a[i][j]!=0:
```

```
            bl=1
            break

print("Matrix is ", a)
if bl==0:
    print("Matrix is upper triangular ")
else:
    print("Matrix is not upper triangular ")
```

Python code explanation

The provided Python code checks whether a given matrix **a** is an upper triangular matrix. An upper triangular matrix is a square matrix in which all elements below the main diagonal (including the diagonal) are zero. Initially, the matrix is declared as **a = [[1, 1, 1], [10, 11, 12], [0, 0, 1]]**. The **bl** variable will determine whether the matrix is upper triangular. An outer loop iterates over the rows of the matrix. It runs three times since there are three rows in the 3x3 matrix. An inner loop starts and goes through the matrix's columns inside the outer loop. It runs up to the current row index **i**, checking only the elements below the diagonal. If **a[i][j] != 0**, a non-zero element is found below the main diagonal; hence, the matrix is not upper triangular. So, **bl** is set to **1**. The loop terminates using a **break** statement. Finally, outside the loop, if **bl == 0**, it prints that the matrix is upper triangular; otherwise, it prints that the matrix is not upper triangular.

C code

C code for the program is as follows:

```
#include <stdio.h>
int main() {
    int a[3][3] = {{1,1,1},{0,1,1},{0,0,1}};
    int bl = 0;

    for (int i = 0; i < 3; i++) {
        for (int j = 0; j < i; j++) {
            if (a[i][j] != 0) {
                bl = 1;
                break;
            }
        }
```

```
        if (bl == 1) {
            break;
        }
    }
    if (bl == 0) {
        printf("Matrix is upper triangular\n");
    } else {
        printf("Matrix is not upper triangular\n");
    }
    return 0;
}
```

C code explanation

The C code checks whether a given matrix **`a`** is an upper triangular matrix. An upper triangular matrix is a square matrix in which all elements below the main diagonal (including the diagonal) are zero. Initially, the matrix is assigned some values. The **`bl`** variable will determine whether the matrix is upper triangular. An outer loop iterates over the rows of the matrix. It runs three times since there are three rows in the 3x3 matrix. Inside the outer loop, it starts an inner loop that iterates over the columns of the matrix. It runs up to the current row index **`i`**, checking only the elements below the diagonal. If **`a[i][j] != 0`**, a non-zero element is found below the main diagonal; hence, the matrix is not upper triangular. So, **`bl`** is set to **`1`**. The loop terminates using the break statement. Finally, outside the loop, if **`bl == 0`**, it prints that the matrix is upper triangular; otherwise, it prints that the matrix is not upper triangular.

Program 5.11: Check if matrix is symmetric

Input a matrix and check whether it is symmetric or not.

Sample input output

Test case #1:

Input: `[[1, 2, 3, 4], [3, 4, 5, 7], [5, 6, 7, 1]]`

Output:

```
Original Matrix [[1, 2, 3, 4], [3, 4, 5, 7], [5, 6, 7, 1]]
Transposed Matrix [[1, 3, 5], [2, 4, 6], [3, 5, 7], [4, 7, 1]]
not Symmetric
```

Test case #2:

Input: `[[1, 2, 3], [2, 3, 4], [3, 4, 6]]`

Output:

```
Original Matrix [[1, 2, 3], [2, 3, 4], [3, 4, 6]]
Transposed Matrix [[1, 2, 3], [2, 3, 4], [3, 4, 6]]
Symmetric
```

Algorithm

To run the above program, the following steps are needed to be followed:

1. `Start`
2. `Let a be a matrix`
3. `bl= 0`
4. `Iterate for i = 0 to 2`
   ```
   Iterate   for j = 0 to i - 1
             if a[i][j] is not equal to a[j][i]
             set bl to 1
             break out of inner loop
   ```
5. `if bl is equal to 0`
   ```
             print " Matrix is symmetric"
             else
             print " Matrix is not symmetric "
   ```
6. `Stop`

Flowchart

Figure 5.11 illustrates the program in the form of a flowchart:

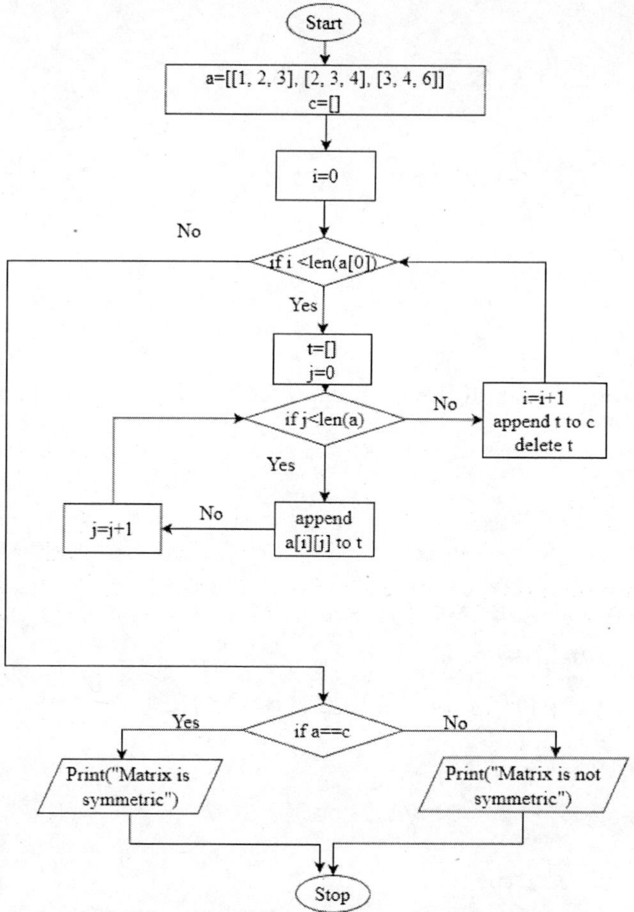

***Figure 5.11**: Flowchart illustrating the program 5.11*

Python code

Python code for the program is as follows:

```
a=[[1, 2, 3], [2, 3, 4], [3, 4, 6]]
c=[]
for i in range(0, len(a[0])):
    t=[]
    for j in range(0, len(a)):
        t.append(a[j][i])
    c.append(t)
    del t
```

```
print("Original Matrix",a)
print("Transposed Matrix",c)

if a==c:
    print("Symmetric")
else:
    print("not Symmetric")
```

Python code explanation

The code checks whether a given matrix **a** is a symmetric matrix. A symmetric matrix is a square matrix with symmetric elements concerning the main diagonal. In other words, if you were to fold the matrix along its main diagonal, the elements on one side of the diagonal would match the elements on the other side. Initially, the matrix is assigned some values. Using the nested for loop, another matrix is created such that the row elements of **a** become the column elements of matrix **c**. So, the matrix **c** is the transposed matrix of **a**. Now, if **a** and **c** are the same, the matrix **a** is symmetric. Otherwise not.

C code

C code for the program is as follows:

```
#include <stdio.h>
int main() {
    int a_s[3][3] = {{5,5,5},{0,5,5},{0,0,5}};
    int bl = 0; int i, j;

    for (ii = 0; ii < 3; ii++) {
        for (jj = 0; jj < ii; jj++) {
            if (a_s[ii][jj] !=a_s[jj][ii]) {
                bl = 1;
                break;
            }
        }
        if (bl == 1) {
            break;
        }
    }
```

```
    if (bl == 0) {
        printf("Matrix is symmetric \n");
    } else {
        printf("Matrix is not symmetric \n");
    }
    return 0;
}
```

C code explanation

The code checks whether a given matrix **a_s** is symmetric. A symmetric matrix is a square matrix with symmetric elements for the main diagonal. In other words, if you were to fold the matrix along its main diagonal, the elements on one side of the diagonal would match the elements on the other side. Initially, the matrix is assigned some values. The **bl** variable will determine if the matrix is symmetric. An outer loop iterates over the rows of the matrix. It runs three times since there are three rows in the 3x3 matrix. Inside the outer loop, it starts an inner loop that iterates over the columns of the matrix. It runs up to the current row index **ii**, checking only the elements below the diagonal. If **a_s[ii][jj] != a_s[jj][ii]**, it means that elements are not the same along the main diagonal fold, and hence, the matrix is not symmetric. So, **bl** is set to **1**. The loop terminates using a **break** statement. Finally, outside the loop, if **bl == 0**, it prints that the matrix is symmetric; otherwise, it prints that the matrix is not symmetric.

Program 5.12: Print 2-D pattern 1

Print the patterns (with n rows) as shown:

$				
$	$			
$	$	$		
$	$	$	$	
$	$	$	$	$

Sample input output

Test case #1:

Input: 5

Output:

$				
$	$			
$	$	$		
$	$	$	$	
$	$	$	$	$

Algorithm

To run the above program, the following steps are needed to be followed:

1. `Start`
2. `Enter a number as nn`
3. `Iterate for ii =1 to nn`

    ```
    Iterate for jj = 1 to ii
    Print "$"
    Print newline
    ```

4. `Stop`

Flowchart

Figure 5.12 illustrates the program in the form of a flowchart:

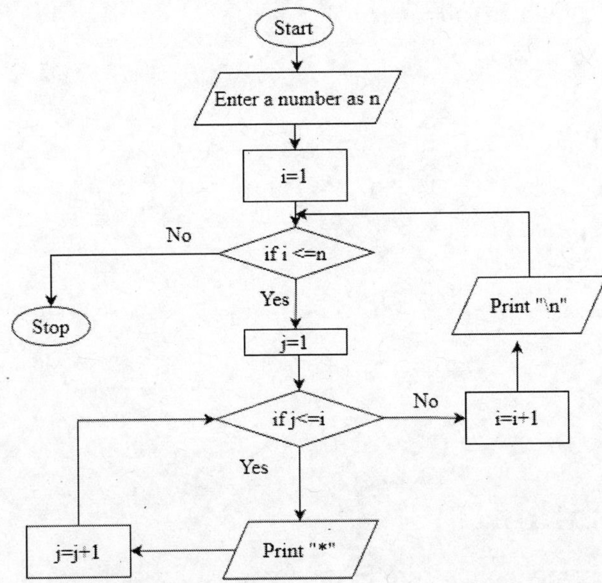

***Figure 5.12**: Flowchart illustrating the program 5.12*

Python code

Python code for the program is as follows:

```
nn= int(input("Enter a number"))
for ii in range(1,nn+1):
    for jj in range(1, ii+1):
     print("$", end=" ")
    print("\n")
```

Python code explanation

The number of rows is taken as input from the user and stored in **nn**. The first loop runs **n** times, with **ii** taking on values from **1** to **nn**. The second loop runs **ii** times, with **jj** taking on values from **1** to **ii**. Inside the second loop, an asterisk is printed without a newline character (**end=" "** means to end the **print** statement with a space instead of a newline). After the second loop completes, a newline character is printed to move to the next row.

C code

C code for the program is as follows:

```
#include <stdio.h>
int main() {
    int nn;
    printf("Enter a number: ");
    scanf("%d", &nn);

    for (int ii = 1; ii <= nn; ii++) {
        for (int jj = 1; jj <= ii; jj++) {
            printf("$ «);
        }
        printf("\n");
    }
    return 0;
}
```

C code explanation

This C code uses the same logic as the Python code to print a triangle of asterisks with n rows. The **scanf()** function reads the user input for **n**, and the **printf()** function displays the asterisks and newline characters. The **`for`** loops work the same way as in the Python code, with the variables **`ii`** and **`jj`** taking on the values necessary to create the correct pattern of asterisks.

Program 5.13: Print 2-D pattern 2

Print the patterns (with n rows) shown:

1				
2	2			
3	3	3		
4	4	4	4	
5	5	5	5	5

Sample input output

Test case #1:

Input: 5

Output:

1				
2	**2**			
3	**3**	**3**		
4	**4**	**4**	**4**	
5	**5**	**5**	**5**	**5**

Algorithm

To run the above program, the following steps are needed to be followed:

1. **`Start`**
2. **`Enter a number as nn`**
3. **`Iterate for ii =1 to nn`**

   `Iterate for jj = 1 to ii`

   `Print ii`

   `Print newline`
4. **`Stop`**

Flowchart

Figure 5.13 illustrates the program in the form of a flowchart:

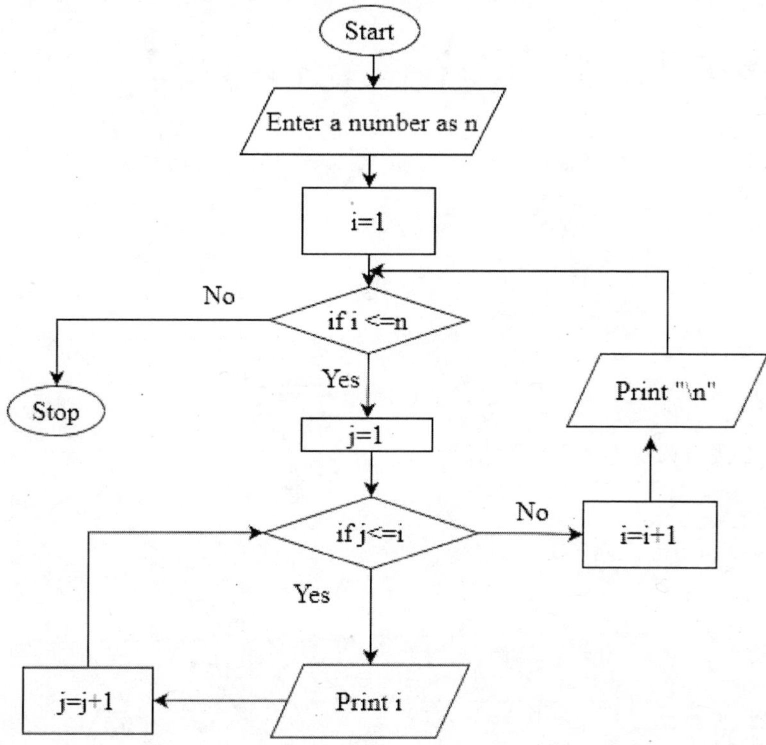

***Figure 5.13**: Flowchart illustrating the program 5.13*

Python code

Python code for the program is as follows:

```
nn= int(input("Enter a number"))
for ii in range(1,nn+1):
    for jj in range(1, ii+1):
        print(ii, end=" ")
    print("\n")
```

Python code explanation

The program is the same as the previous one, and the only difference is that instead of **$**, the value of **ii** is printed.

C code

C code for the program is as follows:

```
#include <stdio.h>
int main() {
    int nn;
    printf("Enter a number: ");
    scanf("%d", &nn);

    for (int ii = 1; ii <= nn; ii++) {
        for (int jj = 1; jj <= ii; jj++) {
            printf("%d ", ii);
        }
        printf("\n");
    }
    return 0;
}
```

C code explanation

The program is the same as the previous one, and the only difference is that instead of **$**, the value of **`ii`** is printed.

Program 5.14: Print 2-D pattern 3

Print the patterns (with n rows) shown:

1				
1	2			
1	2	3		
1	2	3	4	
1	2	3	4	5

Sample input output

Test case #1:

Input: 5

Output:

1				
1	2			
1	2	3		
1	2	3	4	
1	2	3	4	5

Algorithm

To run the above program, the following steps are needed to be followed:

1. `Start`
2. `Enter a number as nn`
3. `Iterate for ii =1 to n`

   ```
   Iterate for jj = 1 to ii
   Print jj
   Print newline
   ```
4. `Stop`

Flowchart

Figure 5.14 illustrates the program in the form of a flowchart:

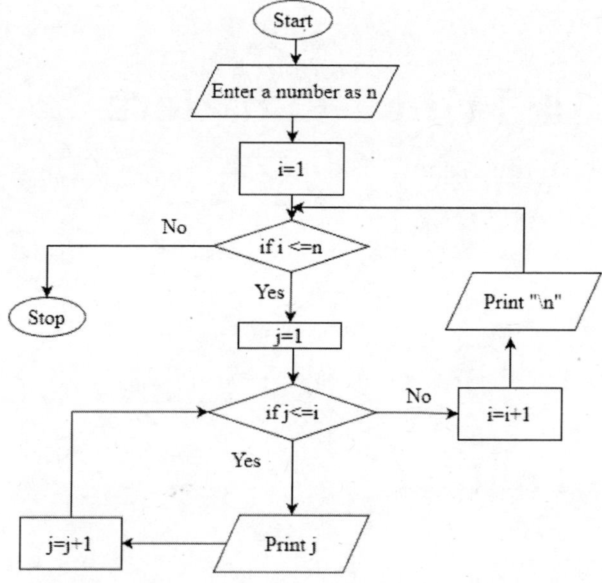

***Figure 5.14**: Flowchart illustrating the program 5.14*

Python code

Python code for the program is as follows:

```
nn= int(input("Enter a number"))
for ii in range(1,nn+1):
    for jj in range(1, ii+1):
        print(jj, end=" ")
    print("\n")
```

Python code explanation

The program is the same as the previous one, and the only difference is that instead of the same value in the whole row, the value of **jj** is now printed to print **1,2,3**,....

C code

C code for the program is as follows:

```
#include <stdio.h>
int main() {
    int nn;
    printf("Enter a number: ");
    scanf("%d", &nn);
    for (int ii = 1; ii <= nn; ii++) {
        for (int jj = 1; jj <= ii; jj++) {
            printf("%d ", jj);
        }
        printf("\n");
    }
    return 0;
}
```

C code explanation

The program is the same as the previous one, and the only difference is that instead of the same value in the whole row, the value of **jj** is now printed to print **1,2,3**,....

Program 5.15: Print 2-D pattern 4

Print the patterns (with n rows) shown:

$	$	$	$	$
$	$	$	$	
$	$	$		
$	$			
$				

Sample input output

Test case #1:

Input: 5

Output:

$	$	$	$	$
$	$	$	$	
$	$	$		
$	$			
$				

Algorithm

To run the above program, the following steps are needed to be followed:

1. `Start`
2. `Enter a number as n`
3. `Iterate for ii =1 to n`

```
Iterate for jj = 1 to n-ii+1
Print "$"
Print newline
```

4. `Stop`

Flowchart

Figure 5.15 illustrates the program in the form of a flowchart:

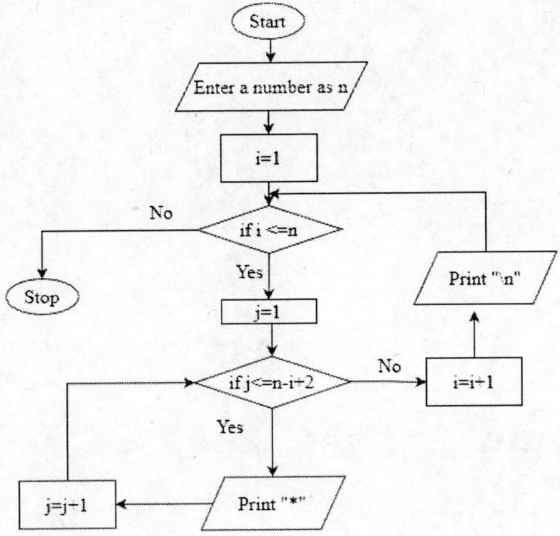

Figure 5.15: Flowchart illustrating the program 5.15

Python code

Python code for the program is as follows:

```
n= int(input("Enter a number"))
for ii in range(1,n+1):
    for jj in range(1, n-ii+2):
     print("$", end=" ")
    print("\n")
```

Python code explanation

It should be observed that the pattern is reversed as compared to the previous program. Hence, the inner loop executes **`n-ii+1`** times for each value of **`i`**. The rest of the logic remains the same.

C code

C code for the program is as follows:

```
#include <stdio.h>
int main() {
    int n;
    printf("Enter a number: ");
    scanf("%d", &n);
```

```
    for (int ii = 1; ii <= n; ii++) {
        for (int jj = 1; jj <= n-ii+1; jj++) {
            printf("$ «);
        }
        printf("\n");
    }
    return 0;
}
```

C code explanation

It should be observed that the pattern is reversed as compared to the previous program. Hence, the inner loop executes **n-ii+1** times for each value of **i**. The rest of the logic remains the same.

Program 5.16: Print 2-D pattern 5

Print the patterns (with n rows) shown:

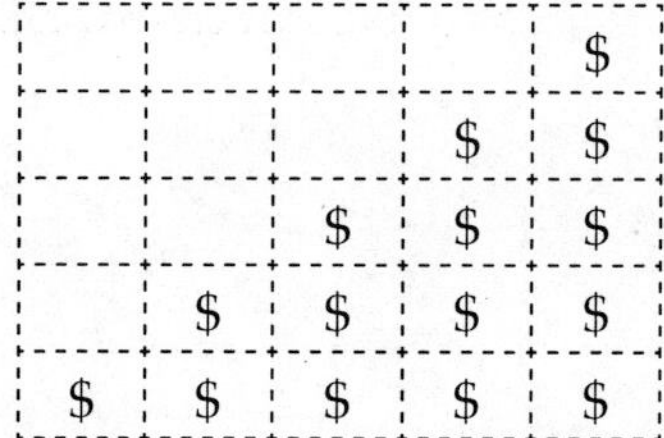

Sample input output

Test case #1:

Input: 5

Output:

				$
			$	$
		$	$	$
	$	$	$	$
$	$	$	$	$

Algorithm

To run the above program, the following steps are needed to be followed:

1. `Start`
2. `Enter a number as n`
3. `Iterate for i =1 to n`

```
    Iterate for j = 1 to n-i+1
    Print " "
    Iterate for k = 1 to i
    Print "$"
```

4. `Print newline`
5. `Stop`

Flowchart

Figure 5.16 illustrates the program in the form of a flowchart:

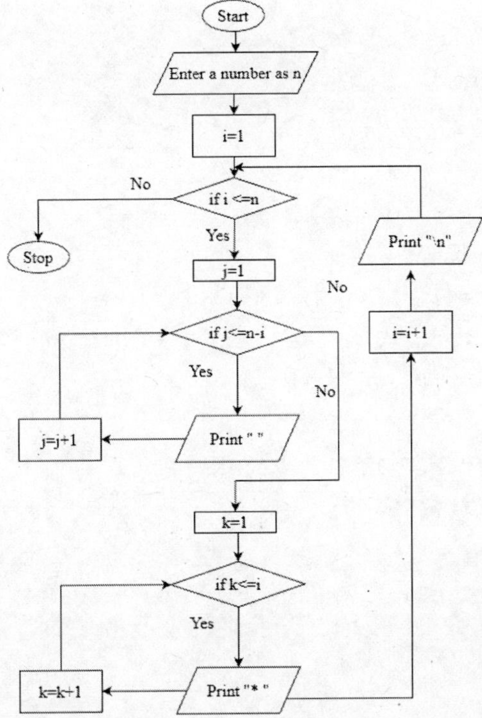

***Figure 5.16**: Flowchart illustrating the program 5.16*

Python code

Python code for the program is as follows:

```
n= int(input("Enter a number"))
for i in range(1,n+1):
    for j in range(1, n-i+1):
     print(" ", end=" ")
    for k in range(1, i+1):
     print("$", end=" ")
    print("\n")
```

Python code explanation

Here, the pattern is right aligned. That means a blank space needs to be printed before printing the character. Hence, inside the outer loop, there are two inner loops consecutively. The first inner loop prints the blank space followed by **$**, to be printed by the second for-loop for each iteration.

C code

C code for the program is as follows:

```
#include <stdio.h>
int main() {
    int n;
    printf("Enter a number: ");
    scanf("%d", &n);
    for (int i = 1; i <= n; i++) {
        for (int j = 1; j <= n-i; j++) {
            printf("  ");
        }
        for (int k = 1; k <= i; k++) {
            printf("$ «);
        }
        printf("\n");
    }
    return 0;
}
```

C code explanation

Here, the pattern is right aligned. That means a blank space needs to be printed before printing the character. Hence, inside the outer loop, there are two inner loops consecutively. The first inner loop prints the blank space followed by **$**, to be printed by the second for-loop for each iteration.

Program 5.17: Print 2-D pattern 6

Print the patterns (with n rows) shown:

				$				
			$	$	$			
		$	$	$	$	$		
$	$	$	$	$	$	$	$	$

Sample input output

Test case #1:

Input: 5

Output:

				$				
			$	$	$			
		$	$	$	$	$		
	$	$	$	$	$	$	$	
$	$	$	$	$	$	$	$	$

Algorithm

To run the above program, the following steps need to be followed:

1. `Start`
2. `Enter a number as n`
3. `Iterate for i =1 to n`

```
        Iterate for j = 1 to n-i+1

        Print " "

        Iterate for k = 1 to i
```

```
Print "$"
Iterate for l = 1 to i-1
Print "$"
Print newline
```

4. Stop

Flowchart

Figure 5.17 illustrates the program in the form of a flowchart:

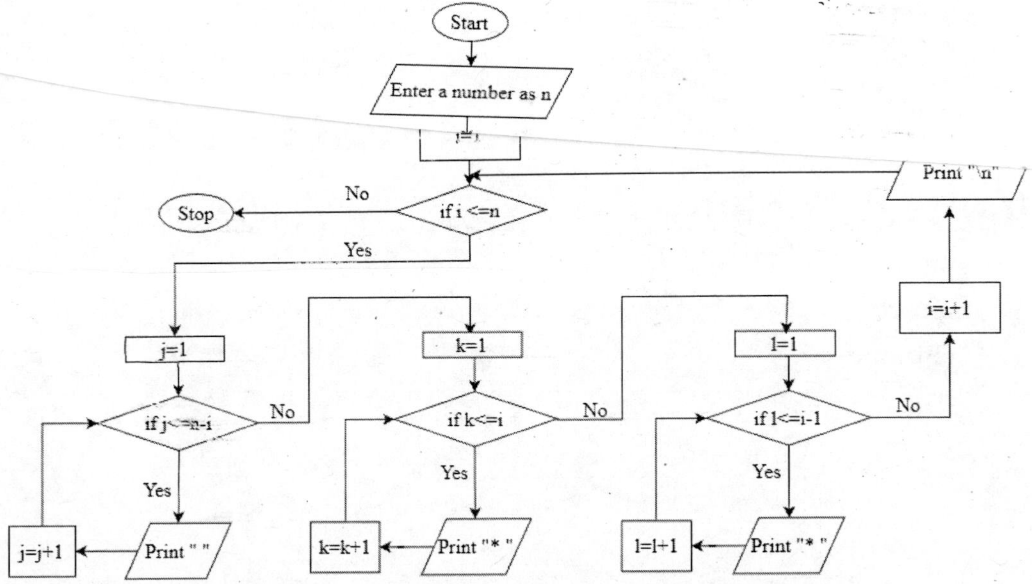

***Figure 5.17**: Flowchart illustrating the program 5.17*

Python code

Python code for the program is as follows:

```
n= int(input("Enter a number"))
for i in range(1,n+1):
    for j in range(1, n-i+1):
     print(" ", end=" ")
    for k in range(1, i+1):
     print("$", end=" ")
```

```
    for j in range(1, i):
     print("$", end=" ")
    print("\n")
```

Python code explanation

In this program, the pattern is center-aligned. The first two inner loops in each row are the same as the previous program to print the blank space, then right-aligned **$**. The third inner for-loop is used to print the remaining **$**.

C code

C code for the program is as follows:

```
#include <stdio.h>
int main() {
    int n;
    printf("Enter a number: ");
    scanf("%d", &n);
    for (int i = 1; i <= n; i++) {
        for (int j = 1; j <= n - i; j++) {
            printf("  ");
        }
        for (int k = 1; k <= i; k++) {
            printf("$ « );
        }
        for (int j = 1; j < i; j++) {
            printf("$ «);
        }
        printf("\n");
    }
    return 0;
}
```

C code explanation

In this program, the pattern is center-aligned. The first two inner loops in each row are the same as the previous program to print the blank space, then right-aligned **$**. The third inner for-loop is used to print the remaining **$**.

Program 5.18: Print 2-D pattern 7

Print the patterns (with n rows) shown:

				1				
			2	2	2			
		3	3	3	3	3		
	4	4	4	4	4	4	4	
5	5	5	5	5	5	5	5	5

Sample input output

Test case #1:

Input: 5

Output:

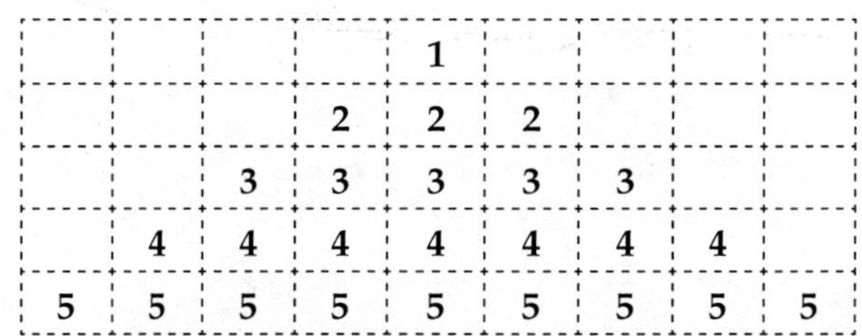

				1				
			2	2	2			
		3	3	3	3	3		
	4	4	4	4	4	4	4	
5	5	5	5	5	5	5	5	5

Algorithm

To run the above program, the following steps are needed to be followed:

1. `Start`
2. `Enter a number as n`
3. `Iterate for i =1 to n`

```
Iterate for j = 1 to n-i

Print " "

Iterate for k = 1 to i

Print i

Iterate for l = 1 to i-1

Print i

Print newline
```

4. `Stop`

Flowchart

Figure 5.18 illustrates the program in the form of a flowchart:

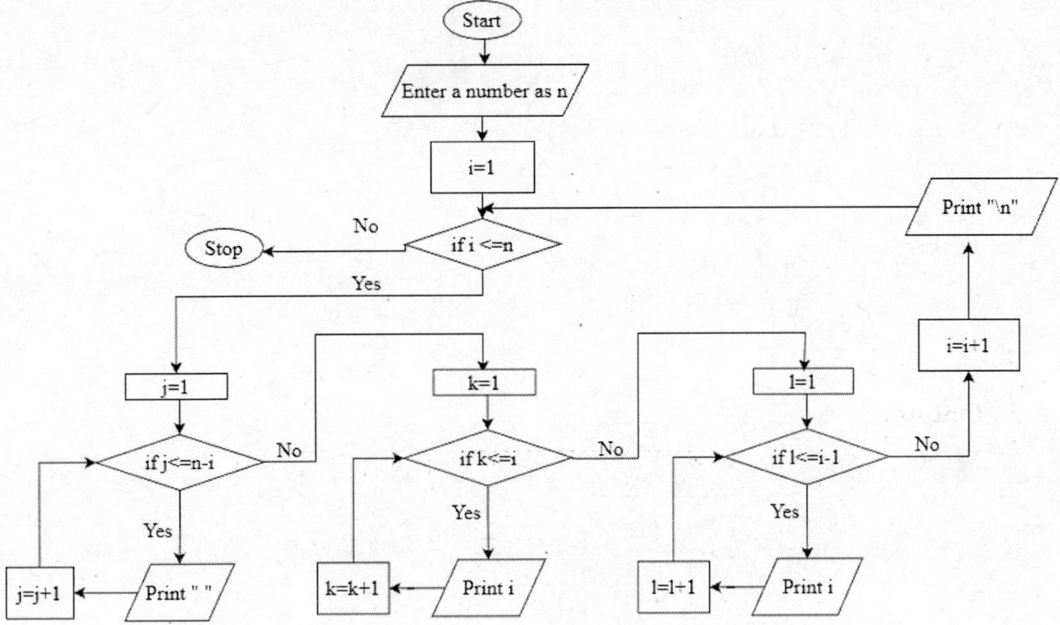

Figure 5.18*: Flowchart illustrating the program 5.18*

Python code

Python code for the program is as follows:

```
n= int(input("Enter a number"))
for i in range(1,n+1):
    for j in range(1, n-i+1):
     print(" ", end=" ")
    for k in range(1, i+1):
     print(i, end=" ")
    for j in range(1, i):
     print(i, end=" ")
    print("\n")
```

Python code explanation

This program is the same as the previous one. The only difference is to print the row number instead of **$**.

C code

C code for the program is as follows:

```c
#include <stdio.h>
int main() {
    int n;
    printf("Enter a number: ");
    scanf("%d", &n);
    for (int i = 1; i <= n; i++) {
        for (int j = 1; j <= n - i; j++) {
            printf("  ");
        }
        for (int k = 1; k <= i; k++) {
            printf("%d ", i);
        }
        for (int j = 1; j < i; j++) {
            printf("%d ", i);
        }
        printf("\n");
    }
    return 0;
}
```

C code explanation

This program is the same as the previous one. The only difference is to print the row number instead of **$**.

Program 5.19: Print 2-D pattern 8

Print the patterns (with n rows) shown:

				1				
			1	2	1			
		1	2	3	2	1		
	1	2	3	4	3	2	1	
1	2	3	4	5	4	3	2	1

Sample input output

Test case #1:

Input: 5

Output:

				1				
			1	2	1			
		1	2	3	2	1		
	1	2	3	4	3	2	1	
1	2	3	4	5	4	3	2	1

Algorithm

To run the above program, the following steps are needed to be followed:

1. `Start`
2. `Enter a number as n`
3. `Iterate for i =1 to n`

```
Iterate for j = 1 to n-i

Print " "

Iterate for k = 1 to i

Print k

Iterate for l = 1 to i-1

Print k-1

Print newline
```

4. `Stop`

Flowchart

Figure 5.19 illustrates the program in the form of a flowchart:

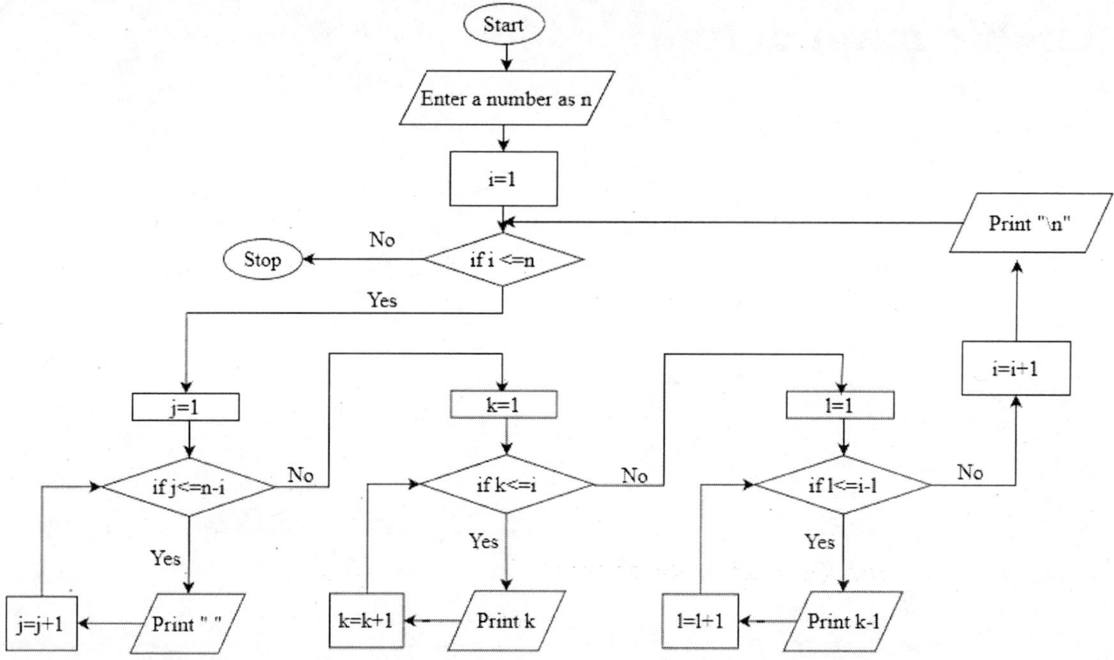

***Figure 5.19**: Flowchart illustrating the program 5.19*

Python code

Python code for the program is as follows:

```
n= int(input("Enter a number"))
for i in range(1,n+1):
    for j in range(1, n-i+1):
     print(" ", end=" ")
    for k in range(1, i+1):
     print(k, end=" ")
    for l in range(1, i):
     print(k-l, end=" ")
    print("\n")
```

Python code explanation

This program is the same as the previous one. The only difference is to print the column number instead of **$**.

C code

C code for the program is as follows:

```
#include <stdio.h>
int main() {
     int n, i,j,k,l;
     printf("Enter a number: ");
     scanf("%d", &n);

     for (i = 1; i <= n; i++) {
          for ( j = 1; j <= n - i; j++) {
               printf("  ");
          }
          for (k = 1; k <= i; k++) {
               printf("%d ", k);
          }
          for (l = 1; l < i; l++) {
               printf("%d ", k-l-1);
          }
          printf("\n");
     }
     return 0;
}
```

C code explanation

This program is the same as the previous one. The only difference is to print the column number instead of **$**.

Program 5.20: Print 2-D pattern 9

Print the patterns (with n rows) shown:

5	5	5	5	5	5	5	5	5
	4	4	4	4	4	4	4	
		3	3	3	3	3		
			2	2	2			
				1				

Sample input output

Test case #1:

Input: 5

Output:

5	5	5	5	5	5	5	5	5
	4	4	4	4	4	4	4	
		3	3	3	3	3		
			2	2	2			
				1				

Algorithm

To run the above program, the following steps are needed to be followed:

1. `Start`
2. `Enter a number as n`
3. `Iterate for i =1 to n`

```
Iterate for j = 1 to i-1

Print " "

Iterate for k = 1 to n-i+1

Print n-i+1

Iterate for l = 1 to n-i

Print n-i+1

Print newline
```

4. `Stop`

Flowchart

Figure 5.20 illustrates the program in the form of a flowchart:

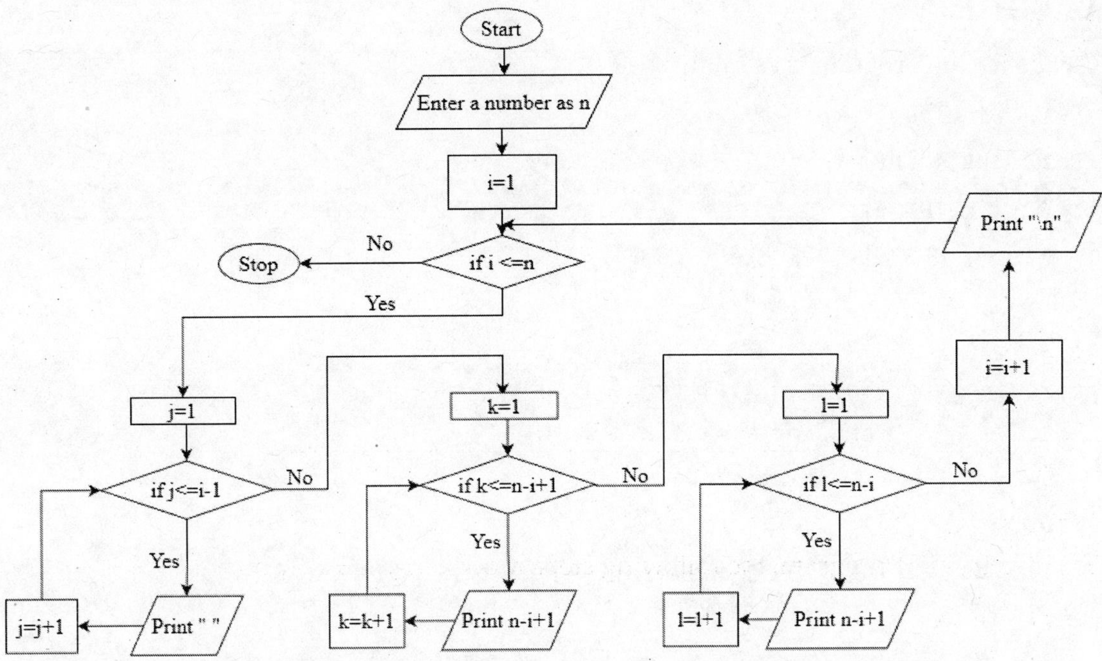

Figure 5.20: Flowchart illustrating the program 5.20

Python code

Python code for the program is as follows:

```
n= int(input("Enter a number"))
for i in range(1,n+1):
    for k in range(1, i):
     print(" ", end=" ")
    for j in range(1, n-i+2):
     print(n-i+1, end=" ")
    for l in range(1, n-i+1):
     print(n-i+1, end=" ")
    print("\n")
```

Python code explanation

The program is similar to the earlier program. So, the same logic is applied.

C code

C code for the program is as follows:

```
#include <stdio.h>
int main() {
    int n;
    printf("Enter a number: ");
    scanf("%d", &n);

    for (int i = 1; i <= n; i++) {
        for (int k = 1; k < i; k++) {
            printf(" ");
        }
        for (int j = 1; j <= n - i + 1; j++) {
            printf("%d ", n - i + 1);
        }
        for (int l = 1; l < n - i + 1; l++) {
            printf("%d ", n - i + 1);
        }
        printf("\n");
    }
    return 0;
}
```

C code explanation

The program is similar to the earlier program. So, the same logic is applied.

Conclusion

This chapter has discussed complex logic building using various programming constructs like flowcharts, algorithms, and coding. With the help of several examples, the different flavors of multiple steps, conditional logic, loops, lists, and matrices are presented. In the next chapter, real-world problems will be discussed with the help of a good number of solved examples.

Points to remember

- `Math.h` library includes the basic functions of math in C Programming. The `counter` module in Python is C.
- A list (in Python) or array (in C) is a collection of homogenous elements that can be accessed using indices.
- A matrix is a 2-D array represented with the help of rows and columns.
- Logic to display various patterns can be developed by visualizing the pattern as a matrix.

Questions

1. Check if the reversed number is greater than the number.
2. Check if the input number is palindrome or not.
3. Given n numbers, find the first pair of two neighboring elements with the same sign. For example, *l1= {1, -1, -5, 2, 3, -8}*, output is *(-1, -5)*.
4. Check whether a given number is an Armstrong number or not. [Example: A 3-digit number N is an Armstrong number if *N=X^3+Y^3+Z^3*, where X, Y, and Z are individual digits of the number N].
5. Input a matrix and print its transpose.
6. Convert Base 2 number to Base 10. (For example, *(101)2 = (5)10*).

CHAPTER 6

Real World Problems

Introduction

In this chapter, the real-world problems/puzzles using various programming constructs (as discussed in previous chapters) are discussed. The main focus of the chapter is to map real-world problems to already-studied concepts. The chapter presents the problems that require intricate design using simple programming constructs. Once the mapping is understood, the programming becomes simple. The chapter discusses creating a logical flow for solving real-world problems, including algorithms and flowcharts, to plan solutions before writing code.

Structure

In this chapter, there are a total of 10 programs, and five sub-sections complement each program:

- Understand the program objective with sample test cases consisting of inputs and outputs. It will give the user an understanding of what kind of user input is expected and what result will be projected for a particular program.
- Understand the program with an algorithm. This will help the user understand the logical flow of real-world problems.
- Visualize the program flow with flowcharts. Program objectives can be understood

easily with the flowchart representation. Users will understand which symbols to use in which context throughout different program's flowchart representations.

- Python source code of each program. Each program's source code in Python programming language is provided to the user so the user can understand the basic operations of the language. An explanation of each code is also provided.
- C implementation of each program. Users can learn the basic concepts of C language with the provided C language code and its explanation for every program.

Objectives

In this chapter, readers will explore techniques for solving real-world problems that often involve multiple sequential steps, intricate combinations of conditional statements and nested loops, and manipulating data structures like lists and functions. The main objective is to demonstrate how a real-world problem can be mapped to already studied concepts. Further, how to utilize simple conditional and loop statements to solve even complex real-world problems.

Program 6.1: Optimize book storage

An almirah can have *m* number of bags, and each bag can hold *n* number of books. Take the capacity of the almirah and bag (m and n) as input from the user. Also, take input the number of books the user has (in variable a). Then, calculate the number of bags and almirahs required to store *a* books.

Sample input output

Test case #1:

Input: `Enter the capacity of the almirah: 5`

`Enter the capacity of the bag: 10`

`Enter the number of books the user has: 79`

Output:

`8 bags and 2 almirahs are required.`

Test case #2:

Input: `Enter the capacity of the almirah: 15`

`Enter the capacity of the bag: 4`

`Enter the Number of books the user has: 987`

Output:

`247 bags and 17 almirahs are required.`

Algorithm

To run the above program, the following steps are needed to be followed:

1. `Start`
2. `Read the capacity of the almirah as cap_al`
3. `Read the capacity of the bag as cap_bag`
4. `Read the number of books the user has as book`
5. `n_bag=ceiling_value(book/cap_bag)`
6. `n_al=ceiling_value(n_bag/cap_al)`
7. `Display n_bag, " bags and ",n_al, " almirahs are required."`
8. `Stop`

Flowchart

Figure 6.1 illustrates the program in the form of a flowchart:

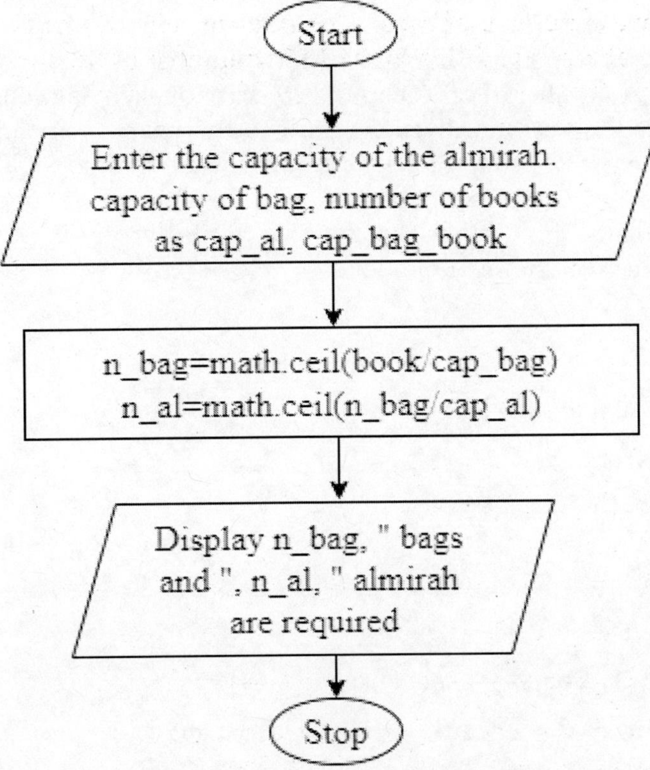

***Figure 6.1**: Flowchart illustrating the program 6.1*

Python code

Python code for the program is as follows:

```
import math

cap_al= int(input("Enter the capacity of the almirah: "))
cap_bag= int(input("Enter the capacity of the bag: "))
book= int(input("Enter the number of books user have: "))
n_bag=math.ceil(book/cap_bag)
n_al=math.ceil(n_bag/cap_al)

print(n_bag, " bags and ", n_al, " almirah are required.")
```

Python code explanation

This Python code calculates the number of bags and almirahs required to store a given number of books based on the input capacities of the bags and almirah. The **`math`** module provides mathematical functions, and it is imported at the beginning of the code to use the **`ceil()`** function later. The user is prompted to enter the almirah's capacity, the bag's capacity, and the total number of books. The total number of bags required is calculated by dividing the total number of books by the capacity of each bag (**`cap_bag`**). The **`math.ceil()`** function rounds up the division result to the nearest whole number, ensuring enough bags to accommodate all the books. Similarly, the number of almirahs required is calculated by dividing the number of bags (**`n_bag`**) by the capacity of each almirah (**`cap_al`**). Finally, based on the input capacities, the code prints the number of bags and almirahs required to store the given number of books.

C code

C code for the program is as follows:

```
#include<stdio.h>
#include<math.h>

int main()
{
int cap_al, cap_bag, book, n_bag, n_al;
printf("Enter the capacity of the almirah: ");
scanf("%d", &cap_al);
```

```
printf("Enter the capacity of the bag: ");
scanf("%d", &cap_bag);

printf("Enter the Number of books user have: ");
scanf("%d", &book);

n_bag=ceil(book/(float)cap_bag);
n_al=ceil(n_bag/(float)cap_al);

printf("%d bags and %d almirah are required.", n_bag, n_al);
return 0;
}
```

C code explanation

This code calculates the number of bags and almirahs required to store a given number of books based on the input capacities of the bags and almirah. The **`math.h`** library provides mathematical functions, and it is imported at the beginning of the code to use the **`ceil()`** function later. The user is prompted to enter the almirah's capacity, the bag's capacity, and the total number of books. The total number of bags required is calculated by dividing the total number of books by the capacity of each bag (**`cap_bag`**). The denominator is typecast to float number to perform real value division. The **`math.ceil()`** function rounds up the division result to the nearest whole number, ensuring enough bags to accommodate all the books. Similarly, the number of almirahs required is calculated by dividing the number of bags (**`n_bag`**) by the capacity of each almirah (**`cap_al`**). Finally, based on the input capacities, the code prints the number of bags and almirahs required to store the given number of books.

Program 6.2: Identify living creatures

Identify a living creature (human, bird, or animal) based on features like the number of legs and feathers.

Sample input output

Test case #1:

> **Input:** `Enter the number of legs: 2`
>
> `Enter if it has feather: y`
>
> **Output:** **`Bird`**

Test case #2:

Input: `Enter the number of legs: 4`

`Enter if it has feather: n`

Output: **`Animal`**

Test case #3:

Input: `Enter the number of legs: 4`

`Enter if it has feather: y`

Output: **`No such creature exists.`**

Algorithm

To run the above program, the following steps are needed to be followed:

1. **`Start`**
2. **`Read the number of legs as l`**
3. **`Read if it has feather:as f`**
4. **`If l == 2:`**
    a. **`if f == 'y':`**
        i. **`Display("Bird")`**
    b. **`else:`**
        i. **`Display("Human")`**
5. **`Else if l == 4:`**
    a. **`if f == 'n':`**
        i. **`Display("Animal")`**
    b. **`else:`**
        i. **`Display("No such creature exists.")`**
6. **`Else:`**
    a. **`Display("No such creature exists.")`**
7. **`Stop`**

Flowchart

Figure 6.2 illustrates the program in the form of a flowchart:

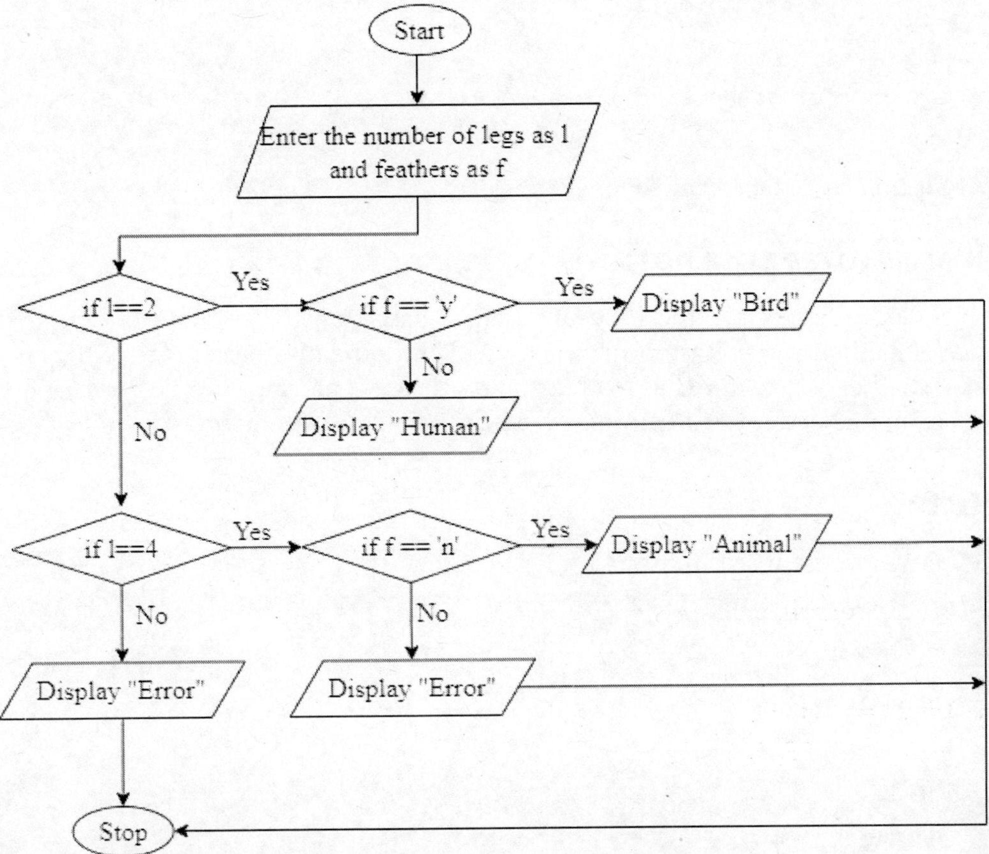

Figure 6.2: Flowchart illustrating the program 6.2

Python code

Python code for the program is as follows:

```
l=int(input("Enter the number of legs:"))
f= input("Enter if it has feather:")
if l == 2:
    if f == 'y':
        print("Bird")
    else:
        print("Human")
elif l == 4:
    if f == 'n':
```

```
            print("Animal")
        else:
            print("No such creature exists.")
else:
    print("No such creature exists.")
```

Python code explanation

The given code determines the type of creature based on the number of legs and the presence of feathers. First, it prompts the user to enter the number of legs of the creature and asks whether the creature has feathers, with the user entering **y** for yes or **n** for no. The type of creature is determined using the nested if- elif-else statements.

C code

C code for the program is as follows:

```
#include<stdio.h>

int main()
{
int l;
char f;

printf("Enter the number of legs: ");
scanf("%d", &l);

fflush(stdin);

printf("Enter if it has feather: ");
scanf(" %c", &f);


if(l == 2)
{
    if (f == 'y')
        printf("Bird");
```

```
    else
        printf("Human");
}
else if(l == 4)
{
    if(f == 'n')
        printf("Animal");
    else
        printf("No such creature exists.");
}
else
 printf("No such creature exists.");
return 0;
}
```

C code explanation

The given code determines the type of creature based on the number of legs and the presence of feathers. First, it prompts the user to enter the number of legs of the creature and asks whether the creature has feathers, with the user entering **`y`** for yes or **`n`** for no. Since the value of the feather is to be read in character, **`fflush()`** function is used before the **`scanf()`** function to clear the input buffer. The type of creature is determined using the nested if- elseif-else statements.

Program 6.3: Identify objects

Take features such as shape and color as input and identify the object based on its shape and color as follows:

Sphere and red:	Tomato
Sphere and orange:	Orange
Cuboid and red:	Brick
Cuboid and orange:	Dustbin

Sample input output

Test case #1:

Input: `Enter the shape of the object (s/ c): s`

`Enter the color of the object (r /o): o`

Output: **`Object is Orange`**

Test case #2:

Input: `Enter the shape of the object (s/ c): c`

`Enter the color of the object (r /o): o`

Output: **`Object is Dustbin`**

Algorithm

To run the above program, the following steps are needed to be followed:

1. **Start**
2. **Read the shape of the object as s**
3. **Read the color of the object as co**
4. **if s== "s":**
    a. **if co == "r":**
        i. **Display("Object is Tomato")**
    b. **Else if co=="o":**
        i. **Display("Object is Orange")**
    c. **Else:**
        i. **Display("Wrong input")**
5. **Else if s == "c":**
    a. **if co == "r":**
        i. **Display("Object is Brick")**
    b. **Else if co=="o":**
        i. **Display("Object is Dustbin")**
    c. **Else:**
        i. **Display("Wrong input")**
6. **Else:**
    a. **Display("Wrong input")**
7. **Stop**

Flowchart

Figure 6.3 illustrates the program in the form of a flowchart:

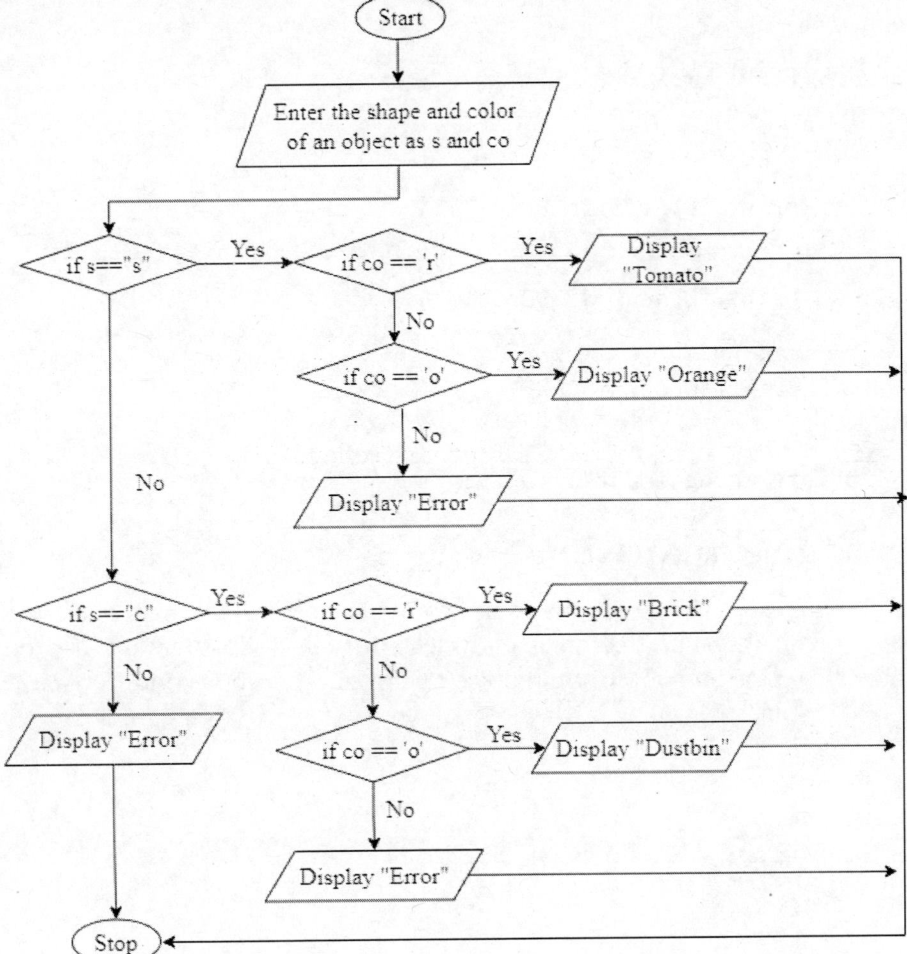

***Figure 6.3**: Flowchart illustrating the program 6.3*

Python code

Python code for the program is as follows:

```
s=input("Enter the shape of the object:")
co= input("Enter the color of the object:")
if s== "s":
    if co == "r":
```

```
        print("Object is Tomato")
    elif co=="o":
        print("Object is Orange")
    else:
        print("Wrong input")
elif s == "c":
    if co == "r":
        print("Object is Brick")
    elif co=="o":
        print("Object is Dustbin")
    else:
        print("Wrong input")
else:
    print("Wrong input")
```

Python code explanation

This code allows a user to input the shape and color of an object and then identify the object based on the given shape and color using a nested if-elif-else statement. It prompts the user to enter the shape and color of the object. Following various conditions, it identifies the object and displays it.

C code

C code for the program is as follows:

```
int main()
{
char s, co;

fflush(stdin);
printf("Enter the shape of the object (s/ c): ");
scanf("%c", &s);

fflush(stdin);
printf("Enter the color of the object (r /o): ");
scanf("%c", &co);
```

```

if(s== 's')
{
    if(co == 'r')
        printf("Object is Tomato");
    else if(co == 'o')
        printf("Object is Orange");
    else
        printf("Wrong input");
}
else if(s == 'c')
 {
    if(co == 'r')
        printf("Object is Brick");
    else if(co == 'o')
        printf("Object is Dustbin");
    else
        printf("Wrong input");
}
else
    printf("Wrong input");

}
```

C code explanation

This code allows a user to input the shape and color of an object and then identify the object based on the given shape and color using a nested if-else if-else statement. It prompts the user to enter the shape and color of the object. Following various conditions, it identifies the object and displays it. Like the previous program, wherever we read a character as input from the user, **`fflush()`** function is used before the **`scanf()`** function to clear the input buffer.

Program 6.4: Rock-paper-scissors

Make a two-player rock-paper-scissors game.

Hint: Ask for player plays (using input), compare them, print out a message of congratulations to the winner, and ask if the players want to start a new game.

The rules of the game are:

- Rock beats scissors
- Scissors beat paper
- Paper beats rock

Player 1	Player 2	Output
Scissor	Scissor	Tie
Scissor	Stone	Player 2
Scissor	Paper	Player 1
Stone	Scissor	Player 1
Stone	Stone	Tie
Stone	Paper	Player 2
Paper	Scissor	Player 2
Paper	Stone	Player 1
Paper	Paper	Tie

Sample input output

Test case #1:

Input: `Enter signs of the game: s for scissor, p for paper, r for stone: s s`

Output: `There is a tie`

Test case #2:

Input: `Enter signs of the game: s for scissor, p for paper, r for stone: s p`

Output: `x is the winner`

Algorithm

To run the above program, the following steps needed to be followed:

1. `Start`
2. `Input x and y`
3. `if (x== "scissor" and y== "paper") or (x== "stone" and y== "scissor") or (x== "paper" and y== "stone") then`
    i. `Print "x is the winner"`

4. **Else if (y== "scissor" and x== "paper") or (y== "stone" and x== "scissor") or (y== "paper" and x== "stone") then**
   i. **Print "y is the winner"**

5. **Else if (x== "scissor" and y== "scissor") or (x== "stone" and y== "stone") or (x== "paper" and y== "paper") then**
   i. **Print "There is a tie"**

6. **Stop**

Flowchart

Figure 6.4 illustrates the program in the form of a flowchart:

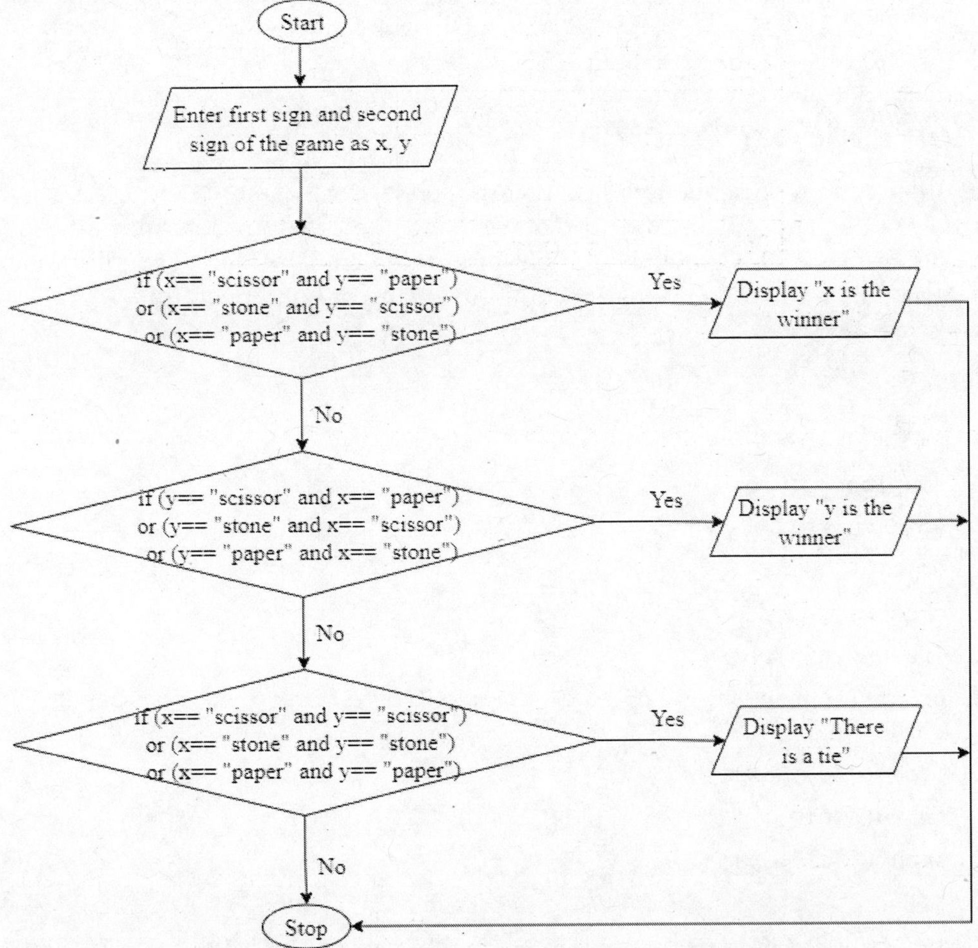

***Figure 6.4**: Flowchart illustrating the program 6.4*

Python code

Python code for the program is as follows:

```
x=input("Enter first sign of the game ")
y=input("Enter second sign of the game ")
if (x== "scissor" and y== "paper") or (x== "stone" and y== "scissor") or (x== "paper" and y== "stone"):
    print( "x is the winner")
elif (y== "scissor" and x== "paper") or (y== "stone" and x== "scissor") or (y== "paper" and x== "stone") :
    print("y is the winner")
elif (x== "scissor" and y== "scissor") or (x== "stone" and y== "stone") or (x== "paper" and y== "paper"):
    print( "There is a tie")
```

Python code explanation

This Python code represents a simple rock-paper-scissors game where the user inputs their choice of signs (scissor, stone, or paper), and the program determines the winner based on the rules of the game using if-elif-else statements. Inside the condition block of an if-statement, various conditions are combined using or/ and operators.

C code

C code for the program is as follows:

```
#include<stdio.h>
void main()
{
char x,y;
fflush(stdin);
printf("Enter signs of the game: s for scissor, p for paper, r for stone: ");
scanf("%c", &x);
fflush(stdin);
scanf("%c", &y);

if ((x== 's' && y== 'p') || (x== 'r' && y== 's') || (x== 'p' && y== 'r'))
  printf( "x is the winner");
```

```
if ((y== 's' && x== 'p') || (y== 'r' && x== 's') || (y== 'p' && x== 'r'))
  printf("y is the winner");
if ((x== 's' && y== 's') || (x== 'r' && y== 'r') || (x== 'p' && y== 'p'))
  printf( "There is a tie");
}
```

C code explanation

This Python code represents a simple rock-paper-scissors game where the user inputs their choice of signs (scissor, stone, or paper), and the program determines the winner based on the rules of the game using if-else if-else statements. Inside the condition block of an if-statement, various conditions are combined using or/ and operators. Like the previous program, wherever we read a character as input from the user, **`fflush()`** function is used before the **`scanf()`** function to clear the input buffer.

Program 6.5: Print hotel bill

Calculate and print the bill for a hotel that provides hourly services of two types: Regular and premium. The rates for the regular services are as follows: base rate: $50 (applicable for 2 hrs). After that, $30 for every hour will be charged. The rate of a private pool for 1 hour is $70.

The rates for the premium services are as follows: base rate: $100 (applicable for 3 hrs). After that, $50 for every hour will be charged. 5% discount on private pool booking if booked for 2 hrs or more.

Ask the user to enter the inputs as a type of service (r – regular, p – premium), booking duration, and private pool required. Generate the bill for the customer.

Sample input output

Test case #1:

Input: `Enter the type of service (r - regular, p - premium): r`

```
Enter the booking duration (in hrs): 7
Private pool required?(y/n): y
Enter duration of pool (in hrs): 5
```

Output:

`The bill amount is 550`

Test case #2:

Input: `Enter the type of service (r - regular, p - premium): p`

```
Enter the booking duration (in hrs): 5
```

```
Private pool required?(y/n): y
Enter duration of pool (in hrs): 8
```

Output:

```
The bill amount is 732.0
```

Algorithm

To run the above program, the following steps are needed to be followed:

1. `Start`
2. `Read the type of service (r - regular, p - premium) as ser`
3. `Read the booking duration (in hrs) as dur`
4. `Read if Private pool required?(y/n) as pool`
5. `if ser == 'r':`
    a. `rate_reg=50`
    b. `if dur > 2:`
        i. `rate_reg = rate_reg+ (dur-2)*30`
    c. `if pool=='y':`
        i. `Read duration of pool (in hrs) as dur_pool`
        ii. `rate_reg = rate_reg+ dur_pool*70`
    d. `Display("The bill amount is ", rate_reg)`
6. `else if ser == 'p':`
    a. `rate_p=100`
    b. `if dur > 3:`
        i. `rate_p = rate_p+ (dur-3)*50`
    c. `if pool=='y':`
        i. `Read duration of pool (in hrs) as dur_pool`
        ii. `if dur_pool<2:`
            1. `rate_p = rate_p+ dur_pool*70`
        iii. `else:`
            1. `rate_p = rate_p+ dur_pool*70*0.95`
    d. `Display("The bill amount is ", rate_p)`

7. **else:**
   a. **Display("Wrong service selected")**

8. **Stop**

Flowchart

Figure 6.5 illustrates the program in the form of a flowchart:

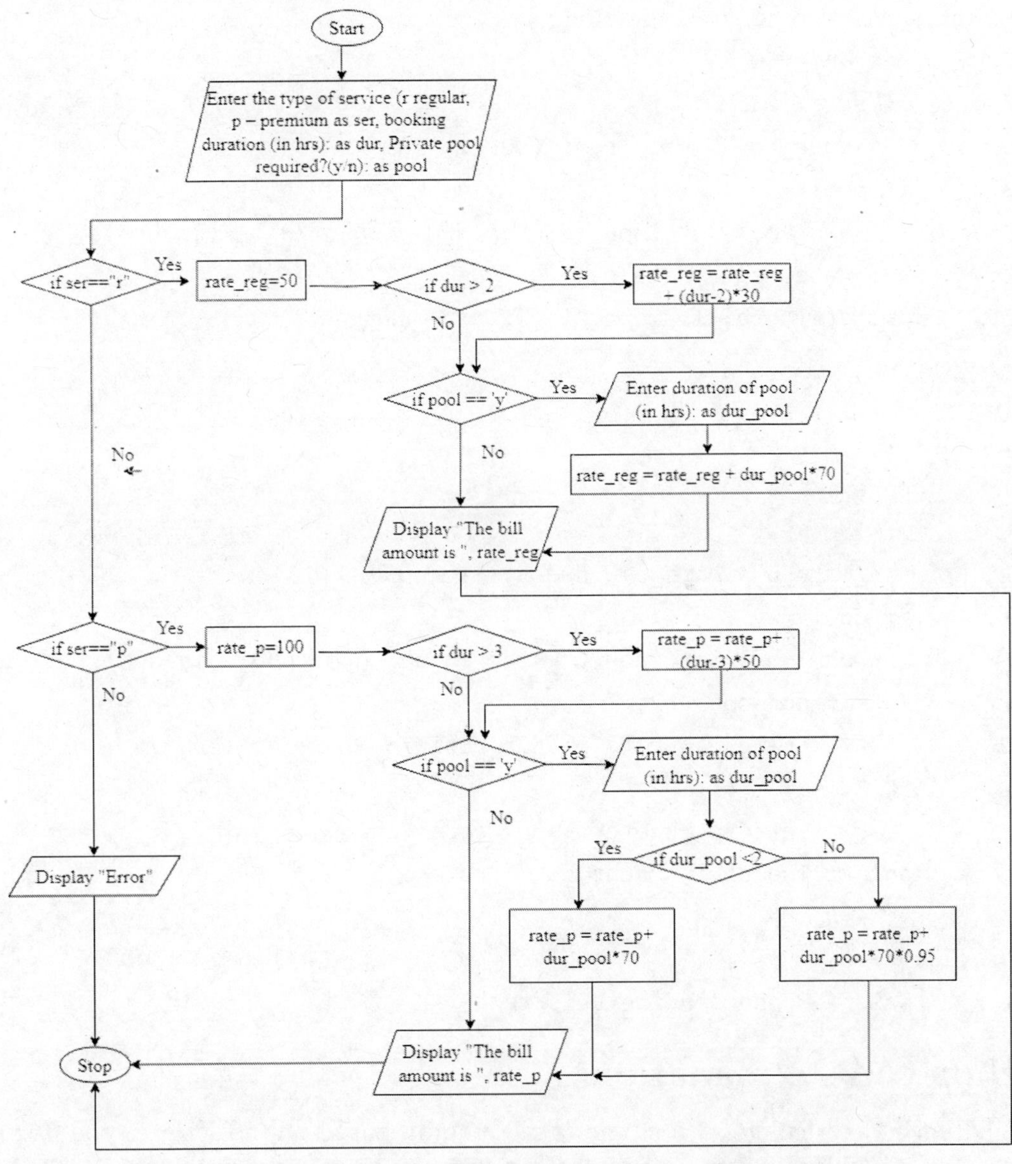

***Figure 6.5**: Flowchart illustrating the program 6.5*

Python code

Python code for the program is as follows:

```
ser=input("Enter the type of service (r - regular, p - premium): ")
dur=int(input("Enter the booking duration (in hrs): "))
pool=input("Private pool required?(y/n): ")
if ser == 'r':
    rate_reg=50
    if dur > 2:
        rate_reg = rate_reg+ (dur-2)*30
    if pool=='y':
        dur_pool=int(input("Enter duration of pool (in hrs): "))
        rate_reg = rate_reg+ dur_pool*70
    print("The bill amount is ", rate_reg)
elif ser == 'p':
    rate_p=100
    if dur > 3:
        rate_p = rate_p+ (dur-3)*50
    if pool=='y':
        dur_pool=int(input("Enter duration of pool (in hrs): "))
        if dur_pool <2:
            rate_p = rate_p+ dur_pool*70
        else:
            rate_p = rate_p+ dur_pool*70*0.95
    print("The bill amount is ", rate_p)
else:
    print("Wrong service selected")
```

Python code explanation

This Python code calculates a customer's bill amount based on the service type (regular or premium), booking duration, and whether a private pool is required. It reads the type of service (regular or premium), the booking duration in hours, and if a private pool is required as input from the user. Using the nested if- elif-else statements, the bill is generated.

C code

C code for the program is as follows:

```
#include<stdio.h>
int main()
{
char ser, pool;
int dur, dur_pool;
float rate_reg, rate_p;
fflush(stdin);
printf("Enter the type of service (r--> regular, p-->premium): ");
scanf("%c", &ser);

fflush(stdin);
printf("Enter the booking duration (in hrs): ");
scanf("%d", &dur);

fflush(stdin);
printf("Private pool required?(y/n): ");
scanf("%c", &pool);

if(ser == 'r')
{
    rate_reg=50;
    if(dur > 2)
        rate_reg = rate_reg+ (dur-2)*30;
    if(pool=='y')
      {
      printf("Enter duration of pool (in hrs): ");
      scanf("%d",&dur_pool);
      rate_reg = rate_reg+ dur_pool*70;
```

```
        }
    printf("The bill amount is %f", rate_reg);
}
else if(ser == 'p')
{
    rate_p=100;
    if(dur > 3)
        rate_p = rate_p+ (dur-3)*50;
    if(pool=='y')
    {
        printf("Enter duration of pool (in hrs): ");
        scanf("%d",&dur_pool);
        if(dur_pool <2)
            rate_p = rate_p+ dur_pool*70;
        else
            rate_p = rate_p+ dur_pool*70*0.95;
    }
    printf("The bill amount is %f", rate_p);
}
else
    printf("Wrong service selected");

return(0);
}
```

C code explanation

This code calculates a customer's bill amount based on the service type (regular or premium), booking duration, and whether a private pool is required. It reads the type of service (regular or premium), the booking duration in hours, and if a private pool is required as input from the user. Using the nested if-else if-else statements, the bill is generated. **`fflush()`** function is used before reading a character value as input.

Program 6.6: Find fewest denominations

Take the amount from the user and print the minimum number of notes required. Let the denominations be 500, 100, 50, 20, 10, 5, 2, 1.

For example:

Input: `amount: 576`

Output: **`Total number of notes: 500: 1, 100: 0, 50: 1, 20: 1, 10: 0, 5: 1, 2: 0, 1: 1`**

Sample input output

Test case #1:

Input: `Enter the amount 985`

Output: **`500: 1, 100 : 4, 50 : 1, 20 : 1, 10 : 1, 5 : 1, 2 : 0, 1 : 0,`**

Test case #2:

Input: `Enter the amount: 772`

Output: **`500 : 1, 100 : 2, 50 : 1, 20 : 1, 10 : 0, 5 : 0, 2 : 1, 1 : 0,`**

Algorithm

To run the above program, the following steps are needed to be followed:

1. **`Start`**
2. **`deno=[500, 100, 50, 20, 10, 5, 2, 1]`**
3. **`Read the amount as a_m`**
4. **`d_freq=[]`**
5. **`s=a_m`**
6. **`for i= 0 to len(deno)`**
   a. **`Append(s//deno[i]) as d_freq`**
   b. **`s=s%deno[i]`**
   c. **`Display(d_freq[i])`**
7. **`for i= 0 to len(deno)`**
   a. **`Display(deno[i], ":", d_freq[i], end=", ")`**
8. **`Stop`**

Flowchart

Figure 6.6 illustrates the program in the form of a flowchart:

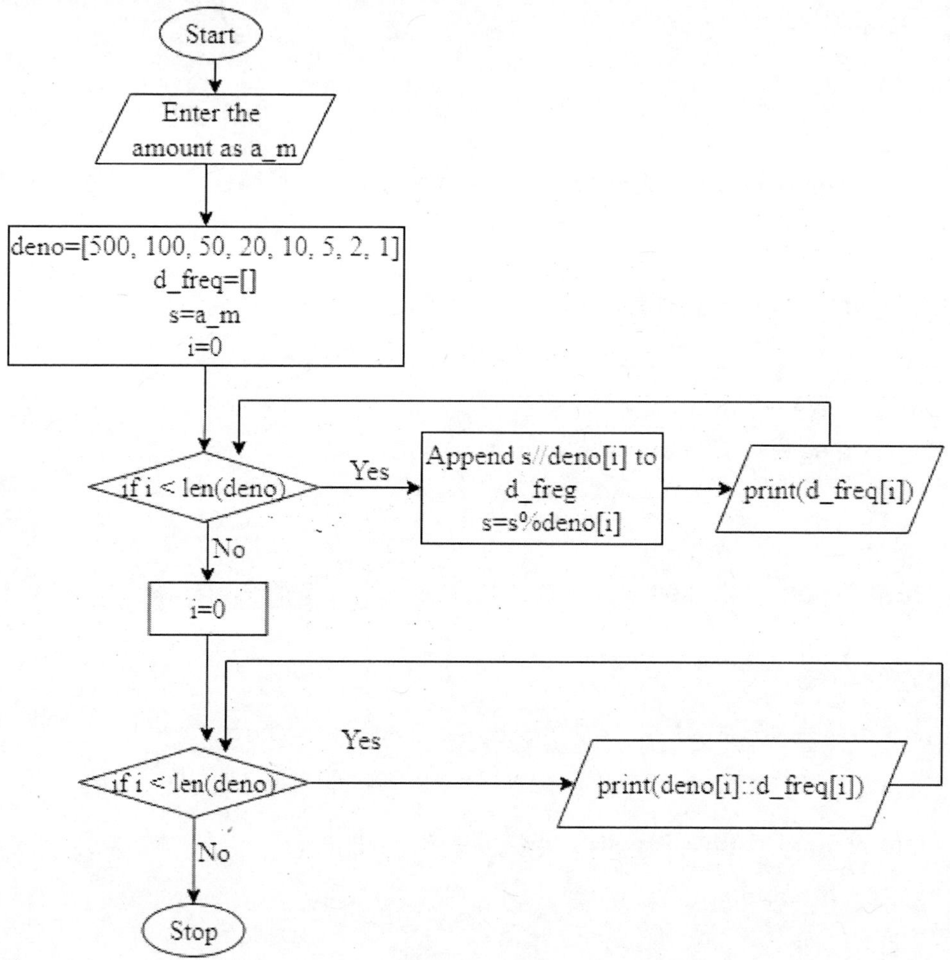

***Figure 6.6**: Flowchart illustrating the program 6.6*

Python code

Python code for the program is as follows:

```
deno=[500, 100, 50, 20, 10, 5, 2, 1]
a_m=int(input("Enter the amount"))
d_freq=[]
s=a_m

```

```
for i in range(0, len(deno)):
    d_freq.append(s//deno[i])
    s=s%deno[i]

for i in range(0, len(deno)):
    print(deno[i], ":", d_freq[i], end=", ")
```

Python code explanation

This Python code snippet is designed to calculate the minimum number of denominations (bills/coins) required to represent a given amount (**a_m**) using a predefined list of denominations (**deno**).

It prompts the user to enter an amount and stores the input as an integer in the variable **a_m**. An empty list **d_freq** stores the frequency of each denomination. Variable s will be used to keep track of the remaining amount as the code calculates the denominations. The **for** loop iterates through the denominations in descending order and calculates how many times the current denomination (**deno[i]**) can be used in the remaining amount (**s**) and appends that value to the **d_freq** list. It then updates the remaining amount (**s**) after subtracting the amount represented by the used denominations. Finally, it displays the number of denominations required to represent the given amount, using the denominations specified in the **deno** list.

C code

C code for the program is as follows:

```
#include<stdio.h>

int main()
{

int deno[8]={500, 100, 50, 20, 10, 5, 2, 1};
int a_m, s, i, d_freq[8];

printf("Enter the amount: ");
scanf("%d", &a_m);

s=a_m;
```

```
for(i=0; i<8; i++)
{
    d_freq[i]=s/deno[i];
    s=s%deno[i];
}
for(i=0; i<8;i++)
    printf("%d : %d;  ", deno[i], d_freq[i]);
return(0);
}
```

C code explanation

This C code snippet is designed to calculate the minimum number of denominations (bills/coins) required to represent a given amount (**a_m**) using a predefined array of denominations (**deno**).

It prompts the user to enter an amount and stores the input as an integer in the variable **a_m**. An array **d_freq** stores the frequency of each denomination. Variable s will be used to keep track of the remaining amount as the code calculates the denominations. The **for** loop iterates through the denominations in descending order and calculates how many times the current denomination (**deno[i]**) can be used in the remaining amount (**s**) and appends that value to the **d_freq** array. It then updates the remaining amount (**s**) after subtracting the amount represented by the used denominations. Finally, it displays the number of denominations required to represent the given amount using the denominations specified in the **deno** array.

Program 6.7: Assign class rank

Take the percentage marks of ten students as input from the user and assign them class rank.

Sample input output

Test case #1:

Input: `Enter the percentage marks: 90`

`Enter the percentage marks: 50`

`Enter the percentage marks: 32`

```
Enter the percentage marks: 76

Enter the percentage marks: 46

Enter the percentage marks: 98

Enter the percentage marks: 12

Enter the percentage marks: 23

Enter the percentage marks: 56

Enter the percentage marks: 77
```

Output: **`Students in order of their ranking are [6, 1, 10, 4, 9, 2, 5, 3, 8, 7]`**

Algorithm

To run the above program, the following steps are needed to be followed:

1. **`Start`**
2. **`n=10`**
3. **`m_l=[]`**
4. **`m_s=[]`**
5. **`for ii =0 to n-1:`**
    a. **`Read the percentage marks as m`**
    b. **`Append m to m_l`**
    c. **`Append ii+1 to m_s`**
6. **`for jj= 0 to n-2`**
7. **`for ii = 0 to n-jj-2`**
8. **`if m_l[ii] <m_l[ii+1]:`**
    a. **`swap(m_l[ii],m_l[ii+1])`**
    b. **`swap(m_s[ii],m_s[ii+1])`**
9. **`Display ("Students in order of their ranking are", m_s)`**
10. **`Stop`**

Flowchart

Figure 6.7 illustrates the program in the form of a flowchart:

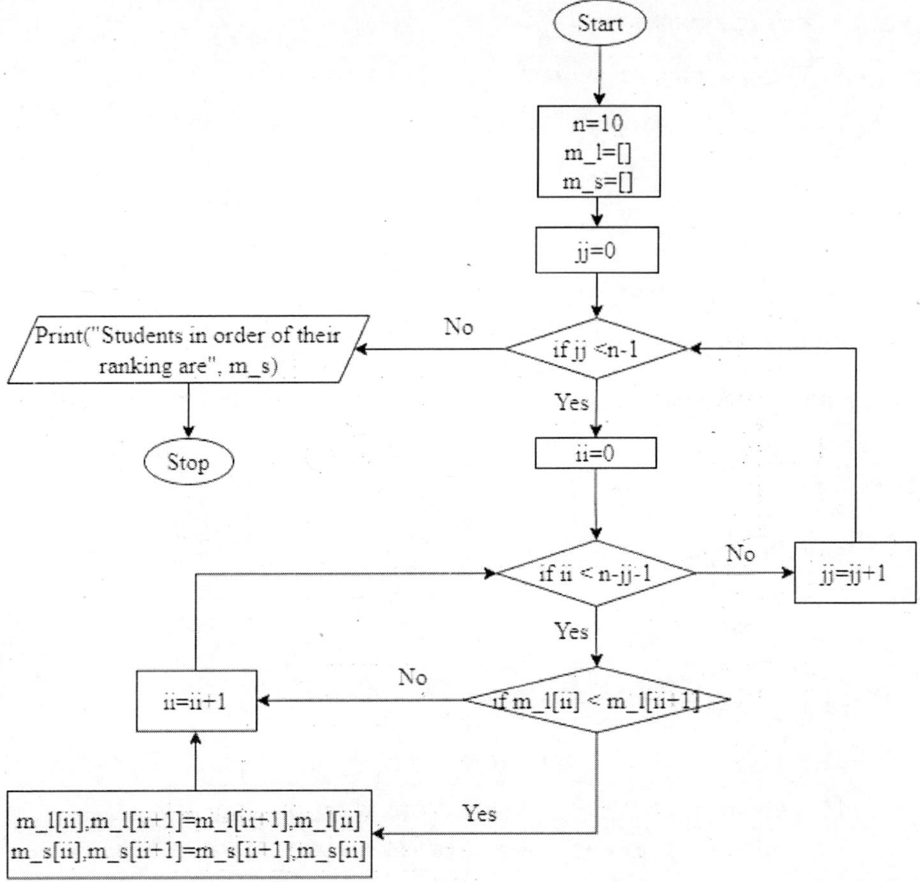

***Figure 6.7**: Flowchart illustrating the program 6.7*

Python code

Python code for the program is as follows:

```
n=10
m_l=[]
m_s=[]
for ii in range (0, n):
    m_l.append(int(input("Enter the percentage marks: ")))
    m_s.append(ii+1)

for jj in range(0,n-1):
    for ii in range(0, n-jj-1):
```

```
        if m_l[ii] < m_l[ii+1]:
            m_l[ii],m_l[ii+1]=m_l[ii+1],m_l[ii]
            m_s[ii],m_s[ii+1]=m_s[ii+1],m_s[ii]

print("Students in order of their ranking are", m_s)
```

Python code explanation

This Python code takes input for the percentage marks of **10** students and assigns each student a rank. It initializes an empty list **m_l** to store the percentage marks of the students and an empty list **m_s** to store the enrollment numbers of the students, which are assigned from **1** to **10**.

The first marks of **10** students are taken as input from the user using a for-loop and stored in the **m_l** list. Then, marks are sorted in descending order using the sorting program discussed in *Chapter 5, Complex Problem Solving*. The enrollment numbers are also swapped with marks to keep them in sync. Finally, it prints enrollment numbers in rank order.

C code

C code for the program is as follows:

```
#include<stdio.h>

int main()
{
int n=10;
int m_l[10];
int m_s[10];
int ii, jj, t;

printf("Enter the percentage marks of 10 students: ");
for(ii=0; ii<n; ii++)
{
    scanf("%d", &m_l[ii]);
    m_s[ii]=ii+1;
}

```

```
for(jj=0; jj<n-1; jj++)
    {
        for(ii=0; ii<n-jj-1; ii++)
    {
        if(m_l[ii] < m_l[ii+1])
        {
            t=m_l[ii];
            m_l[ii]=m_l[ii+1];
            m_l[ii+1]=t;

            t=m_s[ii];
            m_s[ii]=m_s[ii+1];
            m_s[ii+1]=t;
        }
    }
    }
printf("Students in order of their ranking are ");
for(ii=0; ii<n; ii++)
{
   printf("%d ", m_s[ii]);
}
return(0);
}
```

C code explanation

This Python code takes input for the percentage marks of **10** students and assigns each student a rank. It initializes an empty array **m_l** to store the percentage marks of the students and an empty array **m_s** to store the enrollment numbers of the students who are assigned from **1** to **10**.

The first marks of **10** students are taken as input from the user using a for-loop and stored in the **m_l** array. Then, marks are sorted in descending order using the sorting program discussed in *Chapter 5, Complex Problem Solving*. The enrollment numbers are also swapped with marks to keep them in sync. Finally, it prints enrollment numbers in the order of rank.

Program 6.8: Minimize the difference

Take marks of n students and input from the user. Obtain a subset of m students to minimize the difference between the highest and lowest scorers in that subset.

For example:

Input:

`Let marks[] = {50, 70, 10, 90, 20, 100, 30} and m = 3`

Output:

`Subset is {10, 20, 30}`

`Difference is 20`

Sample input output

Test case #1:

Input: `Enter the number of students: 6`

```
Marks: 70
Marks: 10
Marks: 90
Marks: 20
Marks: 100
Marks: 30
Enter the group size: 3
```

Output: **`Subset is [10, 20, 30]`**

Test case #2:

Input: `Enter the number of students: 5`

```
Marks: 3
Marks: 7
Marks: 8
Marks: 10
Marks: 14
Enter the group size: 2
```

Output: **`Subset is [7, 8]`**

Algorithm

To run the above program, the following steps are needed to be followed:

1. `Start`
2. `st_l=[]`
3. `Read the number of students as nn`
4. `for ii =0 to nn-1`
    a. `Read marks as m`
    b. `Append m to st_l`
5. `Read the group size as mm`
6. `for jj= 0 to nn-2`
    a. `for ii = 0 to nn-jj-2`
        i. `if st_l[ii] >st_l[ii+1]:`
            1. `swap(st_l[ii],st_l[ii+1])`
7. `diff=[]`
8. `min_no=max(st_l)`
9. `ind=nn`
10. `for jj0 to nn-mm`
    a. `Appendst_l[jj+mm-1]-st_l[jj] to diff`
    b. `if diff[jj] <min_no:`
        i. `min_no=diff[jj]`
        ii. `ind=jj`
11. `Display("Subset is ", st_l[ind: ind+mm])`
12. `Stop`

Flowchart

Figure 6.8 illustrates the program in the form of a flowchart:

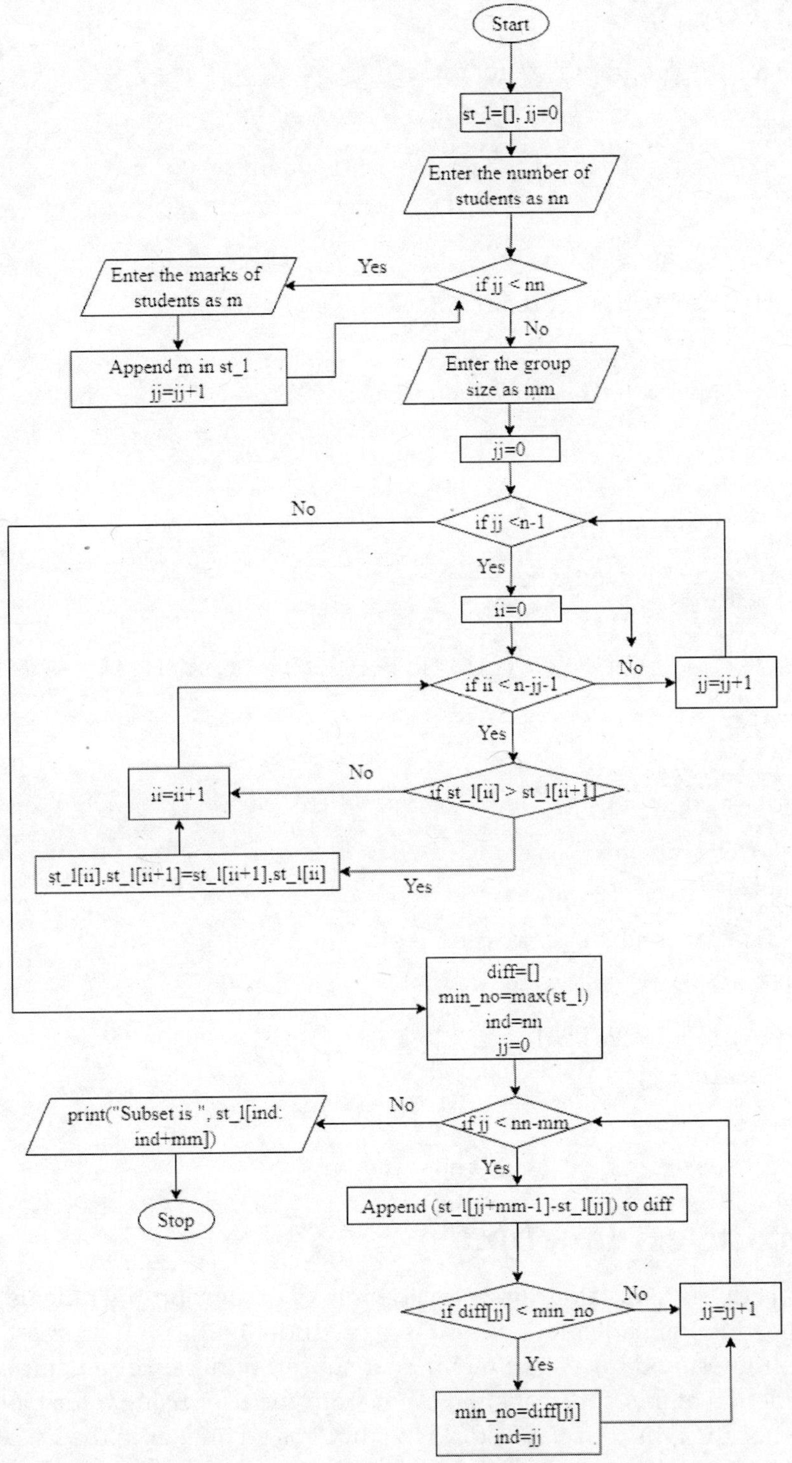

***Figure 6.8**: Flowchart illustrating the program 6.8*

Python code

Python code for the program is as follows:

```
st_l=[]
nn=int(input("Enter the number of students: "))
for ii in range(0, nn):
    st_l.append(int(input("Marks: ")))
mm=int(input("Enter the group size: "))
for jj in range(0,nn-1):
    for ii in range(0, nn-jj-1):
        if st_l[ii] > st_l[ii+1]:
            st_l[ii],st_l[ii+1]=st_l[ii+1],st_l[ii]
diff=[]
min_no=max(st_l)
ind=nn
for jj in range(0,nn-mm):
    diff.append(st_l[jj+mm-1]-st_l[jj])
    if diff[jj] < min_no:
        min_no=diff[jj]
        ind=jj
print("Subset is ", st_l[ind: ind+mm])
```

Python code explanation

This Python code snippet takes input for the marks of a group of students and a group size and then finds and displays the subset of students that minimizes the difference between the highest and lowest scorers in that subset. It initializes an empty list **`st_l`** to store the students' marks and reads the input from the user using a for-loop. It prompts the user to enter the group size and stores the input as an integer in the variable **`mm`**. Then, sorting is carried out on the students' marks using the code discussed in *Chapter 5, Complex*

Problem Solving. Then, the code calculates the difference in marks between each group of **mm** students and finds the group with the smallest range.

C code

C code for the program is as follows:

```
#include<stdio.h>

int main()
{

int st_l[100];
int nn, ii, jj, mm, min_no, diff[100], ind, t;

printf("Enter the number of students: ");
scanf("%d", &nn);
printf("Enter Marks of the students: ");
for(ii=0; ii<nn; ii++)
    scanf("%d", &st_l[ii]);

printf("Enter the group size: ");
scanf("%d", &mm);

for(jj=0; jj<nn-1; jj++)
    {
    for(ii=0; ii<nn-jj-1; ii++)
    {
        if(st_l[ii] > st_l[ii+1])
        {
            t=st_l[ii];
            st_l[ii]=st_l[ii+1];
            st_l[ii+1]=t;
        }
    }
```

```
    }
min_no=200;
ind=nn;
for(jj=0; jj<(nn-mm); jj++)
{
    diff[jj]=st_l[jj+mm-1]-st_l[jj];
    if(diff[jj] < min_no)
    {
        min_no=diff[jj];
        ind=jj;
    }
}
printf("Subset is ");
for(jj=ind; jj<ind+mm; jj++)
{
    printf("%d ", st_l[jj]);
}
return(0);
}
```

C code explanation

This C code snippet takes input for the marks of a group of students and a group size and then finds and displays the subset of students that minimizes the difference between the highest and lowest scorers in that subset. It declares an array **`st_l`** to store the students' marks and reads the input from the user using a for-loop. It prompts the user to enter the group size and stores the input as an integer in the variable **`mm`**. Then, sorting is carried out on the students' marks using the code discussed in *Chapter 5, Complex Problem Solving*. Then, the code calculates the difference in marks between each group of **`mm`** students and finds the group with the smallest range.

Program 6.9: Convert decimals to different bases

The number system is a mathematical representation of a number in an understandable machine format. For instance, Binary numbers are used by computers to perform various arithmetic operations. Octal numbers are used to set file permissions in UNIX operating systems. Your task is to take a decimal number and the desired base (from **2** to **9**) as inputs from the user and convert the decimal number to the required base representation.

For example:

Input: `5,2`

Output: **`101`**

Sample input output

Test case #1:

Input:

`Enter the decimal number: 56`

`Enter the required base: 2`

Output: **`The base 2 representation of 0 is 111000`**

Test case #2:

Input:

`Enter the decimal number: 97`

`Enter the required base: 8`

Output: **`The base 8 representation of 0 is 141`**

Test case #3:

Input:

`Enter the decimal number: 284`

`Enter the required base: 5`

Output: **`The base 5 representation of 0 is 2114`**

Algorithm

To run the above program, the following steps are needed to be followed:

1. **`Start`**
2. **`bina = 0`**
3. **`i = 1`**
4. **`Read the decimal number as nn`**
5. **`Read the required base as bb`**
6. **`if bb<2 or bb > 9:`**
    a. **`Display("Base should be between 2 to 9")`**
    b. **`Quit the program`**

7. **Repeatnn != 0 :**
    a. **re = nn % bb**
    b. **nn = nn//bb**
    c. **bina += re * i**
    d. **i *= 10**
8. **Display("The base ", bb, " representation of ", nn, " is ", bina)**
9. **Stop**

Flowchart

Figure 6.9 illustrates the program in the form of a flowchart:

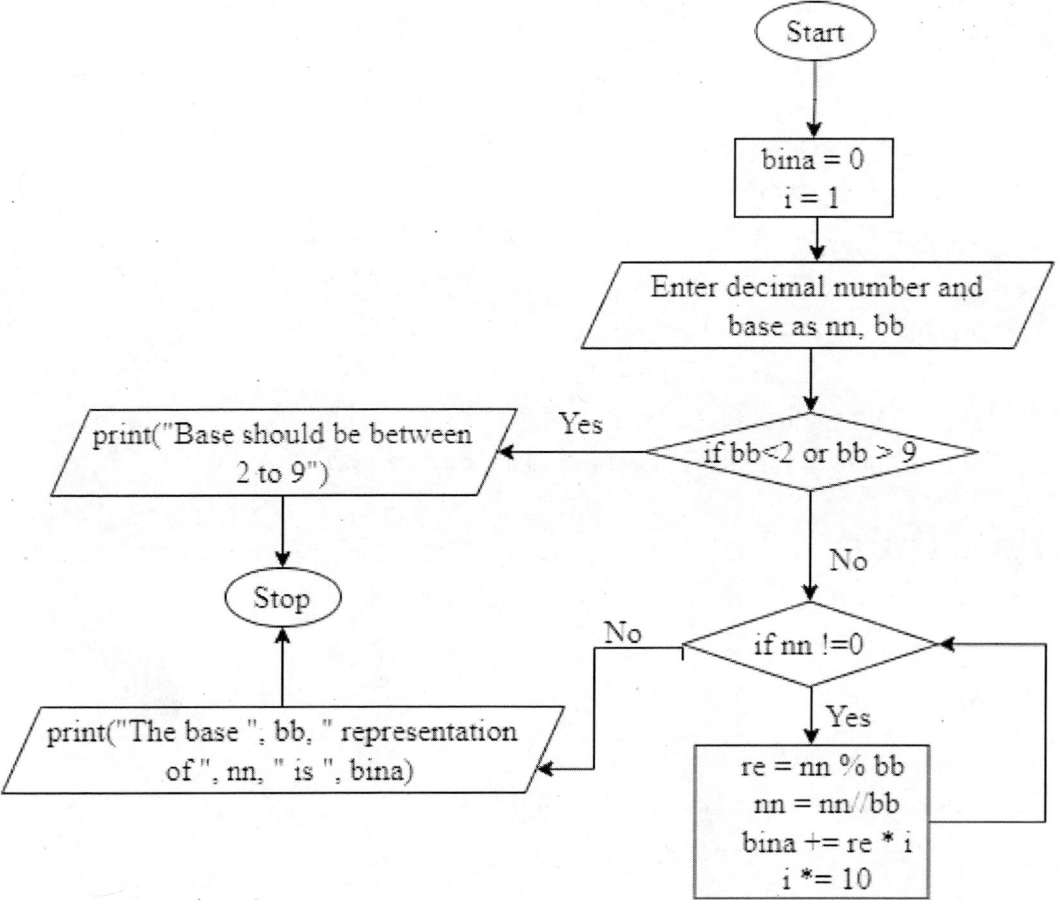

***Figure 6.9**: Flowchart illustrating the program 6.9*

Python code

Python code for the program is as follows:

```
bina = 0
i = 1
nn=int(input("Enter the decimal number: "))
bb=int(input("Enter the required base: "))
if bb<2 or bb > 9:
    print("Base should be between 2 to 9")
    exit(0)
while nn != 0 :
    re = nn % bb
    nn = nn//bb
    bina += re * i
    i *= 10
print("The base ", bb, " representation of ", nn, " is ", bina)
```

Python code explanation

The Python code takes the decimal number and the base of the number as input and converts the decimal number to the equivalent representation in the desired base. The logic behind the conversion is the successive division of the number and recording of the remainder. The program will only work from base 10 to base between **2** to **9** conversions. The first base value is checked. The program will terminate with an appropriate error message if it is less than **2** or greater than **9**. Otherwise, it will keep dividing the number with the base until it becomes **0**. The remainder is recorded in every division. Finally, all the remainder are combined to form one number by multiplying them by **10**.

C code

C code for the program is as follows:

```
#include<stdio.h>
#include<stdlib.h>
```

```
int main () {
  // variable to store the result
  long bina = 0;
  int re, i = 1;
  int nn, bb;
  printf("Enter the decimal number: ");
  scanf("%d", &nn);

  printf("Enter the required base: ");
  scanf("%d", &bb);

  if(bb<2 || bb > 9)
  {
      printf("Base should be between 2 to 9");
      exit(0);
  }
 // Loop to convert to binary
  while (nn != 0) {
        // get remainder of nn divided by base
    re = nn % bb;
        // divide nn by base
    nn = nn/bb;
        // multiply remainder by i
    // add the product to bin
    bina += re * i;
        // multiply i by 10
    i *= 10;
  }

  printf("The base %d representation of %d is %ld", bb,nn,bina);

return 0;
}
```

C code explanation

The C code takes the decimal number and the base of the number as input and converts the decimal number to the equivalent representation in the desired base. The logic behind the conversion is the successive division of the number and recording of the remainder. The program will only work from base 10 to base between **2** to **9** conversions. The first base value is checked. The program will terminate with an appropriate error message if it is less than **2** or greater than **9**. Otherwise, it will keep dividing the number with the base until the number becomes **0**. The remainder is recorded in every division. Finally, all the remainder are combined to form one number by multiplying them by **10**.

Program 6.10: Password validation and encryption

Validate and encrypt the password as per the following conditions:

1. Length of the password should be between 8-12 characters. It should contain the alphabet, digits, and special characters.
2. For encryption, replace alphabets with a 6-bit binary number such that the first bit represents lower case (by 0) or upper case (by 1), and the remaining 5 bits are the binary encoding. For example: *a→ 000001, B→ 100010* and so.
3. Replace digits as *0-A, 1-B, 2-C, 3-D, 4-E, 5-F, 6-G,7-H, 8-I, 9-J*
4. Keep the special characters as it is

For example:

Password: `@Ab_%%82`

Encrypted Password: **`@100001000010_%%IC`**

Sample input output

Test case #1:

Input: `Enter your password: @as09$%$%`

Output: **`The encrypted password is  @000001010011101111J$%$%`**

Test case #2:

Input: `Enter your password: A@gh1`

Output: `Length of the password should be between 8-12 characters.`

Test case #3:

Input: `Enter your password: Coding11`

Output: **`The password must contain at least one uppercase alphabet, lowercase alphabet, digits, and special characters.`**

Algorithm

To run the above program, the following steps are needed to be followed:

1. `Start`
2. `Read your password p_s`
3. `encry_ps=""`
4. `Ac=0`
5. `ac=0`
6. `nc=0`
7. `sc=0`
8. `if len(p_s) < 8 or len(p_s) > 12:`
    a. `Display("Length of the password should be between 8-12 characters." )`
    b. `Quit the Program`
9. `for each character ii ofp_s:`
    a. `if ord(ii) in range(65,91):`
        i. `Ac=1`
    b. `else if ord(ii) in range(97, 123):`
        i. `ac=1`
    c. `else if ord(ii) in range(48, 58):`
        i. `nc=1`
    d. `else if ord(ii) in range(33,127):`
        i. `sc=1`
10. `if not(Ac==1 and ac==1 and nc==1 and sc==1):`
    a. `Display("Password must contain atleast one uppercase alphabet, lowercase alphabet, digits and special characters.")`
    b. `Quit the program`
11. `for each character ii ofp_s:`
    a. `if ord(ii) in range(65,91):`
        i. `x="1"`

ii. `x1=bin(ord(ii)-65+1)`

iii. `x2=x1[2:]`

iv. `for h = 1 to 5-len(x2)+1):`

1. `x=x+'0'`

v. `x=x+x2`

vi. `encry_ps=encry_ps+str(x)`

b. **`else if ord(ii) in range(97, 123):`**

i. `x="0"`

ii. `x1=bin(ord(ii)-97+1)`

iii. `x2=x1[2:]`

iv. `for h = 1 to 5-len(x2)+1):`

1. `x=x+'0'`

v. `x=x+x2`

vi. `encry_ps=encry_ps+str(x)`

c. **`else if ord(ii) in range(48, 58):`**

i. `encry_ps=encry_ps+chr(ord(ii)+17)`

d. **`else if ord(ii) in range(33,127):`**

i. `encry_ps=encry_ps+ ii`

12. **`Display("The encrypted password is ", encry_ps)`**

13. **`Stop`**

Flowchart

Figure 6.10 illustrates the program in the form of a flowchart:

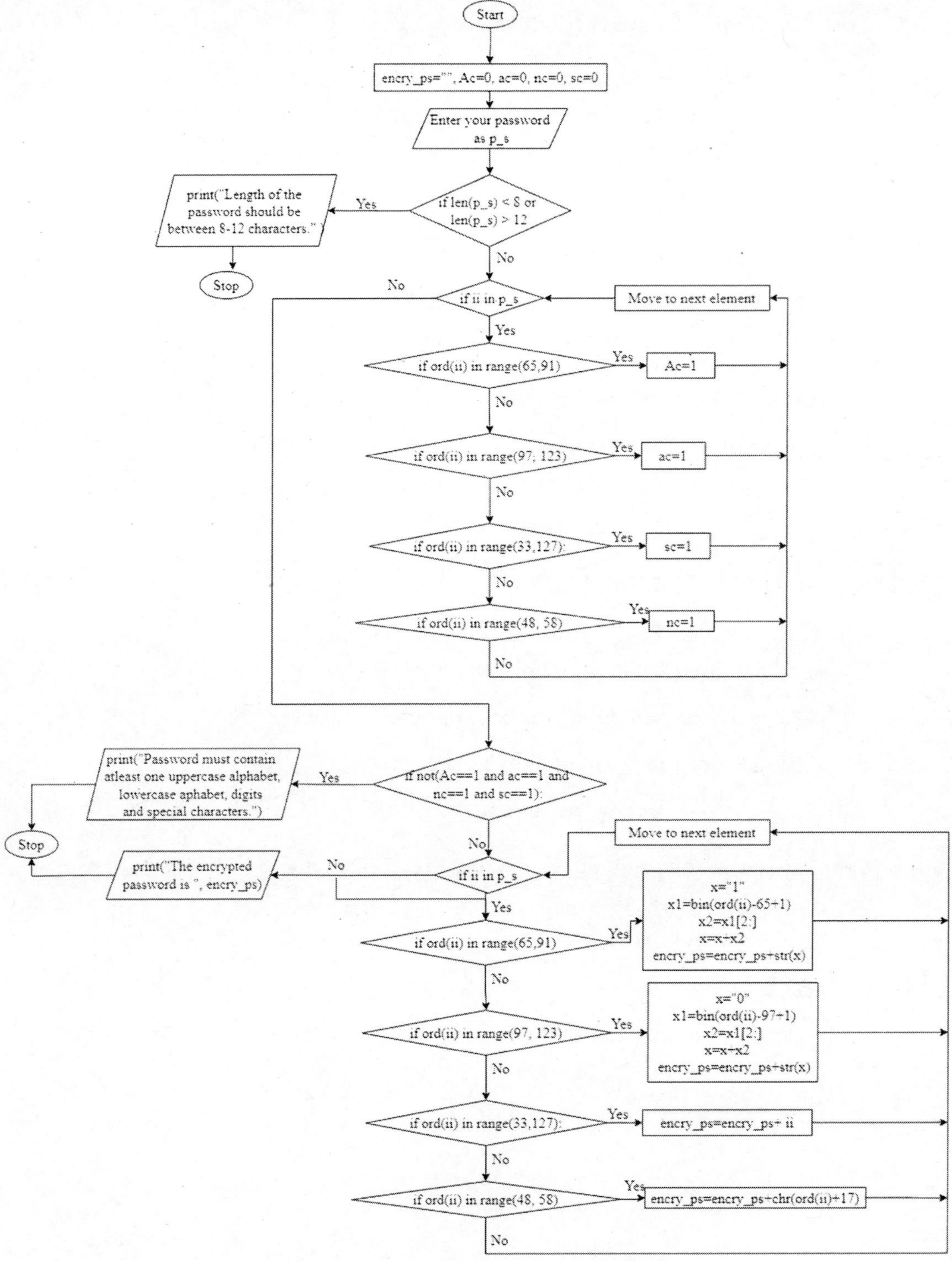

***Figure 6.10**: Flowchart illustrating the program 6.10*

Python code

Python code for the program is as follows:

```
p_s=input("Enter your password: ")
encry_ps=""
Ac=0
ac=0
nc=0
sc=0
if len(p_s) < 8 or len(p_s) > 12:
    print("Length of the password should be between 8-12 characters." )
    exit()
for ii in p_s:
    if ord(ii) in range(65,91):
        Ac=1
    elif ord(ii) in range(97, 123):
        ac=1
    elif ord(ii) in range(48, 58):
        nc=1
    elif ord(ii) in range(33,127):
        sc=1

if not(Ac==1 and ac==1 and nc==1 and sc==1):
    print("Password must contain atleast one uppercase alphabet, lowercase aphabet, digits and special characters.")
    exit()
for ii in p_s:
    if ord(ii) in range(65,91):
        x="1"
        x1=bin(ord(ii)-65+1)
        x2=x1[2:]
        for h in range(1,5-len(x2)+1):
            x=x+'0'
        x=x+x2
```

```
        encry_ps=encry_ps+str(x)
    elif ord(ii) in range(97, 123):
        x="0"
        x1=bin(ord(ii)-97+1)
        x2=x1[2:]
        for h in range(1,5-len(x2)+1):
            x=x+'0'
        x=x+x2
        encry_ps=encry_ps+str(x)
    elif ord(ii) in range(48, 58):
        encry_ps=encry_ps+chr(ord(ii)+17)
    elif ord(ii) in range(33,127):
        encry_ps=encry_ps+ ii

print("The encrypted password is ", encry_ps)
```

Python code explanation

This Python code prompts the user to input a password and then encrypts the password based on specific criteria. It prompts the user to input a password, stores the input in the variable, and initializes an empty string **encry_ps** to store the encrypted password. The variables **Ac**, **ac**, **nc**, and **scare** are initialized to **0** and are used to track whether the password contains at least one uppercase alphabet, one lowercase alphabet, one digit, and one special character, respectively. The code checks the length of the password and whether it contains at least one character from each category (uppercase, lowercase, digit, and special character). If these conditions are not met, an error message is printed, and the program exits. If the password meets the length and character type requirements, the code encrypts the password using specific rules. Finally, the encrypted password is printed to the console. Here, the function **len()** returns the length of the string. Function **ord()** returns the **ASCII** value of the character. **ASCII** value of uppercase alphabets is from 65-90, lowercase (97-122), digits (48-57), and others are treated as special characters. **Bin()** is a predefined function in Python to obtain the binary equivalent of any decimal number.

C code

C code for the program is as follows:

```
#include<stdio.h>
#include<string.h>
#include<stdlib.h>
```

```

int ord(char s)
{
    return((int)s);
}

void bin (int nn, int ss[]) {
  // variable to store the result
  long bina = 0;
  int re, i = 1;
  int j=0;
 // loop to convert to binary
  while (nn != 0) {
        // get remainder of n divided by 2
    re = nn % 2;
        // divide n by 2
    nn /= 2;
        // multiply remainder by i
    // add the product to bin
    bina += re * i;
        // multiply i by 10
    i *= 10;
    ss[j]=re;
    j=j+1;
      //printf("in func=%c\n", ss[j-1]);
  }
  while(j<6)
  {
     ss[j]=0;
     j=j+1;
  }
  //ss[j]='\0';
  //printf("in func=%d\n", strlen(ss));
```

```

//return bina;
}

int main()
{
char encry_ps[100]="";
char p_s[13];
int Ac=0;
int ac=0;
int nc=0;
int sc=0;
int ii, h;

fflush(stdin);
printf("Enter your password: ");
scanf("%s", p_s);

if(strlen(p_s) < 8 || strlen(p_s) > 12)
    {
        printf("Length of the password should be between 8-12 characters." );
        getch();
        exit(0);
    }
for(ii=0; ii< strlen(p_s); ii++)
{
    if (ord(p_s[ii]) >=65 && ord(p_s[ii]) <=90)
        Ac=1;
    else if (ord(p_s[ii]) >=97 && ord(p_s[ii]) <=122)
        ac=1;
    else if (ord(p_s[ii]) >=48 && ord(p_s[ii]) <=57)
        nc=1;
    else if (ord(p_s[ii]) >=33 && ord(p_s[ii]) <=126)
```

```
            sc=1;
}
if (!(Ac==1 && ac==1 && nc==1 && sc==1))
    {
   printf("Password must contain atleast one uppercase alphabet, lowercase aphabet, digits and special characters.");
    getch();
    exit(0);
    }

for(ii=0; ii< strlen(p_s); ii++)
{
     if (ord(p_s[ii]) >=48 && ord(p_s[ii]) <=57)
        {
        encry_ps[strlen(encry_ps)]=p_s[ii]+16;
        }
    else if (ord(p_s[ii]) >=65 && ord(p_s[ii]) <=90)
       { char xx[7]="";
        int xx2[6];
        long xx2_int;
        bin(ord(p_s[ii])-65+1, xx2);
        xx2[5]=1;
        int h1;
        for(h1=0; h1<=5; h1++)
            xx[h1]=xx2[h1]+48;
        xx[h1]='\0';
        strrev(xx);
        strcat(encry_ps,xx);
       }
    else if (ord(p_s[ii]) >=97 && ord(p_s[ii]) <=122)
       { char xa[7]="";
        int xa2[6];
        bin(ord(p_s[ii])-97+1, xa2);
        xa2[5]=0;
```

```
            for(h=0; h<=5; h++)
                xa[h]=xa2[h]+'0';
            xa[h]='\0';
            strrev(xa);
            strcat(encry_ps,xa);
        }
    else
        {
        encry_ps[strlen(encry_ps)]=p_s[ii];
        }
}
printf("The encrypted password is %s", encry_ps);

return(0);
}
```

C code explanation

This C code prompts the user to input a password and then encrypts the password based on specific criteria. It prompts the user to input a password, stores the input in the variable, and initializes an empty string **encry_ps** to store the encrypted password. The variables **Ac**, **ac**, **nc**, and **scare** are initialized to **0** and are used to track whether the password contains at least one uppercase alphabet, one lowercase alphabet, one digit, and one special character, respectively. The code checks the length of the password and whether it contains at least one character from each category (uppercase, lowercase, digit, and special character). If these conditions are not met, an error message is printed, and the program exits. If the password meets the length and character type requirements, the code encrypts the password using specific rules. Finally, the encrypted password is printed to the console. Here, the function **strlen()** returns the length of the string. **Strrev()** is used to reverse the string. **Strcat()** is used to concatenate two strings. All these string functions are defined in **string.h** library. The function is defined as **ord()**, which returns the **ASCII** value of the character. **ASCII** value of uppercase alphabets is from 65-90, lowercase (97-122), digits (48-57), and others are treated as special characters. **Bin()** is a defined function in Python to obtain the binary equivalent of any decimal number. Unlike Python, **ord()** and **bin()**are not the predefined function. So, they are defined in the program.

Conclusion

The chapter has discussed real-world problems/puzzles using various programming constructs like flowcharts, algorithms, and coding. With the help of several examples, the different flavors of multiple steps, conditional logic, loops, lists, and functions are presented.

Points to remember

- **`Math.h`** library includes the basic functions of math in C Programming. The **`counter`** module in Python is math.
- **`String.h`** is the C library where various string-related functions are already defined.
- Predefined functions can be called to include the corresponding libraries.
- Users can also define the functions which can be called in the program.

Questions

1. Convert any base number to Base 10.
2. Display the enrollment number of the student who scored the highest marks in the exam.
3. Ask the user to input 10 phone numbers. Then, take a phone number as input from the user and check if it exists in the list.
4. Sort elements at even index in increasing and odd index in decreasing order
5. Given a set of n nuts of different sizes and n bolts of different sizes. There is a one-one mapping between nuts and bolts. Your task is to match nuts and bolts. Constraint: Comparison of a nut to another nut or a bolt to another bolt is not allowed. It means a nut can only be compared with a bolt, and a bolt can only be compared with a nut to see which one is bigger/smaller.

Code Bundle and Coloured Images

Please follow the link to download the
Code Bundle and the ***Coloured Images*** of the book:

https://rebrand.ly/eaal7hm

The code bundle for the book is also hosted on GitHub at
https://github.com/bpbpublications/Code-Factory
In case there's an update to the code, it will be updated on the existing GitHub repository.

We have code bundles from our rich catalogue of books and videos available at **https://github.com/bpbpublications**. Check them out!

Index

V

W